JOURNAL FOR THE STUDY OF THE OLD TESTAMENT SUPPLEMENT SERIES
97

Editors
David J.A. Clines
Philip R. Davies

BIBLE AND LITERATURE SERIES
27

General Editor
David M. Gunn

Assistant General Editor
Danna Nolan Fewell

Consultant Editors
Elizabeth Struthers Malbon
James G. Williams

Almond Press
Sheffield

To
Scott Hafemann

THE UNITY
of
THE TWELVE

Paul R. House

The Almond Press · 1990

Bible and Literature Series, 27

General Editor: David M. Gunn
(Columbia Theological Seminary, Decatur, Georgia)
Assistant General Editor: Danna Nolan Fewell
(Perkins School of Theology, Dallas, Texas)
Consultant Editors: Elizabeth Struthers Malbon
(Virginia Polytechnic Institute & State University, Blacksburg, Virginia)
James G. Williams
(Syracuse University, Syracuse, New York)

Copyright © 1990 Sheffield Academic Press

Published by Almond Press

Editorial direction: David M. Gunn
Columbia Theological Seminary
P.O. Box 520, Decatur
GA 30031, U.S.A.

Almond Press is an imprint of
Sheffield Academic Press Ltd
The University of Sheffield
343 Fulwood Road
Sheffield S10 3BP
England

Typeset by Sheffield Academic Press and
Printed in Great Britain
by Billing & Sons Ltd
Worcester

British Library Cataloguing in Publication Data
House, Paul R.
    The unity of the twelve.
    1. Bible. O.T. Minor Prophets.—Critical studies
    I. Title   II. Series   III. Series
    224.906

ISSN 0309-0787
ISSN 0260-4493
ISBN 1-85075-250-8

CONTENTS

PREFACE

This book was written during the 1986-87 academic year at Taylor University. Many excellent works on the minor prophets have appeared since then which would have enhanced my research. Hopefully the materials included in this project are representative of today's main currents in minor prophet studies.

Many people deserve thanks for their help with this book. David Gunn, the editor of this series, helped me clarify my aims for the project and offered valuable suggestions at critical stages of my writing. I appreciate his interest in seeing literary analysis of the Old Testament grow as a discipline. David Orton and the editorial staff at Sheffield Academic Press have done their usual good job.

My colleagues at Taylor University were supportive of this publication. Mrs Rita Koch, Mrs Sharon Gretillat, and Mrs Nancy Gore typed the manuscript. The members of the Religion Department continue to tolerate my views with a maximum of courtesy. They are all valued colleagues and friends.

Becky, my wife, and Molly, my daughter, continue to support my writing efforts and, as always, they added joy to the work process.

More than anyone else, my friend, and then-colleague, Scott Hafemann encouraged me to finish this book. Practically every day I wrote he affirmed my efforts. Though he has not read a word of this manuscript, he has impacted it in a significant way. To this friend the book is dedicated.

For these and other kindnesses I am very grateful.

Paul R. House
Upland, Indiana

Chapter 1

INTRODUCTION

A Brief History of Minor Prophets Interpretation

One of the obvious gaps in Old Testament studies is the absence of work on the so-called minor prophets, or book of the twelve. Some of these prophets, such as Amos, Hosea and Micah, have received a great deal of critical attention, while others, like Obadiah, Nahum and Zephaniah, are rarely treated outside of commentary series. Beyond the individual books, there is even less literature on the book of the twelve itself. Relatively few scholars discuss why these prophecies are placed together.

Even writers who attempt to survey the shape or shaping of the Twelve often appear puzzled or frustrated in their efforts. Most note that the twelve prophecies have long been considered one book. Why they have been so designated is a mystery. Brevard Childs observes:

> Unfortunately, the historical factors at work in the collecting and ordering of the prophetic books remain very obscure (cf. ch. II), and one is largely dependent upon the implications which have been drawn from internal evidence of growth. Even such an obvious problem as explaining how twelve independent prophetic collections were united into a single book has remained unresolved although various forces at work in the process have been correctly observed by R.E. Wolfe, K. Budde, W. Rudolph, and others (1980: 308-309).

Most of the advances Childs mentions are in the area of compilation and redaction. Even these examples of progress are more effective with single books than with the corpus as a whole.

Some obvious elements of order in the twelve have been noticed. Chronological data provided in the prophecies themselves show that a measure of historical sequence is maintained. Six of the twelve (Hosea, Amos, Micah, Zephaniah, Haggai and Zechariah) note the kings reigning during their careers. But as H.W. Wolff observes 'a separate investigation of each of the remaining six books is required to account for... specific placement within the framework' (1974: 3). Writing about Joel, Wolff continues:

> Hence, in view of the absence of chronological data in the book of Joel, those who arranged the Hebrew collection of the Twelve Prophets must have used other criteria to determine its position between Hosea and Amos. These criteria must have been self-evident to them, just as obvious as the temporal references in the superscriptions (1974: 3).

Wolff then suggests that Joel is tied to Amos by verbal agreements, certain parallel rubrics, and the fact that Amos 1.3–2.16 carries out the judgment promised in Joel 4 (1974: 3).

Linguistic elements link other books as well. It has long been assumed that there is a strong connection between the uses of משא in Zech. 9.1, Zech. 12.1, and Mal. 1.1. Ronald Pierce observes that beyond such syntactic correspondences lie thematic likenesses that bind Haggai, Zechariah and Malachi (1984: 401). Certainly even more such parallels exist among other parts of the Twelve, but few if any clues as to the significance of the Twelve's overall configuration have emerged.

No doubt one of the reasons for this gap in prophetic studies has been that critics have emphasized historical analyses for the past century. These analyses have elucidated many of the facts *behind* the text, such as historical situation, order of compilation, *Sitz im Leben*, etc. Even the nature of prophecy and the psyche of the prophets have been explored with some success. What has been neglected, almost forgotten in fact, is the nature of the final, written form of the prophetic books themselves. Such an oversight seems strange when one observes that the canonical form of prophetic books is the main resource for all the above-mentioned studies.

It is instructive to note how prophecy has been treated in the past so questions can arise about future interpretation. In this way the old can inform the new. Beyond general research into prophecy there must be some exploration of minor-prophet discussions. Perhaps from these commentaries some patterns will emerge that can further our understanding of how twelve different prophecies could have come to be considered one book.

A brief survey of approaches to prophecy in general during the past century demonstrates how written prophecy has been slighted in scholarly research. Immediately following Wellhausen's *Prolegomena to the History of Israel* (1869) the tendency of critics was to explore the prophets through source-critical means. Since Wellhausen claimed that the prophets were the true progenitors of Israel's ethical, monotheistic religion, scholarly efforts focused on the attempt to uncover the original words of the prophets so the foundation of Israelite faith could emerge. Books were broken into sections, sections into sentences, and sentences into words, always with the purpose of dating each layer and separating 'authentic' and 'non-authentic' statements. Passages judged authentic were, of course, of higher historical value than their later counterparts.

Almost as influential in the overall scheme of Old Testament research as Wellhausen, and probably more important in prophetic studies, was Bernhard Duhm. He also focused on the prophets' role as agents of change in Israelite religion, as Robert R. Wilson summarizes:

> Like Ewald, Duhm saw the major significance of the prophets in their theology, which raised the level of Israelite religion to new moral and ethical heights. The prophets broke sharply with the ancient Israelite religious traditions, particularly those of the patriarchal period, and were powerful forces in shaping a religion free of superstitious cultic and magical practices (1980: 3).

Duhm also popularized the practice of dividing Isaianic authorship into two or more hands through his 1892 work on Isaiah. Thus Duhm directs his readers behind the prophetic text to show the situation and redaction of the books. The final forms of the prophecies are not deemed as important as these issues.

Perhaps the most representative example of early source criticism in English is the influential International Critical Commentary series. The goal of these works was to apply historical-critical methods to the entire Bible. Most of the early volumes reflect a definite bias towards source criticism. John Skinner and S.R. Driver utilized the tenets of the documentary hypothesis to dissect Genesis and Deuteronomy respectively, and such writers as George Buchanan Gray (Isaiah) and William Rainey Harper (Amos and Hosea) did similar work on the prophets. Gray argued for the diversity of Isaianic authorship, though his commentary does not cover the entire book of Isaiah. Harper was originally engaged to write on all the minor prophets, but was unable to finish this task before his death. While a number of able historical scholars completed the work on the Twelve, there is very little variation in their approach to the books. Textual, historical and stylistic concerns are covered, and exegetical comments are made. Once more there is a great emphasis on 'authentic' and 'spurious' oracles. After breaking the text into pieces there is no attempt, however, to unite the fragments. Nor is there any notion of describing and interpreting the Twelve as a whole.

Doubtlessly the source critics made a significant contribution to prophetic studies. Their surveys of the world in which the prophets lived advanced critical knowledge of why the prophets preached, the times in which they preached, and the original audience to whom they preached. A better grasp of the historical milieu of the prophets can only aid interpretation. Still, the effects of source criticism have not all been positive. These scholars began the tendency to treat the Old Testament prophetic books as collections of disparate pericopae rather than unified works. So much energy has now been expended on *dividing* the prophetic writings that the vision of a unified prophetic canon has almost completely disappeared.

Gustav Hölscher moved criticism from the compilation of texts to the psychology of prophetic experience. Though he acknowledged the extreme value of original oracular utterances Hölscher wanted to go one step further and recover the process of how the prophets delivered their original messages.

Duhm had noted that Old Testament prophets probably had ecstatic experiences and then brought forth their inspired sayings, citing biblical references and New Eastern parallels as evidence for this position. Hölscher did more comparative studies and concluded that prophetic preaching was at heart an ecstatic experience. Ronald Clements offers an excellent summary of Hölscher's methods when he writes:

> Hölscher examined the various phenomena associated with ecstatic and visionary experiences: a sense of heightened awareness, loss of bodily feeling, concentration of thought, uncontrolled bodily actions, dreams, hallucinations, hypnotic visions, experiences of dumbness, amnesia and paralysis. All of these he related to specific actions designed to induce such ecstatic experience through music, dancing and various cultic and mantic rites (1976: 57).

Many of these experiences were traced in Old Testament prophecy. The prophets were thereby seen as individuals who participated in a widespread phenomenon that spanned the Near East.

A more recent advocate of the psychological approach to prophecy is Johannes Lindblom. Like Hölscher, Lindblom believes prophetic utterance initially came when the inspired prophet was totally under the influence of a deity. He claims that

> in religious ecstasy, consciousness is entirely filled with the presence of God, with ideas and feelings belonging to the divine sphere. The soul is lifted up into the exalted region of divine revelation, and the lower world with its sensations momentarily disappears (1965: 5).

Lindblom also describes how these ecstatic utterances came to be written, but even in this area of his work he emphasizes the oracular nature of the books (1962: 220ff.). Through this tendency Lindblom focuses attention on pre-textual matters. What is important to him is how the prophetic books were formed—not what they are in their *final* form.

The psychology-of-experience approach to prophecy continued the tendency begun by source criticism to feature elements other than the text itself. It is the prophet and his experience that take precedence over the prophet's writing.

Hölscher's ideas have led to a better understanding of the prophet's cultural context, but they do not illuminate canonical prophecy in a greatly significant way.

Another group of scholars that both learned from and reacted to source criticism was the early form critics. These scholars basically accepted the tenets and conclusions of Wellhausen and his followers, but felt the form original prophetic utterances took needed to be recognized. Hermann Gunkel believed that the prophetic books were collections of sermons, teachings and sayings of the prophets. It was not enough, for Gunkel, to note that prophecy was originally an oral form, however, so he sought to classify the prophetic oral traditions. Gunkel identified a number of types (Gattungen) of prophetic utterances, and said these 'promises, threats, admonitions, warnings, hymns, laments, liturgies and allegories all became established forms of speech which the prophets employed to develop and expound their message' (Clements 1976: 61). Larger written units are collections of smaller oral types. For instance, Gunkel discovered a psalm type in Nahum 1.2-8 that serves as an introduction to the rest of the book. Brevard Childs notes that 'Gunkel's contribution lay in his first drawing attention to the exact idiom of the psalm and thus enabling the interpreter to hear the text with a new precision' (Childs 1980: 443).

One of Gunkel's chief goals was to use the form of an oracle to discover the life situation (*Sitz im Leben*) that spawned individual messages. Thus there was a very definite historical motivation behind his literary analyses. Just as adept at suggesting historical situations for prophecies as Gunkel was Sigmund Mowinckel. Mowinckel used form criticism to tie the prophets to the temple cult of Israel. From psalms used in the cult the prophets learned various forms they adapted for their own purposes. Mowinckel thinks that

> in the prophets too we find many psalm-like passages. Some-
> times the collectors of their prophecies, the later prophet-dis-
> ciples, have given expression to the song of joy which the
> congregation is to sing, when once salvation has become a
> fact. Sometimes they themselves exhorted the congregation
> to break into praise for the salvation which already sends its
> rays into the age. More often they used the psalm form as an

effective garb for the prophecy. Jeremiah laments on behalf of the people... Deutero-Isaiah fashions his salvation prophecy as a hymn to Yahweh... (1979: 40).

It is plain in Mowinckel's studies that even if the prophets are ecstatics, they also use oral forms that were extant in their day. Thus, the prophet uses the lament to mourn an event or a psalm of joy to celebrate an event. The form of the literature verifies the situation of the prophet and people.

Form criticism makes a solid contribution to prophetic studies when it focuses on the style of written prophecy. It is quite helpful to analyze the various pericopae in a careful, consistent way. Many elements of the artistry of written prophecy emerge through such exploration. Unfortunately, too much of form criticism is merely a prelude to historical declarations. The literature becomes just a door that leads once more, *behind* the text. While form-critical scholars offer some helpful analytical methods, their emphasis on pre-textual matters does not help illuminate written prophecy. They also tend to deal with parts of books rather than larger blocks of material.

Gerhard von Rad became the most influential proponent of a different approach to prophecy during the middle of this century. It was his opinion that the canonical prophetic writings reflect a long history of received traditions, therefore this method was called tradition or traditio-historical criticism. Rather than viewing the prophets as innovative pioneers of a new religion, as Wellhausen and others had done, von Rad observed the long history of Israelite faith and claimed that the prophets' oracles were shaped to reflect their hearers' understanding of that history. No definitive traditions affect all the prophets, but careful study of each book can offer clues to the main tradition reshaped by individual prophets. Von Rad says:

What is the common factor in the message of these prophets? The first characteristic is that they have their roots in the basic sacral traditions of the early period. Certainly, there are very great differences in the way in which the individual prophets draw upon the old traditions. One has only to compare the extremely different, though contemporary, prophets Hosea and Isaiah, the former of whom takes his stand on the old Israel-Covenant tradition, while the latter does not even

> seem to have knowledge of this, and appeals exclusively to
> the Zion-David tradition (1967: 11).

Tradition critics sought to trace, then, the influence of particular traditions in each of the prophets.

What is significant about tradition criticism is that it acknowledges the validity of religious faith before the prophets. Rather than innovators, the prophets stand in a long line of ethical, monotheistic belief. As von Rad notes, some of these traditions stretch clear back to the initial election of Israel, and, as H.W. Wolff realizes, some go back to the wisdom circles (1974: xxiv). Even if such traditions are reshaped there is a conscious effort to shape utterances from existing ideas. In von Rad's studies there is also an effort to show that prophecy has a certain content (1967: 11-14). Certainly, written prophecy is illuminated by the recognition of its content. Still, there is more concern for the shaping and reshaping of prophecy than for its final form. The nature and unity of the completed traditions are left for further analysis by other writers.

In his work *Prophecy and Society in Ancient Israel* Robert R. Wilson combines the ideas of Wellhausen, Hölscher, Lindblom and von Rad in an effort to define the prophet's role in Israelite society. Wilson uses anthropological, sociological and theological data in his study. He attempts to transfer tendencies from other cultures that relate to Israel's situation to the discussion of prophecy. The conclusion of the study is 'that prophets seem to have played a central role in Israelite society in the premonarchial period but took on peripheral functions after the rise of the monarchy' (1980: 298). Wilson also believes that, as traditional prophecy gradually ceased, apocalyptic materials began to emerge. Thus, appreciation for the prophet and his office was lost after the exile.

Wilson's work revises some older theories about the prophets and notes how the prophets impacted their societies. None of the acts, speeches or writings of the prophets were produced in some sociological vacuum. The prophets related to their times. With the risk of being repetitious, though, it must be said that much of what Wilson discusses is non-textual or at least pre-textual. All the prophetic works we really have within the Israelite tradition are in the canon. It is time for some effort to be made to recognize the fixed forms of the prophets and *their* role in society.

Some of the interests already expressed about written prophecy are covered by canonical criticism. The main thrust of canonical criticism is to take the present form of the Hebrew canon and understand in what ways 'the texts served a religious function in closest relationship to the worship and service of God whom Israel confessed to be the source of the sacred word' (Childs 1980: 73). Therefore both the Old Testament and its relationship to living faith are discussed. Brevard Childs further defines canonical criticism when he writes:

> Canonical analysis focuses its attention on the final form of the text itself. It seeks neither to use the text merely as a source for other information obtained by means of an oblique reading, nor to reconstruct a history of religious development. Rather, it treats the literature in its own integrity. Its concern is not to establish a history of Hebrew literature in general, but to study the features of this peculiar set of religious texts in relation to their usage within the historical community of ancient Israel (1980: 73).

Even within this context the canonical critics do not cast off the historical elements of the Old Testament. The history of the nation is interwoven with the history of the text in a way that makes the study of both necessary.

Various canonical studies of the prophets have appeared, mostly in article form. Many of these studies center on the unified message of written prophecy rather than on pre-textual matters. In his essay 'Patterns in the Prophetic Canon' Ronald Clements claims that canonical prophecy offers a unified message of coming judgment and eventual salvation. This unified message is what is unique about the prophets— not their social or psychological backgrounds. In fact, Clements argues:

1. The prophets were interpreted in relation to their message, not the special experiences of God which they encountered. Hence it was the message that was regarded as inspired, and the inspiration of the prophet was inferred from this.

2.	This message concerned the destruction and restoration of Israel, but special emphasis was attached to the latter...

3.	This message of restoration allowed great flexibility of interpretation as regards time, circumstances, and the particular form which Israel would assume in the time of its salvation (1977: 45).

Clements therefore shifts the uniqueness of prophecy from the men to their message.

Both Brevard Childs and Joseph Blenkinsopp agree with the basic conclusions of Clements. Blenkinsopp, however, uses canonical discoveries to reconstruct the redactional history of the prophets, to date the final form of the prophetic canon and to chart the rise of apocalyptic writing (1977: 96-123). By so doing he makes canonical prophecy a tool to settle once more some pre-textual issues. Childs displays some of these tendencies in his *Introduction to the Old Testament as Scripture*, but normally he does emphasize that canonical analysis can provide a way out of many of the impasses that have arisen in historical criticism. Thus, for Childs, it is more productive to discuss, for instance, the canonical significance of Isaiah 40–44 than to argue its authorship, date, origin, etc. So Childs tries to bridge the gaps between the historical and canonical approaches without losing his distinctive ideas about the final form of the text.

Quite obviously a thoroughgoing canonical approach to prophecy is a revolutionary change from most of the older methods. The most fundamental difference is that generally canonical critics deal with written prophecy instead of the background of that prophecy. These critics realize that it is the prophetic message that has been most important to the community of faith in the Old Testament and to the Christian Church as well. Their methods open the way for studies that arise out of issues in the text. Written prophecy can now be highlighted.

Finally, some of the new literary approaches to prophecy must be mentioned. Several studies of narrative and poetry have appeared, but precious few literary critical works on prophecy have been published. Except in a very scattered way

structuralist and reader-response critics have not yet contributed to prophetic studies. The field has thereby been left to
rhetorical and formalistic scholars. Even these analyses are in
a very beginning stage and need to be supplemented by more
work.

James Muilenburg coined the phrase 'rhetorical' criticism
in his 1969 article 'Form Criticism and Beyond'. Basically
Muilenburg's method is to analyze the components of speech
into paragraphs, sentences and phrases so the overall artistry
of a text can emerge. Muilenburg's work has inspired a number of rhetorical analyses of prophetic books, pericopae and
phrases. For each published work there is probably at least one
unpublished dissertation using this method. The problem with
rhetorical criticism, at least for this book, is that it is more
effective with short passages than books or groups of books.
The various syntactical gems of a pericope do not always lead
to an overall grasp of a group of pericopae. Though rhetorical
critics deal well with the final text, their approach cannot be
the only way of looking at the Twelve.

John D.W. Watts has produced the longest literary-critical
commentary on a prophetic book. His work on Isaiah 1–33 in
the Word Biblical Commentary attempts to show the unity of
Isaiah 1–33 by treating the text as a drama. The material is
divided into acts, scenes, and speeches. Various characters are
introduced, and plot is charted. This innovative approach
illuminates every aspect of the written prophecy, thus making
a real contribution to prophetic studies. More such commentary work needs to be done if the literary-critical approach is
to make a significant impact on prophetic analysis.

A book that has treated a minor prophet through literary-
critical means is my *Zephaniah—a Prophetic Drama*. This
work surveys genre criticism, does a close reading of Zephaniah, and concludes that Zephaniah is a drama cast in a comic
prophetic mode. The unity of the book is recognized, including
the so-called 'addition', 3.14-20. As in Watts' book, the important thing is the final form of the prophecy, and the final form
is a unified construction—not a collection of disparate but
related pericopae.

While more literary-critical studies of the prophets are
needed, the work already done proves the usefulness of the

method. Literary critics deal with the text to reveal its artful-
ness and multiplicity of meaning. Every aspect of a book is
explored to find the keys of meaning in texts. Robert Alter
offers a good definition of literary criticism when he writes:

> By literary analysis I mean the manifold varieties of
> minutely discriminating attention to the artful use of lan-
> guage, to the shifting play of ideas, convention, tone, sound,
> imagery, syntax, narrative viewpoint, compositional units,
> and much else; the kind of disciplined attention, in other
> words, which through a whole spectrum of critical
> approaches has illuminated, for example, the poetry of
> Dante, the plays of Shakespeare, the novels of Tolstoy (1981:
> 12-13).

In other words, the literary critic seeks to explicate every
aspect of the final, written form of biblical texts. A methodology
for a literary study of the minor prophets will be suggested
later in this chapter.

Like the canonical critics, literary scholars provide new
ways of looking at prophecy. The literature is examined, not
the pre-history of the literature. Looking at the Bible's literary
aspects is no more harmful than tracing its historical background, life situations, or theological perspectives. The Bible is
still a God-inspired book, and is recognized as such. What is
sought in literary analysis is the results of how that inspired
Book is shaped as literature. I hope that a look at the literary
aspects of the minor prophets will yield results about their
unity that have escaped the researches that use other methods.

Before moving to other issues, it is proper to note the
significant achievements of conservative scholarship in
prophetic studies. Since the reformation conservatives have
tried to chart the historical backgrounds, philological patterns,
theological concerns, and life situations of the prophets. Their
careful research has produced a wealth of material related to
these areas. This method of research is normally called the
grammatical-historical approach, as befits its interest in textual and historical matters.

Martin Luther and John Calvin are really the fathers of
this method. Both wrote commentaries on the prophets that
reflected definite expositional and theological concerns, but the

foundations of their studies were historical backgrounds and philological discussions. They chart the author, date and situations of the various books, then offer comments on individual verses. Even critical scholars have followed their agenda to a great extent.

Scores of treatments of the prophetic books have come from grammatical-historical scholars since the nineteenth century. Much valuable interpretative data has arisen from these researches. In these works two very clear viewpoints have arisen. The first of these tendencies is to react to non-traditional commentaries. R.K. Harrison's massive *Introduction to the Old Testament* is a prominent example of skillful reactive criticism. Harrision charts in tremendous detail the notions of non-traditional scholars concerning date, authorship, setting, etc. He then very carefully argues for such conservative ideas as the unity of Isaiah and an early date for Daniel. Very few of the higher-critical scholars display Harrison's familiarity with the wide spectrum of Old Testament studies. As editor of the New International Commentary on the Old Testament, Harrison is exercising a strong influence on new studies of the prophets.

At least as significant as the reactive strain of grammatical-historical critics is the tendency of other conservative writers to note more critical analyses and then produce a historical, textual presentation in the tradition of Luther and Calvin. John Oswalt's recent commentary *Isaiah 1–39* in the New International Commentary on the Old Testament series is a good representative of such treatments. Oswalt argues for the unity of Isaiah's authorship, but focuses on theological and exegetical questions. It is not the main purpose of the commentary to face and refute opinions with which he disagrees. Rather, Oswalt attempts to place Isaiah in its historical context, translate the text, and offer comments on the text. Like Harrison, Oswalt's work is extremely thorough and valuable.

As is true of most of the approaches to prophecy surveyed above, conservative scholarship has added greatly to prophetic studies. Exegetical commentaries deal very seriously with the text and have displayed a consistent ability to uncover what a text means today by showing what it meant in the past. Despite this excellence, grammatical-historical scholars, like their non-traditional counterparts, are more effective when dealing with small portions of a text. A book's larger picture, or the picture of a series of books, is rarely a major concern. Pericopae are elucidated without the book's overall scheme coming into focus. There is therefore room for explorations of the anatomy of whole books and groups of books.

As may be expected, treatments of the minor prophets have reflected the trends of prophetic studies in general. Each school of thought has contributed to a better understanding of the prophets. Source critics have pointed out the diverse nature of written prophecy. Various strands of thought may exist in books, even if these strands are from the same hand. Thus, the work of the writers featured in the International Critical Commentary is valuable because it forced interpreters to explore the possible unity or disunity of books. In short, these commentators declared that the minor prophets are complex books. More recent scholars like James Luther Mays have continued the process of separating 'non-authentic' and 'authentic' oracles. So important to Mays is this process that he writes, 'an account of the mission and message of Micah depends upon a decision about which of the sayings collected in the books derive from him' (1976: 12). Therefore the interpretation of the minor prophets hinges on its redactional layers since each passage is best understood in its historical context.

Of course the problem with source-critical analyses is they tend to atomize books. Prophecies cannot be treated as unities, source critics claim, because most books are collections of oracles from different authors living in various time periods. If no single book is a unity, then it is nonsense to call the minor prophets the *book* of the twelve. In fact the number twelve should be multiplied to include the number of redactors who handled these prophecies. Obviously a sense of unity must arise from another method of analysis.

Psychological studies of the minor prophets have also sought to demonstrate the diversity of prophecy. Scholars like Hölscher and Lindblom have tried to show that Israel's prophets are not unique, but rather have the same kinds of experiences as the prophets in neighboring countries. Their prophecies were given when a spirit of ecstasy fell upon them, a phenomenon that also supposedly occurred in places other than Israel. Even the written, canonical prophecies reflect this ecstatic context, since they are collections of speeches uttered during a prophet's lifetime and messages added to the collections long after the original prophets were dead.

Several criticisms of psychological analyses deserve mention. First, these scholars, like source critics, use the text as a way of getting back to the situation of the prophet. The written literature does not receive attention because of its own inherent value. Second, the uniqueness of the prophetic office is lost. Certainly other nations had prophets, but Hebrew prophets claimed to have a special word from Yahweh, the God of all the earth. All Biblical faith hinges at least partly on the truth of this claim. Third, psychological criticism is a very subjective discipline. Otto Kaiser makes this point very clearly when he writes:

> There is a limit to the possibilities of psychological analysis imposed by the nature of the sources. For the prophets were concerned not to describe their extraordinary situations and experiences, but to carry out the commission given to them. For this reason any psychological inquiry is dependent largely on analogical deductions and circumstantial evidence, in which the comparative material must be taken from our own period (1977: 210).

Form criticism and rhetorical analysis at first glance offers more hope to one exploring the possible unity of the minor prophets because both methods assume the importance of the written text. Both disciplines examine and explicate pericopae in an extremely thorough fashion. Very few analyses of the minor prophets could hope to surpass H.W. Wolff's commentaries on Hosea, Joel, and Amos in linguistic and theological insight. Claus Westermann's *Basic Forms of Prophetic Speech* likewise offers an excellent survey of the typical kinds of oracles found in the prophets.

Ironically, their emphasis on exhaustive treatments of individual paragraphs keep form and rhetorical scholars' from noting the overall picture of books. They feel a prophetic book is a series of loosely connected speeches at best, and virtually unconnected speeches at worst. No notion of unity can come from this attitude save what is found within small units of speech. It is again nonsense to speak of twelve books displaying unity in any comprehensive sense. Just as ironic is the fact that the methodologies of form and rhetorical criticism can help provide data from short passages that will lead to the perception of unity in larger prophetic sections. If a single pericope can be illuminated by careful observation, then so can a book or group of books.

Though tradition critics also tend to attempt to use a book to get back to the people behind the text, their desire to trace common biblical traditions brings some notion of unity to the prophetic corpus. Common traditions lead to common writing. When several prophetic books utilize similar ideas their message becomes a coherent whole.

Gerhard von Rad has noted various themes and traditions that run throughout the minor prophets. No motif is more prevalent than the Day of Yahweh, as von Rad claims in *The Message of the Prophets* (1967: 95). God's cataclysmic day of judgment permeates the Twelve, constantly reminding the reader of its punishing and restoring nature. As a regular feature in several books, the Day of Yahweh helps unify the teachings of the canonical prophets. Other overriding themes serve the same purpose.

Beyond the recognition of unifying traditions like the Day of Yahweh in the minor prophets, von Rad's most significant contribution to an understanding of the unity of these books is his emphasis on common literary elements in the prophetic canon. Even in the midst of what he feels is great diversity among the prophets von Rad finds enough coherence in them to declare:

> Nevertheless, however bewildering the ease with which the prophets pass from one form of address to another, there are two constant factors which never fail to find a place with them all. The one is Yahweh's new work for Israel which he allowed the prophet to read off the horizon of world-history. The other is the election tradition, within which the prophet and his hearers alike stand (1967: 101).

Election, however, is constantly tempered with punishment promises to remind Israel and the nations to be holy. Von Rad explains that the comfortable words of the tradition are, however, both called in question by the prophet's message of judgment and reconverted by him into an anti-typical new form of prediction. Thus, tensions created by three factors bring the prophet's *kerygma* into being. These are: the new eschatological word with which Yahweh addresses Israel, the old election tradition, and the personal situation, be it one which incurred penalty or one which needed comfort, of the people addressed by the prophet (1967: 101).

Two elements, then, a new eschatological word for the prophet's original audience and the divine choosing of Israel, are located by von Rad in most, if not all, of the minor prophets. These twin themes are seen as the very essence of the prophetic message. If the essence of prophecy is thematic and can be traced throughout the Twelve, then there is the possibility that unity in the minor prophets can be demonstrated. Certainly more evidence must surface, but von Rad's comments are a step in the right direction.

No one could correctly claim that von Rad's main critical purpose was to tie the prophets together. What he was really concerned with was the discovery of traditions that help explain the compilation and redaction of the prophetic books. This attempt to get behind the text is not helpful to the present study. Still, the very notion that some traditions appear in all prophecy contributes somewhat to the search for other possible traces of overarching unity in the Twelve.

Despite its valuable contribution to an understanding of the background of the prophets, sociological analysis does not ultimately lead to a view of the interrelatedness of the minor prophets. As may be expected, sociological criticism fails to note the unique nature of biblical prophecy in much the same way as psychological analysis. It also contains many subjective elements. Robert Wilson's careful explanation of northern and southern sociological patterns in the Twelve may explain some of the diversity of the books. The recognition of various regional traditions behind the books, though, makes it probable that each individual prophecy has national, regional, and local sociological influences behind them. Therefore, once again the unity of the literature is exploded, and once again the pre-history of the text takes precedence over the canonical writings themselves. Even where this approach is correct it is not able, because it is not its intention, to explain the canonical-literary likenesses of the minor prophets.

As was mentioned above, canonical criticism seeks to deal with the prophecies as we have them and to explain the significance of their final form. Brevard Childs' *Introduction to the Old Testament as Scripture* discusses both the concept of the former and latter prophets and the canonical shape of individual books. He does not claim to explain the significance of the form of the Twelve, though he does comment on the final canonical shaping of the individual books. Childs asserts that the various orders of the major prophets in the canon argues against any discernible purpose for the present configuration of the 15 prophetic books (1980: 310). This idea may be true for the general position of individual prophecies, but the fact remains that the Twelve were almost always ordered in ancient times as they are today. Childs may not deal with the canonical unity of the minor prophets as a whole, but his approach does make it possible for the question of whether these books constitute a coherent body of literature to be posed.

Ronald Clements' 'Patterns in the Prophetic Canon' is a significant article because it illuminates the canonical shape of the Twelve in several ways. First, the piece argues that the essence of prophecy is located in its message rather than in some aspect of its pre-history (1977: 45). Second, Clements says that the prophetic corpus is a unified construction. Third, he observes that this unity comes from the prophet's emphasis on punishment and restoration. Clements states that

> it is rather precisely the element of connectedness between the prophets, and the conviction that they were all referring to a single theme of Israel's destruction and renewal, which has facilitated the ascription to each of them of the message of hope which some of their number had proclaimed after 587 BC. In this way the collection of the various prophetic sayings into books, and of these books into collections, has been a process which was concerned to present the wholeness of the prophetic message, not an attempt to preserve separately the *ipsissima verba* of individual prophetic personalities (1977: 48-49).

Finally, Clements' serious attempt to find patterns in the prophetic portion of the canon, like Childs' work, leads to further research. Some steps have been taken towards recognizing binding elements in the minor prophets, and the way has been cleared for further exploration.

Canonical critics must be commended for trying to see the prophets as a group instead of a series of unconnected oracles. They have made it possible to talk seriously of written prophecy instead of what lies behind written prophecy. Only when this method becomes a mere tool of source and redaction criticism does it lose its distinctiveness. Though canonical analysis does not finally answer the problem of the Twelve's unity, it does ask the right questions about that unity and offers some suggestions for finding the needed answers.

Like canonical critics, literary scholars treat the text as it now exists. Little if any effort is expended on extensive explorations of authorship, date, redaction or historical setting. These elements of the Old Testament are not considered unimportant, but are just not major concerns in a literary analysis of scripture. When historical judgments are mixed with literary comments both areas can suffer. Perhaps the major difficulty with John Watts' work on Isaiah is that too many historical statements are made in this thoroughgoing literary-critical analysis. It is not really necessary to make declarations about date and redaction when the main focus of a study is to demonstrate the unified nature of Isaiah.

Even with some minor flaws, Watts makes some tremendous contributions to literary works on the prophets. Perhaps the largest of these contributions is that Watts shows it is possible to find unified literary patterns in a major prophet. That Isaiah 1–33 can function as a drama means its characters, plot, structure, and themes form a symmetrical whole. Another advance is that the dramatic form in no way obscures the theology of Isaiah. In fact, it is unfolded in a very clear fashion. Finally, the dramatic approach to Isaiah is a very effective way to illuminate the character of Yahweh, Isaiah and Israel. Therefore, there is no doubt that much that is vital to Isaiah's prophecy emerges in Watts' commentary. His ability to demonstrate unity, theological clarity, and character development offers hope that similar success will come in a study of the minor prophets.

Besides my book on Zephaniah, there are almost no literary studies of individual books in the Twelve. Some other writing on the prophets, however, has appeared. Robert Alter discusses the nature of prophetic poetry in *The Art of Biblical Poetry*. Alter's book is quite instructive, for it explains how poetry works in prophecy. For Alter, Old Testament poetry is more than a series of parallel lines that have no clear relationship. Each set of parallel statements leads to another, more informative, set of lines. Prophetic couplets are thus closely interlinked parts of a poetic argument or narrative. The prophets achieve arguments and stories chiefly by having verbal connections between neighboring couplets, but also by using these likenesses as a springboard to the next part of the prophecy. To illustrate his idea of how a line becomes a story Alter presents Joel 2.1-19 and comments:

> The poet here is less interested in an illusion of seamless temporal progression than in a steady, solemn advance— spatially, from the distant mountains up to and over the walls of the city and into the houses—marked by a mounting drumbeat, and for this the model of incremental repetition is particularly apt: they run, they dance, they run, they scale a wall, they go; indeed, they go, they swarm, they run, they scale, they come in at the windows like thieves (1985: 43).

Beyond his analysis of how poetic prophecy utilizes 'incremental repetition', Alter contributes to the study of the minor prophets through his exploration of the major modes of prophetic poetry. He contends that

> the overarching purpose is reproof (and not, I would contend, prediction), and this general aim is realized through three related poetic strategies: (1) direct accusation; (2) satire; (3) the monitory evocation of impending disaster (1985: 141).

All three basic modes are meant to bring hearers to repentance. Alter's explication of these types is thorough and convincing, and will be consulted later in this book. At this point, however, it suffices to say that Alter's serious look at the prophets provides several new avenues of understanding prophecy. The most glaring omission in Alter's three categories is the absence of the many examples of hope and restoration in the prophets. Certainly, reproof and judgment are major motifs in the prophetic canon, but they are counterbalanced by promises of forgiveness and reconciliation.

Despite the presence of the above-mentioned literary-critical works, it is obvious that the field is wide open for more writing in this area. Literary criticism can illuminate the prophetic literature in a number of ways, but is particularly able to demonstrate the unity of single books, as is evidenced in Watts' *Isaiah 1–33*. It is also a good methodology for exploring the possible areas of unity in groups of books like the Pentateuch, the historical books, and the prophets. Perhaps literary-critical methods will be as successful in demonstrating the unity of the Twelve as other types of analysis have been in declaring its diversity.

What has been learned, then, from this brief overview of scholarship on prophecy in general and the minor prophets in particular? First, all types of criticism recognize the historical fact of the present form of the Twelve. They further note that the Twelve were considered a single book by the ancient community of faith, and posit that the date of the books and catchwords in the books explain somewhat the present configuration. Still, there is no convincing theory of how, or if, the twelve books function as one unified, canonical construction. Second, most studies of the Twelve focus on their diversity rather than their unity. What has been stressed is the many elements that combined to create the canonical text we possess. That canonical text itself has not received much attention. Third, the work completed on the prophets has been quite exhaustive. If new insight is to be gained it must probably arise from a fresh approach. Finally, this overview proves that the unity of the minor prophets remains an unsolved critical question. Maybe it is unsolved because it has not been explored, but it is unsolved nonetheless.

Since the significance of the canonical shape of the Twelve is as yet undiscovered, there is a need for work in this area. If there are overriding elements of unity in the Twelve the whole notion of biblical prophecy will be illuminated. Likenesses in the minor prophets could help explain how the community of faith defined prophecy and how it affected them. Quite obviously the interpretation of prophecy would thereby be improved both for the academy and for the church. A last benefit of unity in prophecy would be a better understanding of the Old Testament. Unity, where it can truly be demonstrated, can provide a balance to the constant claim of diversity that comes from so many biblical scholars.

Methodology

If the normally accepted methods of approaching the prophets have either not considered or not discovered the unity of the Twelve, then some new tool of analysis must be sought. As one might assume from my previous comments, two methodologies offer promise for discovering possible unity in the minor prophets. The first, canonical criticism, asks the right questions to discover unity, while the second, literary criticism, provides the actual means of uncovering unity. Both methodologies deal with the canonical text, look for symmetry rather than diversity, and take seriously the notion that unity in a group of books is possible. Both tend to deal with literature, too, instead of historical backgrounds.

The very presence of *canonical* analysis allows the interpreter of the Twelve to wonder why the books are ordered as they are. Further, *the* question is not how the books came to be arranged as they are, but is how they are to be understood as they now appear. Of course the presupposition behind these queries is that there is some significance in canonical shaping. That significance can only arise, though, from the text itself and not from theories of how or why prophets and redactors worked as they did. In other words, the final literary product is the only indication of the importance of the order of the prophecies. The final literary product must therefore receive the most critical attention if unity is to emerge.

Despite its ability to pose the problem this study seeks to solve, canonical criticism is not the best methodology to explore the question of unity in the Twelve. While unity is a canonical concern, it is also a major facet of literary criticism. Canonical scholars often use their findings to get behind the text to the history of the literature, which is a tendency literary critics avoid. Another problem with canonical analysis is that its major proponents (e.g. Childs) deal more carefully with individual books than larger sections of scripture. Ronald Clements is an exception to this generalization, but his work typifies literary criticism at several points, especially when he urges 'devoting more attention than has usually been given to the literary structure and "patterns" of the written prophetic collections' (1977: 43-44). In fact, Clements' work is the strongest argument that literary analysis can help answer questions raised by canonical criticism, for when he speaks of canonical unity he bases his claims on a study of literary plots and themes. This book does not reject canonical criticism, rather it attempts to begin with the observations of that methodology and then demonstrate the literary strands that justify those observations.

Several types of literary analysis have been utilized recently in biblical studies. Among these methodologies are structuralism, reader-response criticism, psychological analysis, poetic studies, narratology, formalism, archetypal criticism, comparative-literature approaches, rhetorical analysis, and genre studies. Because I surveyed many of these critical approaches in *Zephaniah—a Prophetic Drama*, and because other writers have provided similar overviews, I will not write detailed summaries of each type of analysis. Instead I will note the methodologies that are pertinent to the present work. Only those that advance an understanding of unity in large blocks of literature will be used.

Since structuralism and rhetorical analysis are most effective when applied to small units of literature they will not be used in this book. These two methodologies are not invalid means of approaching texts, but they are not very helpful when attempting to draw together aspects of twelve prophecies. Psychological criticism and reader-response analysis are likewise rejected, but for a different reason. Both types emphasize something besides the text itself. The former tries to understand the psyche of the author, while the latter focuses on how literature affects its readers. A comparative-literature approach, though informative for other kinds of inquiries, does not aid this work because this type of criticism needs the final results of a close reading before it can compare one piece of literature to another. Perhaps the Twelve could be part of a comparative approach after this study, but at this point the necessary data does not exist.

The remainder of the above-mentioned approaches contribute something to any full-scale literary exploration of individual or multiple artistic pieces. Most important for this work is American formalism, or what is commonly referred to as New Criticism, which began as a reaction to non-textual critical approaches like historical analysis. John Crowe Ransom, Allen Tate, Cleanth Brooks and Robert Penn Warren are the most famous of the early formalists. They believed literary pieces were valuable because of what they said instead of for the historical setting or psychological aspects behind the work. In short, the text has life and value in and of itself. Therefore the interpretation of a work must begin with its literary elements.

Formalistic analyses normally begin with a close reading of the text in question. Such artistic aspects as themes, motifs, plots, characterization, setting, imagery and point of view are scrutinized so what the text says and how it says it can emerge. Once the individual parts have been examined, the whole piece is then better understood. Every creative work is a whole made up of parts, but that wholeness must be kept primary lest the overarching beauty of a text disappear. At no time should the formalistic close reading cause the disintegration of the literature it seeks to illuminate. Thus, formalism dissects texts in order to achieve a unified picture of those texts.

Many of the current trends in narratology coincide with the basic tenets of formalism. Studies of types of narrators and audiences, distances between the two, sincerity and possibilities of both, or the positions (moral, historical, etc.) of either help explain the intricacies of plot, characterization, mode, etc. Only when the author's treatment of his creative world and proposed reader is clarified can the interpreter make declarative statements about the meaning of an individual text. Narrative theories also show how a literary work holds together as a unit. If some common narrative techniques occur frequently in a work then one of the keys of the piece's unity has been uncovered.

Studies of how poetry functions as art are direct descendants of formalism. The early formalists spent a great deal of time analyzing the intricacies of verse, and were particularly successful in describing how each word, phrase, image, etc. in poems creates an artistic whole. Since then the whole field of poetic exposition has been enriched by this methodology. Indeed even studies of biblical poetry are indebted to the formalists, for when Robert Alter, for example, explores Old Testament verse it is through a formalistic methodology, as he states, 'For the most part, I proceed through close readings of specimens of the poetry because that seemed to me the best way to recover a sense of the intricate artistry of the poems' (1985: ix). It is therefore prudent to use formalistic techniques as a way of better understanding the verse sections of the Twelve. Close readings of minor prophets' texts could help reveal some unifying elements in the poetics of these twelve books.

Archetypal criticism may also aid this study, since the clear depiction of recurring symbols in literature points to unity in texts. Northrop Frye has demonstrated in both *The Anatomy of Criticism* and *The Great Code* that there are several dominant motifs in the Bible. Such common symbols include Heaven and Hell, God and Satan, and Creation and Judgment. Frye very correctly argues that some of these themes are in both the Old and New Testaments, which further reveals their ability to unify sacred texts. Such overarching archetypes appear in the Twelve. Ideas like the Day of Yahweh, the remnant, restoration, and human sin move through the minor prophets, clarifying and expanding their meanings with every fresh repetition. Such notions also tie the books together, thus making these many prophecies present a unified picture.

Finally, genre studies are vital to this book as well. Before any literature can be properly interpreted its literary type must be uncovered. C.S. Lewis states:

> The first qualification for judging any piece of workmanship from a corkscrew to a cathedral is to know *what* it is—what it was intended to do and how it is meant to be used... The first thing is to understand the object before you: as long as you think the corkscrew was meant for opening tins or the

cathedral for entertaining tourists you can say nothing to the
purpose about them (1959: 1).

The debate about the nature of prophecy surveyed above is
related to the issue of genre, since scholars have argued over
what prophecy really is. What is still a very open question is
what *written* prophecy *is*. If all the Twelve share common
elements of the same genre—prophecy—then, inevitably,
certain unifying generic aspects exist. Various sub-genres
might also appear that tie the Twelve together. On the other
hand, a wide diversity in these areas could argue against any
strong sense of symmetry in the books.

From the methodologies mentioned some basic conclusions
surface. One is that the final, fixed form of the Twelve has
value in and of itself. These texts are the basis for any real
understanding of Old Testament prophecy; indeed they are
practically the only primary sources we have concerning the
prophets. What is most important for this study, then, is to
understand the content of the minor prophetic books. A second
conclusion is that the Twelve *could* be a unified, coherent
whole. It is inexcusable to assume before the fact that their
final form is diverse because their origins are diverse. These
prophecies must have the opportunity to speak for themselves.
In short, this work assumes that the canonical question of the
significance of the ordering of the minor prophets may be
answered if proper literary methods are applied to the
prophecies.

Since a literary piece's genre is a major factor in its analysis,
chapter two explores the notion of the prophetic genre and any
sub-genres that may grow from that genre. 'What is
prophecy?' is the question this section hopes to answer, and
beyond that query hopes to discover how this definition affects
the Twelve. Sub-genres are compared to see if they help unify
all the books.

Chapter 3 uses the generic information to help delineate the
structure of the Twelve. The definition of prophecy in Chapter
2 helps immensely in seeing how the prophecies have been
woven together. Theological ideas like sin, punishment, and
restoration are noted as major structural devices. There is
definitely some overlap in the framework of the Twelve, but

the overlap serves to demonstrate the validity of the framework itself.

Plot is explored in Chapter 4 as a natural outworking of the structure of the minor prophets. Structure and plot must certainly work as one lest a text lose its focus, and this analytical tenet is as true in the Twelve as it is in any piece of literature. If the plot and framework of these books are not reconcilable, then the group is hardly a unity. The dynamics of plot are discussed, as well as the validity of discussing a story line in the prophetic corpus.

Once genre, structure and plot are outlined, it is necessary to proceed to study the inner workings of a text. Chapter 5 begins this process by examining characterization in the minor prophets. Two main characters, or types of characters, are the focal points of this section. Yahweh is portrayed in various ways in these texts. How God is presented is, of course, vital to their theological emphases. This presentation is also important, though, to the unity of the Twelve, since a stylized portrayal of the Lord may reflect a strong literary pattern. The second type of character that receives major attention in this chapter is the prophet. Prophets serve Yahweh and listeners-readers in a number of ways. They may be messengers for or co-revelators with Yahweh, or serve as exhorters and condemners for the people. How the prophets are portrayed again reveals the theology and literary techniques of the final form of the Twelve. Any unity of characterization across the minor prophets is significant, especially when that unity coincides with the group's genre, structure and plot. Less important figures who appear in the prophecies are also examined, but Yahweh and the prophets themselves must logically take precedence.

Perhaps no other subject in literary studies has created more discussion in the last twenty years than that of narration. How authors tell their stories, shape their poems, and present their messages is an extremely important consideration in the interpretation of literature. Chapter 6 utilizes recent works on narration in an effort to chart, if possible, the narrative voice of the minor prophets. Such subjects as the Twelve's implied author and audience are considered, as are the narrative worlds of the individual books. The aim of this section is to discover if the Twelve itself projects an overriding narrative voice. Any notion of the group's unity depends in a large degree upon how clearly a coherent narrative voice can be discerned in these texts.

Finally, Chapter 7 summarizes the study by drawing together the areas of unity in the Twelve and by noting places where unity does not exist. Implications for the interpretations of the books are noted, as well as pathways for further research. I hope that this work can help stimulate interest in the unified nature of the minor prophetic literature. For too long scholarship has stressed the ways in which the prophetic writings fail to hold together. Otto Kaiser sums up this attitude when he claims:

> If a prophetic book is judged by modern literary standards, in spite of the arrangement by subject matter which editors have attempted to introduce, it will often seem more like accumulated chaos than a planned whole. The lack of a reliable criterion for original speech units, the minimal number of descriptions of situation (which are often in any case secondary), the lack of chronological order, and the arrangement of individual sayings, which is often only by catchwords, mean that the expositor dealing with the original unity of a speech, its authorship and date must start by freeing himself entirely from the tradition given in the book, and base his view on his own work (1977: 292).

Such a negative view must be allowed to be the final word on this literature. A new approach to the material may indeed yield ways of seeing whole books and collections instead of fragments poorly pieced together.

Chapter 2

THE GENRE OF THE TWELVE

Introduction

As was clearly stated in Chapter 1, despite the great volume of scholarly writing on prophecy that has appeared, there have been very few attempts to properly define 'prophecy' and 'prophetic' as literary terms. This omission is quite surprising in view of the fact that the compilers of the Old Testament canon evidently felt the prophetic books reflected an individual genre. The prophets' separation from the Law and the Writings supports this conclusion. Admittedly, it could be argued that there is some canonical blurring of generic distinction when Joshua through Kings is designated 'former prophets' and Isaiah through Malachi is termed 'latter prophets'. Historical divergences cannot account totally for the two names, since there is some parallel material in both kinds of prophecy. This book is, obviously, most concerned with the latter prophets, so the generic definition that is presented comes from those books. Why one section is separated from the other, and indeed why so-called historical books like Samuel and Kings are called prophecy at all, must wait for further research.

Since the Old Testament portrays prophecy as a particular type of literature, surely some understanding of that type must be attempted. Such an understanding would definitely aid a discussion of the unity of the Twelve since that unity exists nowhere if not in the books' literary form. Two items are necessary when approaching the prophetic genre. First, a concise definition of genre is needed. Too often genre has meant whatever a critic wanted it to mean at any given point in a discussion. Second, a way to apply the definition of genre to the prophets must emerge. Without this practical concern generic studies of prophecy will become as splintered as their historical predecessors.

C. Hugh Holman points out the need for precise ideas about genre, which he defines as

> a term used in literary criticism to designate the distinct types of categories into which literary works are grouped according to form or technique or, sometimes, subject matter. The term comes from French, where it means 'kind' or 'type'. In its customary application, it is used loosely, since the varieties of literary 'kinds' and the principles on which they are made are numerous (1972: 239).

Holman's contention that genres are distinguishable by their various forms and subject matters is certainly correct. He is also right when he says these distinctions are usually very loosely applied. Quite often, in fact, they are applied almost at random. Nearly every type of literature is seen as a genre unto itself instead of a part of a larger whole. Holman sums up the problem when he adds:

> The traditional *genres* include such 'kinds' as tragedy, comedy, epic, lyric, pastoral. Today a division of literature into *genres* would also include novel, short story, essay, and, perhaps, radio or television play. The difficulty resulting from the loose use of the term is easily illustrated: novel designates a *genre*, but so does picaresque novel; lyric designates a *genre*, but so does sonnet, as do both elegy and pastoral elegy (1972: 239).

Surely Holman's point is that more precise categories of genre can and should be forwarded. The above-mentioned notion of genre leads one to believe that, since each individual artistic piece is unique and valuable, each new literary work constitutes a genre. To borrow from Holman's illustration, *Don Quixote* could belong to a picaresque novel of the land genre and *Huckleberrry Finn* to a picaresque novel of the river genre. If so, genre studies really cease to matter.

Perhaps a good place to seek a cohesive definition of genre is in the writings of Aristotle, one of the fathers of genre analysis. Holman states that form and subject matter help set apart genre, which is a claim made by Aristotle. When he wrote his definition of genre in *Poetics*, Aristotle primarily mentioned poetic types because these were the major artistic forms of his age. His methodology is still excellent, however, for examining both prose and poetic forms. He writes:

> I propose to treat of Poetry in itself and of its various kinds, noting the essential quality of each; to inquire into the number and nature of the parts of which a poem is composed; and similarly into whatever else falls within the same inquiry (1974: ch.1, 31).

This statement demonstrates that Aristotle is convinced that the best way to describe a piece's genre is to examine its literary 'parts'. In this way he prefigures the formalists' emphasis on close reading. If one is to analyze the parts of a composition, what parts should be discussed? Aristotle lists three areas that separate genres:

> Epic poetry and Tragedy, Comedy also and Dithyrambic poetry, and the music of the flute and of the lyre in most of their forms, are all in their general conception modes of imitation. They differ, however, from one another in three respects—the medium, the objects, the manner or mode of imitation, being in each case distinct (1974: 31).

By 'medium' Aristotle means the kind of language a writer employs. In other words, whether an author writes in poetry, prose, or both. Further, if he composes poetry what kind of rhythm-meter he employs is important. Quite interesting is the fact that Aristotle believes poetry and prose may be mixed, and poets may make use of more than one meter in a composition. Such mixed forms can coexist in genres that have more static forms. He concludes:

> There is another art which imitates by means of language alone, and that either in prose or verse—which verse, again, may either combine different meters or consist of but one kind... There are, again, some arts which employ all the means above mentioned—namely, rhythm, tune and meter (1974: 32).

Thus, genres may be distinguished by their usage of a single linguistic form or a combination of linguistic forms.

Aristotle's second feature, objects of imitation, points to the content of a literature, to the idea 'that we must represent men either as better than in real life, or as worse, or as they

are' (1974: ch. 2, 32). When the characters are thus drawn
their morals, motivations, strengths, faults, prejudices, etc.
become apparent. Portraying the hero, for instance, as better
than other human beings can create tragedy, while the presentation of the hero as inferior to others may indicate the
comedic genre. Very obviously, then, the subject matter, as
revealed in characters, themes, and plots, helps separate
varying types of literature.

Lastly, the manner or mode of imitation refers to narration.
Aristotle's concept of narration sums up the major genres:

> For the medium being the same, and the objects the same,
> the poet may imitate by narration—in which case he can
> either take another personality as Homer does, or speak in
> his own person, unchanged—or he may present all his
> characters as living and moving before us (1974: ch. 3, 33).

Epics normally are narrated by some person chosen by the
author, lyrics are narrated by the author himself, and dramas
are narrated (if that is a good term for what happens in plays)
through direct presentation. Again, the value of Aristotle's category is clear. The author's use of first person, third person, or
direct narration affects the nature of the literature. There is
some overlap among forms, but some types of narration are
definitely more effective when used in certain specific genres.

Aristotle's three means of defining major literary forms
offer a concrete methodology for exploring various genres.
Even prose narrative, a genre yet undeveloped to any extent in
Aristotle's era, can be analyzed according to these criteria.
That the prose genre must be added to the three classical
forms of epic, lyric, and drama has been an opinion held for
some time. The presence of such prose sub-types as the novel,
short story, and novella make this assertion necessary.
Though prose narration often intersects with other genres,
especially drama, it constitutes its own genre because it does
differ from epic, lyric, and drama in its medium, content, and
manner of imitation. In short, prose entails a means of presentation quite foreign to its classical counterparts. Northrop
Frye explains this vital distinction when he asserts that

> we have to speak of the *radical* of presentation if the distinc-
> tions of acted, spoken, and written word are to mean any-

> thing in the age of the printing press. One may print a lyric
> or read a novel aloud, but such incidental changes are not
> enough in themselves to alter the genre. For all the loving
> care that is rightfully expended on the printed texts of
> Shakespeare's plays, they are still radically acting scripts,
> and belong to the genre of drama (1967: 247).

It is therefore safe to conclude that Aristotle's three aspects of
genre are present in prose narrative, but are packaged, or presented, in a new way.

Perhaps at this point a brief summary of the preceding
conclusions is prudent. According to Aristotle, an individual
genre is defined as a type of literature whose combination of
medium, content, and narration differs significantly from
other types of literature. Northrop Frye calls this combination
of factors a literary piece's 'presentation'. Any of the three
elements could overlap with those of other genres, but the
combination or presentation of the three characteristics are
unique. Four rather broad categories arise from this definition:
epic, lyric, drama and prose fiction or narration. It must be
assumed, however, that other genres could develop if their
manner of presentation differs from that of the classical literary forms.

Because the proposed definition only creates broad generic
forms, some method of describing the various writings that
agree in form but diverge in substance is necessary. In other
words, the term 'sub-genre' needs a definition. Sub-genres are
vital to the whole discussion of literary types because they
grow out of their larger counterparts, offering diversity to
established forms. They are also important in that they bring
order to the study of genres. If the excesses noted by Holman
are avoided, it is only by understanding that each new variation on an older form is just a variation and not an entirely
new artistic category. Proper interpretations of literature are
more probable when a work is studied in the context of its literary tradition than if it is examined in isolation.

One way to define sub-genre is to realize that sub-genres
arise when authors take aspects of existing genres and develop
them in some unique way. For example, Shakespeare created
his version of the sonnet by adapting the Italian sonnet for his
own purposes. Similarly, it seems that dramatic comedy

appeared first as a reaction to its tragic counterpart. This way of looking at the notion of sub-genre emphasizes the creative nature of literature without rejecting all means of coherent interpretation. A sub-genre therefore exhibits the characteristics of its genre, but also displays some variation of its genre.

Just how many sub-genres are possible is an open question. Again, some critics choose to allow for as many sub-types as there are works of literature. Such methods must be rejected on the grounds that sub-genres, like genres, must have some frame of reference or they are not open to responsible commentary. Alastair Fowler reflects on these matters by observing:

> There naturally arises the question of how far sub-division should be taken. For we need not regard the absence of literary terms for the sub-genres as setting a limit. We need not confine ourselves to recognizing only those forms that our predecessors happened to name. However, subdivision beyond a certain stage becomes unwieldy, if only because it leads to as many subgenres as poems... (1982: 113).

Fowler's comments evidence a desire to allow a maximum of freedom in generic distinctions without allowing those distinctions to become meaningless. It is best to conclude that sub-genres consist of a number of largely similar works within a particular genre.

Thus, a sub-genre is a significant variation of an individual genre that has enough counterparts to allow sufficient comparison and interpretation. Certainly other definitions are possible, but this one allows this study to avoid the trap of the inability to explicate a number of works together. Sub-genres may vary in many ways from their main type. Still, they maintain their identification with their larger grouping through the basic adherence to a specific manner of presentation.

One other facet of genre requires definition before prophecy itself can be explored. Readers are often confused about a text's genre when a generic form appears within another generic type. Snatches of poetry may appear in a novel, or a novel may embody the principles of epic. Prose, or prose-like lines often appear in poetry, especially in modern and contemporary poetry. Or, the reader will notice that a particular mood or atmosphere is prevalent in a literary piece. Joy or gloom, contentment or bitterness, irony or simplicity are evident as the work unfolds. All these tendencies, of the mixing of genre or the existence of a persisting mood, come under the heading of a text's mode, or tone.

'Mode' is the overall attitude of a passage. If the author desires to accentuate a positive conclusion to, for instance, a novel, then aspects of comedy are employed. If a subtle cynicism is in order then irony becomes a major facet of a work. More possibilities exist of course, but these examples illustrate the concept of 'mode' well enough. The main strength of including mode in the generic discussion is that it helps demonstrate how one genre can illuminate another in a creative fashion. Without this concept minor variations within a genre can be mistaken for fundamental changes in the genre of a work. Various shades of authorial subtlety would therefore be lost.

Within any genre, then, there are sub-genres that contain the basic three elements Aristotle mentions, but that achieve some variation of those elements. Different modes may also appear that further explain the meaning of a text. Though these definitions do not and cannot explicate every area of any genre, they do offer a means of charting the basic tendencies of literary forms.

Prophecy as a Genre

Now that a tentative definition for genre, sub-genre, and mode is in place it is possible to discuss the nature of the prophetic genre. At the outset one very basic question must be addressed, which is whether prophecy should be subsumed under classical headings or stand as an individual genre on its own creative merit. While some prophecies reflect definite classical tendencies, prophecy varies enough from the classical types to warrant a generic classification and explanation of its own. Though he finds the classical genres in the Bible, Richard G. Moulton concludes that prophecy is a unique genre. Moulton claims:

> A second consideration must be mentioned as separating Hebrew from other literatures. When a reader turns over the

> pages of the bible, the department which will impress him
> most by its bulk and importance is one that is not founded
> upon any element of universal literature. This is the
> department of Prophecy (1899: 109).

The reason for this independence stems from the fact that

> Biblical Prophecy, in a sense that belongs to no other class of
> literature, presents itself as an actual Divine message. So far
> as form is concerned Prophecy is not distinctive but compre-
> hensive: all types of literature are attracted towards it, and,
> as will be seen at the proper place, the various literary forms
> are fused together into a new form in the Prophetic Rhap-
> sody (1899: 109).

Several cogent arguments for the uniqueness of a prophetic
genre materialize from Moulton's statements. First, he
observes that the rather large number of biblical prophecies,
not to mention their Near Eastern parallels, allows enough
data for the genre to emerge. Second, the constant claim of the
prophets to speak for God ('thus says the Lord') affords it an
unusual manner of presentation. Third, prophecy is a comprehensive genre that employs a number of literary features
to make its point. Its content is unique because of its specific
ethical admonitions, calls to repentance, threats of punishment and promises of future healing. The linguistic medium
and narration are likewise independent, largely because they
consist of a combination of methods.

How does prophecy relate, then, to the classical genres? In
much the same way the traditional types interact with one
another. Prophecy often highlights a narrative or dramatic
mode or point of view, and spawns sub-genres akin to those
found within epic, drama, lyric, and prose narrative. These
genres therefore help define and interpret prophecy without
inhibiting a description of it in any way.

Another issue is how prophecy relates to the rest of the Old
Testament. This problem does not pose *huge* difficulties, however, since the canon itself separates the law, prophets, and
writings. As will be seen, prophecy not only varies from the
law and writing in its historical time frame, but in its literary
nature as well. The fact that the Hebrew canon places Daniel
in the writings rather than in the prophets lends plausibility to
this claim, for it is entirely possible that Daniel is a different lit-

erary type than the latter prophets. There are no compelling biblical reasons, then, to reject the idea that prophecy represents an independent, unique literary genre.

In the rest of this chapter the various aspects of the definitions of genre, sub-genre, and mode will be applied to the minor prophets, and Isaiah, Jeremiah, and Ezekiel where they illuminate the Twelve, to delineate the nature of the written prophetic genre. From this sketch a better view of prophecy will hopefully emerge. Areas of unity among the minor prophets will be noted, as well as possible items of disagreement between the literary types of the books. Again it must be emphasized that some unity must prevail in the literary genre of the Twelve if any overarching unity of the whole body is to become a credible assertion.

1. *Medium: Prose and Poetry*

Both poetry and prose serve as linguistic mediums for prophecy. Such mixing of mediums is not that unusual in genres, particularly in drama where a play may be all in verse, all in prose, or combine the two. Several of Shakespeare's plays serve as examples of the last of these possibilities. Much has been written about the distinct natures of prose and poetry, so I will not attempt a lengthy discussion of those means of expression here. Still, it is necessary to at least chart the basic characteristics of prose and poetry, note how the minor prophets use each medium and draw some conclusions about how such distinctions affect an understanding of the prophetic genre.

Though it is difficult to say with total certitude, perhaps as much as two-thirds of the Old Testament is written in prose. This majority is caused by prose's prevalence in the Law and Former Prophets, and by its predominance in books like Chronicles in the Writings. In the minor prophets, however, prose sections are in the minority. Norman Gottwald writes:

> Lamentations, Obadiah, Micah, Nahum, Habakkuk, and Zephaniah are poetic in their entirety (with the exception of superscriptions). The greater parts of Job, Isaiah, Hosea, Joel, and Amos are poetic, and Jeremiah is about one half poetry (1962: 829).

Thus, of the Twelve only Jonah, Haggai, Zechariah, and Malachi consist mainly of prose, and three of those four, Jonah, Haggai, and Zechariah, contain poetic sections.

As every serious student of Hebrew knows, prose is usually the easier of the two mediums to read and translate. Prose generally adopts a verb–noun–object format, though varying from time to time for emphasis. Hebrew prose is characterized by perfect and imperfect verbs. Quite often the *waw* consecutive is joined to imperfect verbs to create a continuous narrative sequence. Various parts of speech, such as the relative pronoun, appear periodically in prose to help make a text's meaning even clearer. None of these comments are intended to argue that Hebrew prose is bland or simplistic, though, since some of the most intricate and imaginative literature in the Old Testament is prosaic in nature (e.g. Jonah, the Joseph accounts, etc).

Because of its straightforward syntactical pattern, prose is an action-oriented medium. It best unfolds characters, plots, and the importance of those characters and plot. Prose is therefore often explicitly linear in purpose. It is utilized to convey a story from beginning, to middle, to end, doing so in a basically objective fashion. At times these characteristics are molded together in a way that gives tremendous depth and subtlety to characters and situations. Robert Alter recognizes the value of prose when he states:

> Prose narration, affording writers a remarkable range and flexibility in the means of presentation, could be utilized to liberate fictional personages from the fixed choreography of timeless events and thus could transform storytelling from ritual rehearsal to the delineation of the wayward paths of human freedom, the quirks and contradictions of men and women seen as moral agents and complex centers of motive and feeling (1981: 25-26).

Without necessarily agreeing with Alter's conception of biblical history one can still appreciate Alter's emphasis on the beauty and flexibility of prose. It is in no way inferior to its poetic counterpart, as the growing body of literature on Old Testament narrative attests.

In the minor prophets prose serves both in traditional, in the sense of how prose is normally utilized in the Old Testament, and non-traditional ways. Besides conveying the narrative events portrayed in Jonah and Haggai, it also delineates prophetic sermons and visions, which are most often written in poetry in the Twelve. Jonah's story is somewhat like the story of Elijah in Kings that recounts Elijah's fear of Jezebel. Both prophets run away from the scene of most useful service, and though both are still used by God they are fully rebuked by the Lord. Both pout, but at the same time possess great power. Haggai rekindles memories of the accounts in Kings of the building of Solomon's temple. Though the new temple is vastly inferior to the old the people have been obedient to the word of Yahweh in building it. Malachi and Zechariah's books seem rather unconventional, however, when compared to other Old Testament prose narratives. Zechariah does present a sequence of visions (cf. Zech. 1.1; 1.7; 7.1, etc.), but those visions are unusual to say the least. Only in Ezekiel do we find similar types of oracles (e.g. Ezek. 1.1-28). Malachi's series of questions and answers is also fairly unique. His 'narrative' consists of questions that are increasingly pointed as the book nears its completion.

More will be said about prose's function in later sections. It is enough at this point to recognize that prose narrative has a substantial role in the Twelve. Some of the prose passages are fairly standard in nature and some more unique, but all these pericopae fit into the larger scheme of the minor prophets, as will be seen.

A great amount of current scholarly research on Old Testament literature deals with Hebrew poetry. Excellent works have come from critics representing a variety of viewpoints, thereby offering the student of poetry a more comprehensive perspective on the subject than was possible in the past. Even though this multiplicity of concepts about Old Testament verse is a recent phenomenon, most of these studies react to very old ideas.

Over 200 years ago Robert Lowth suggested that Hebrew poetry consists of a series of connected parallel phrases. Lowth set forth three basic kinds of parallels: antithetical, synonymous, and synthetic (1829: xii). The first type refers to any set of two or more poetic lines in which the second phrase states the opposite meaning of the first phrase. For instance, Hos.

8.12 reads, 'I wrote for them the many things of my law/ but they regarded them as something alien'. Synonymous parallelism occurs when a second phrase restates, often in a fuller way, an initial assertion. Hos. 10.2b declares, 'The Lord will demolish their altars/ and destroy their sacred stones'. One key to this type is the use of 'and' to bind together the similar sayings. Lastly, synthetic parallelism is evident when several lines work together to provide a unified synonymous or antithetical construction. This last type is quite obviously, the most nebulous of the three, as Lowth admits (1829: xxi). These three types of parallelism, and indeed the validity of the notion of parallelism, are at the heart of much critical discussion today.

Two schools of thought on parallelism now exist. One group believes parallelism is a very dubious means of locating Hebrew poetry, and thus argues that there is no set way to define Old Testament verse. James Kugel is perhaps the most effective proponent of this idea. He argues that parallelism is embedded in so-called prose passages, that the number of antithetical and synonymous parallels in the Old Testament is relatively small, and that Hebrew poetry is really a process of saying 'A is true, and what's more B is true' (1981: 51). The other group attempts to build on Lowth's foundation, further elaborate on the complexity of Hebrew verse, examine the metaphorical nature of Old Testament poetry and discuss how Old Testament authors use poetry to reflect and to create narrative sequences. Adele Berlin (1985) excels in the first two areas, while Robert Alter (1985) is very helpful in the latter categories. For Berlin and Alter, and for other writers of their mindset, parallelism is a solid basis for linguistic and thematic analysis. Parallelism is a complex subject, but still a viable starting point for Old Testament exegesis and interpretation. This viewpoint is reflected in the present work. Despite Kugel's claim the presence of parallelistic poetry in the Hebrew Bible is evident, though its essence is quite complicated at times. There is still value, as Berlin and Alter show, in distinguishing between prose and poetry.

Poetry appears throughout the minor prophets. It is found in books as different as Obadiah and Habakkuk, and in books as similar as Amos and Micah. Whether the writing contains condemnation or praise, acceptance or dispute, or judgment or forgiveness, poetry serves as the medium for the message.

All in all, the two linguistic mediums of the minor prophets are fairly neutral as far as the evidence for the unity of the Twelve goes. Either medium can be used effectively to convey the Book's message. Still, the fact that poetry is used to proclaim various messages does not argue against unity. Likewise, prose's use in different prophecies does not change the genre of the books to another form. In fact, if anything, their ability to be utilized interchangeably helps create a body of literature whose type and content is basically consistent.

2. *Imitation or Content*

Following Aristotle's pattern, the second generic aspect one needs to address is how the subject is imitated, or what content is evident in a literary type. In all genres this aspect is an extremely important consideration. Certainly within the prophetic canon there is no more serious generic question. If written prophecy is anything, it is a content-oriented body of material. As for the Book of the Twelve, if there is a discernible unified message that emerges from these texts, then there is the distinct possibility that this message ties the minor prophets together into a coherent literary unit.

Though not all past works on the prophets deal with oral, pre-literary prophecy, it is definitely true that a vast majority reflect this practice. It is odd, yet unmistakably true, that the only positive remains of the prophetic tradition—the biblical texts—have been neglected. This section does not attempt to make judgments on the non-textual matters of the Twelve. Rather, it tries to begin to define what 'written prophecy' means. What is important here, again, is the text. Its content will reveal what prophecy is. I may not uncover the most vital parts of written prophecy, but at least my attempt to do so will begin at the most logical place.

Though the latter prophets are a collection of works that span many centuries, reflect various historical situations, utilize numerous linguistic patterns and emphasize several different theological ideas, there is still a basic coherence in their final literary form. This coherence is particularly striking in

the Twelve where familiar characters and themes appear
again and again. One of the few biblical critics who charts the
subject matter of the minor prophets is Davie Napier. In his
Song of the Vineyard: A Guide through the Old Testament,
Napier argues that there are five recurring thematic elements in the prophets.

> If we essay a single broad look at classical prophetism as a
> whole, a number of concepts emerge as most crucial and
> characteristic. The essence of prophetism is embraced in the
> prophets's understanding of (1) Word and symbol, (2) elec-
> tion and covenant, (3) rebellion and judgment, (4) compas-
> sion and redemption, and (5) consummation (1981: 250).

Undoubtedly Napier's list covers the foundational tenets of
written prophecy, so an analysis of the five notions is in order.
Clearer definitions of the ideas are needed, and some revision
of them is also necessary.

'Word and symbol' refers to the prophets' practice of
claiming their messages, their writings, and their symbolic
acts come from God and declare Yahweh's word to Israel. The
traditional formula 'thus says the Lord' appears in all the
minor prophets except Jonah and Habakkuk. God's word and
will is still prominent in those two books, however, since Yahweh speaks directly to both prophets. The Lord tells Jonah to
go to Nineveh, to preach to the people and to have compassion
on the sinful city. He also explains to Habakkuk why the
Chaldeans are sent against Judah. Through either direct
claim or through the prophetic story itself, then, the Twelve
claims divine sanction.

Symbolic actions that embody prophetic messages are more
common in the major books than in their minor counterparts,
but symbolic action is not totally absent in the Twelve. Hosea's
marriage and children are symbolic of the unfaithful nature
of Yahweh's people. It is only through great distress that
Hosea's word to Yahweh's people comes to us. Jonah serves as
a very negative sort of symbol. He, like Israel does so many
times, rejects God's commands and purpose for his life,
thereby serving as a clear picture of an ugly exclusivism
prevalent in his nation. All of Jonah's travails likewise reveal
how the Lord chastises all who disobey. Zechariah's early

visions are highly symbolic in nature, and his later encounters with God include such pictorial acts as taking on the garb of a shepherd and casting thirty pieces of silver to a potter (Zech. 11.4-17). Thus, either by direct word or symbolic deed the minor prophets create a unified sense that the entire corpus is derived from Yahweh. None of the books fails to establish this distinctive.

Napier's second category, election and covenant, demonstrates the importance in prophecy of knowing that Yahweh has the right to expect certain behavior patterns from Israel because He made a covenant with Abraham, led them on the Exodus journey out of Egypt, and offered the nation the blessing of the law. Of course Hosea is the book that declares the election concept most clearly. It states:

> When Israel was a child, I loved him
> and out of Egypt I called my son.
> But the more I called Israel
> the further they went from me.
> They sacrificed to the Baals
> and they burned incense to images.
> It was I who taught Ephraim to walk,
> taking them by the arms;
> but they did not realize
> it was I who healed them (Hos. 11.1-3).

Because of Israel's election the nation was extended a covenant, which it eventually broke. Once more Hosea declares, 'Like Adam, they have broken the covenant—they were unfaithful to me there' (Hos. 6.7).

Most of the other books of the Twelve also employ election and covenant imagery. Even the notion that Israel can say 'Yahweh is *our* God' betrays a belief that this particular nation has a special relationship to the Lord. Joel 1.14, Obad. 17, Jon. 1.9, Nah. 2.2, Hab. 3.13, Zeph. 2.8 and Hag. 1.12 serve as examples of brief comments that leave no doubt that Yahweh has an agreement of major proportions with Israel. Very obvious claims are made in the other books. Amos says the people of Judah 'have rejected the law of the Lord and have not kept his decrees' (Amos 2.4). Like Amos, Micah states that Yahweh has a legal case to bring against His people:

> Hear, O mountains, the Lord's accusation...
> 'My people, what have I done to you?
> How have I burdened you? Answer me.
> I brought you up out of Egypt
> and redeemed you from the land of slavery.
> I sent Moses to lead you,
> also Aaron and Miriam' (Mic. 6.2-4).

God's displeasure with the nation derives from Israel's obvious departure from its covenant. Zechariah's promises of a messianic king coming to Jerusalem (9.9) and prediction of the future reign of God on earth (14.9) indicate the ultimate goal of Yahweh's relationship with Israel. Malachi closes the Twelve by basing his series of questions and answers on the most obvious of all election statements. 'Yet I have loved Jacob, but Esau I have hated' (Mal. 1.2-3). As can be seen even in this brief survey, from the first part of the minor prophets to the last the election and covenant theme permeates the literature thus providing a common thread of proclamation and interpretation. Nothing more needs to be said on this subject at this point in the study, since the prominence of the idea is so self-evident.

Despite their covenant with the Lord, the people of Israel constantly sin against their God. This component of prophecy, along with its twin emphasis judgment, is probably the most prevalent aspect of the minor prophetic literature. In the Twelve, Israel is joined in judgment and condemnation by all other nations who fail to acknowledge the sovereignty of Yahweh. Napier summarizes the sin and inevitable punishment that follows it:

> Israel's alienation from Yahweh is willful and complete, the shocking exhibition of pride and arrogance, which appear all the more reprehensible against the background of such relationships as parent-child (Isa. 1.2ff., for example), or owner-vineyard (Isaiah 5), or even husband-wife (Jer. 2.2-7; Ezek. 16.8-15; and of course Hosea). Israel's rebelliousness is infidelity; its infidelity pride. Prophetism is persuaded that this is the sickness-unto-death not only of Israel but all people. It is the condition which brings Israel, and ultimately the world, under judgment (1981: 252).

Every one of the Twelve decries either the sin of Israel or of one of Israel's neighbors. Hosea and Joel condemn Israel for a variety of reasons, but particularly for the country's falling away from Yahweh (Hos. 4.13; Joel 1.13). Amos writes against both Israel and her neighbors, claiming in an elaborate literary scheme (1.3–2.8) that all people have sinned so greatly that the Lord will not 'turn back' His wrath. Several specific offenses are chronicled by Amos, such as usury, oppression, hypocritical religious practices and complacency. The shortest of the minor prophets, Obadiah, depicts the arrogance of Edom, while Jonah's book describes the sin of Nineveh at the same time as it denounces the prophet's exclusivistic tendencies. Micah summarizes the transgressions of Israel and the nations in a fashion very similar to Amos. Assyria is the target of Nahum's prophecy because of its extreme pride, oppression and cruelty. Zephaniah also condemns Assyria and predicts the downfall of other nations such as Moab, Edom, Philistia and Cush. Judah is likewise threatened. With the exception of Ethiopia, each of the countries is cited for specific crimes. Zephaniah thus functions much like Amos in that Israel is the focus of the book, but the shortcomings of other peoples are mentioned as well. Habakkuk's classic study of theodicy states that God will use Babylon to punish Judah because of the constant disobedience of the covenant people.

Haggai, Zechariah, and Malachi complete the Twelve's chronicling of Israel's sin. In Haggai the sin is the failure to restore the temple of Yahweh. Zechariah's scope is much larger, encompassing the wrongdoing of both people and priest. To close the minor prophets, Malachi utilizes a series of rhetorical questions to prove that the elect nation robs God, is unfaithful to spouses, offers blemished sacrifices and supports disreputable priests. All the evidence in the Twelve points to the inexcusable and constant nature of the sin of the people of Yahweh. Their crimes are made intolerable by the evident graciousness of God's covenant with them. Pictured as equally heinous, however, are the sins of Israel's neighbors. Despite their non-covenantal status they are held accountable for their deeds by the Lord of history.

Following right behind the sins of Israel and the nations is the punishment of those sins. Such judgment is the inevitable result of rejecting the covenant God and mistreating His people. With extreme regularity the Twelve claims that Yahweh's judgment will be meted out on a final day of darkness and gloom which is commonly, and ominously, called the 'day of Yahweh'. This 'day' is described in various ways in the Twelve, but Zephaniah summarizes the fearful nature of that time very cogently. Using Zeph. 1.7-18 as a representative passage of how the prophets portray the day of Yahweh, Gerhard von Rad comments:

> This day is designated as a sacrificial feast which Yahweh prepares for the guests whom he invites. This is a metaphor which we have already met in Isa. 34.6. Its clearest expression occurs in Jer. 46.10: at the great festivals the blood of the victims flows in streams—Yahweh's war against his foes will be equally bloody (1967: 98).

Such is the severity of that day. As for its effect on the recipients of the wrath von Rad further states:

> This day is a day of distress, of darkness and gloom, a day of trumpet-blast and battle-cry against fortified cities. Men will be overcome by fear... they will be unable to save themselves, for the earth is to be consumed with the fire of Yahweh's zealous wrath (1967: 98).

It would be difficult to imagine a more devastating picture of God's answer to the iniquity of Israel and her neighbors.

Even a brief perusal of the Twelve reveals a uniform emphasis on God's judgment of all people. Indeed, judgment is the chief theme of books like Nahum, Habakkuk, and Zephaniah, and it plays a significant role in Joel, Amos, and Obadiah as well. Both Israel and foreign countries are singled out for judgment in individual prophecies, with Nahum and Obadiah focusing on Assyria and Edom, Joel and Habakkuk on Judah, and Amos and Zephaniah on both. More discussion of the judgment motif in the minor prophets would merely be redundant. This prophetic idea is as clear in the literature as the claims about the sin of the nations and the covenant people of Yahweh.

Just as judgment follows sin in the canonical prophets, so forgiveness and restoration come as the natural response of the Lord after the day of Yahweh. One of the oldest scholarly debates related to the Twelve is whether the positive endings on some of the books (e.g. Amos 9.11-15; Zeph. 3.6-20) are part of the original text. Whatever one's conclusions on the subject, one must acknowledge the importance of this hopeful emphasis in the final form of the minor prophets. Their prominence is undeniable. Hos. 14.1-9, Joel 3.17-21, Amos 9.11-15, Obad. 19–21, Mic. 7.15-20 and Zeph. 3.6-20 represent a strong literary tradition that Yahweh will restore Israel and convert the nations after, or through, the day of punishment and cleansing. These shorter passages are buttressed by whole books that highlight various aspects of restoration. For instance Haggai appears to emphasize the restoration of the temple. Zechariah, on the other hand, sets forth the redemption of Jerusalem, while Malachi stresses the ultimate restoration of the ethical fortitude of the covenant people through the ministry of an 'Elijah' to come.

Condemnation is therefore not the last word in the book of the Twelve. Hope is the final message of most of the individual prophecies and of the corpus as a whole. Though the punishment motif is pervasive, it is not conclusive. To argue the opposite is to totally misunderstand the prophetic literature. The final form of the Twelve always assumes that better days are ahead for all people, domestic or foreign, who repent and seek Yahweh.

Napier lists 'consummation' as the final tenet of prophecy. He claims: 'In its ultimate projection, prophetic faith points, if not beyond history, at least to a history radically transformed' (1981: 256). Included in this transformed, new history is the idea that the Gentiles will share in the blessings of Israel. All nations will thereby be united as one in a world ruled by Yahweh. Napier concludes:

> The notion of the historical redemption of Israel alone was never able to contain the prophetic faith or answer prophetism's pressing questions about the meaning of Israel's redemption, the prophetic intensity of feeling and pressure of conviction mark the intent to be universal (1981: 257).

Without a doubt Napier correctly assesses prophecy at this point. Indeed the restoration of the Gentiles is as important as the restoration of the Jews if the fact that Yahweh is Lord of all creation is properly taken into account.

Various segments of the Twelve stress the universal aspect of God's blueprint for salvation and restoration. Jonah's prophecy serves as the clearest example of the Lord's concern for a foreign country. Though Assyria oppressed both Samaria and Judah, Yahweh's rebuke of Jonah is full of compassion for this city that numbers 'more than a hundred and twenty thousand people who cannot tell their right hand from their left' because of their sin (Jon. 4.11). God asks: 'Should I not be concerned about that great city?' Micah's book, though not as tender in its concern for the Gentiles, predicts that in the last days many nations will congregate on the mountain of the Lord (4.1-2), and that when Israel is restored other nations 'will turn in fear to the Lord' (7.17). Still more hopeful is Zephaniah, where Yahweh claims that after the day of the Lord He will 'purify the lips of the peoples, that all of them may call on the name of the Lord and serve Him shoulder to shoulder' (3.9). Presumably, because of this service, the Gentiles will then share in the blessings recounted in the rest of the book. Much like Micah, Zechariah pictures a time when nations punished by Israel will worship Yahweh (14.16).

The minor prophets' portrayal of the Lord's mercy thus stretches to all the earth's people. While not the most vital part of the content of prophecy, it does serve as an important corollary to the restoration of Israel. It also balances the threats of God's wrath against the Gentiles by offering a solution to the problem of sin in those people. Just as with Israel, then, the Lord's future plan for foreign nations is to forge restoration out of the furnace of judgment.

Clearly the content of the minor prophets presents a unified portrait of prophecy that closely parallels the subject matter of Isaiah, Jeremiah, and Ezekiel. All the main elements of the prophetic message are present in the Twelve. Some books, like Micah and Zephaniah, contain all the emphases listed by Napier. Others present one or more of those aspects. The significance of this observation is revealed in at least three ways. First, the constant interfacing of common motifs in the books shows that the books share a common genre. Second, the tendency of some of the books to exhibit only one or a few traits of the prophetic genre points to the possibility that the books may be in their present configuration in order to offer a complete literary treatment of the meaning of prophecy. Finally, the constant common thematic consistency of the Twelve leads to the conclusion that the books have a unified literary content. Such continuity reflects a unity of construction too obvious to be denied. Though obvious, the unified content of prophecy must be understood for further observations on the Twelve to make sense.

3. *Manner of Imitation: Narration*
Aristotle's third criterion for defining a genre, manner of imitation, refers, basically, to whether the narration of a literary piece is told in first or third person. Any kind of narration can relate a particular story, though each has its own unique way of telling that story. As Aristotle explains:

> As we said at the beginning, imitations are to be distinguished under these three headings: means, object, and manner. Thus, in one way, Sophocles is the same kind of imitative artist as Homer, since they both imitate noble men; but in another sense, he resembles Aristophanes, since they both imitate characters as acting and dramatizing the incidents of a story. It is from this, some tell us, that these latter kinds of imitations are called 'dramas' because they present characters who 'dramatize' the incidents of the plot (1974: ch.3, 32).

Thus, no individual genre can claim to be the only genre that can tell a certain story well. Quite the opposite is true. Still, the effect on the reader or audience differs from genre to genre as does the amount of material that can be included on characters, plots, themes, etc.

First-person narration best fits drama because it forces a writer to allow characters to speak for themselves. Nothing can be told about a plot or person unless it is uncovered through a character's speeches or actions. How the dramatist creates words and deeds determines the form of a play. Very different kinds of speeches appear in comedy, for instance, than in tragedy. Yet the basis of the speeches are the same— first-person narration. Northrop Frye notes the problems and possibilities inherent in the narration of drama when he writes that

> drama is a mimesis of dialogue or conversation, and the rhetoric of conversation obviously has to be a very fluid one. It may range from a set speech to the kind of thrust and parry which is called stichomythia when its basis is metrical; and it has the double difficulty of expressing the speaker's character and speech rhythm and yet modifying them to the situation and the moods of other speakers (1967: 269).

How well the dramatist creates and structures the play's speeches determines the quality of the finished literary piece. If the presentation of character and action clash with the play's purpose and generic nature then the drama appears artificial. On the other hand, the dramatist who can mesh first-person presentation, appropriate action, and a logical plot produces a play with telling impact.

Third-person narration enjoys many luxuries not afforded the dramatist. For example, the writer of prose narrative can insert personal opinion about a character or event into a work. Thus, many new possibilities for a story unfold. The narrator may be either reliable or unreliable, all-knowing or limited, sane or insane (as in Faulkner's novels), or biased or unbiased. One character may be presented accurately by the narrator while an opposite character suffers unfairly in comparison. In a third-person narrated plot the author exercises great power over the audience in that the reader only knows what the writer chooses to disclose. That is, of course, unless the author guides the reader to interpret the narrative by reading between the lines. Though this paragraph offers only the barest-bones outline of third-person narration, some of the implications of this narrative technique are still obvious. Perhaps the most basic of these implications, and perhaps the most important as well, is that the narrator, for better or worse, is always a major part of the story. Wayne C. Booth observes:

> In short, the author's judgment is always present, always evident to anyone who knows how to look for it. Whether its particular forms are harmful or serviceable is always a complex question, a question that cannot be settled by an easy

reference to abstract rules... [W]e must never forget that though the author can to some extent choose his disguises, he can never choose to disappear (1961: 20).

Within the minor prophets, both first and third-person narration are utilized. Because of its background in oral discourse, however, first-person speech tends to overshadow third-person accounts. Still, some books, and parts of books, are cast in a non-dramatic format.

Third-person discourse opens the Twelve, recounting in Hos. 1.1ff. the woes of Hosea's home life. Chapter 3 provides a somewhat happy conclusion to that inauspicious beginning by telling how the prophet regains his wife. Most of the remainder of the book displays first-person narration. For all practical purposes Joel is totally dramatic in presentation, as is Obadiah, Nahum, Habakkuk, Micah, Zephaniah and Malachi. Amos' visions in 7.1ff. and 8.1ff. contain third-person patterning, as does the prophet's experience with the priest of Bethel. The significance of third-person narration in Hosea and Amos is apparently that these experiences are the main life events of those prophets contained in the books. Why such experiences are sprinkled into predominantly first-person passages will be explored in chapter six.

Another category of third-person patterning, besides books mostly first-person, is the prophecies that are mainly third-person presentations. Jonah and Haggai represent this type of work. Except for Jonah's psalm uttered from the belly of the whale, both these books relate biographical events told in the third-person. Even Jonah's psalm, however, fits into the story as what the prophet said when in the whale. Thus it is not a dramatic speech in the strictest sense of that term. Haggai and Jonah are unadorned portrayals of what is wrong with Israel (Jonah) and what can be done to correct the people's sin (Haggai). Similar to the third-person sections in Hosea and Amos, Jonah and Haggai are cast in third-person speech because of their biographical and polemical natures. Such biographical and polemical features have a special role in the Twelve.

Zechariah is a third-person book of yet a different stripe. In Zechariah 1–8 a series of visions are presented as dated events in the life of the prophet. Then 9.1–11.3 interrupts this sequence with direct presentations by Yahweh and the prophet. Next, 11.4-17 gives a third-person story that uses Zechariah as a symbol of good and worthless spiritual leaders. Finally, chs. 12–14 offer dramatic speeches on the day of Yahweh and its implications. It is instructive to note that Zechariah's use of third-person accounts is similar to that in Amos, Hosea, and Jonah. Such correllations raise questions about why books from diverse time periods reflect relatively corresponding literary elements.

Except for the regular sprinkling of 'says Yahweh' into the speeches, most of the remaining minor prophets exhibit first-person narration. The patterns and purposes for using that mode of narration vary, but its presence is undeniable. After chapter three, Hosea employs direct speech throughout, with the exception of a 'says Yahweh' note in 11.11. Joel (2.12) and Obadiah (4, 8) use that phrase sparingly too, while Amos (21 times) and Zechariah (20 times) display it regularly. Zephaniah has the term six times, Micah and Nahum twice and Malachi once. In the context of the books, though, the appearances of 'says Yahweh' function more as stage directions, or reader directions, than as indications of narration. Thus, the majority of the Twelve declare their messages through direct speech rather than through narrated actions.

Typically in the Twelve two speakers are evident: Yahweh and the prophet. These characters serve as co-revelators of God's message, with each taking turns giving a word or interpreting the word of the other. Through this process the nature of both Lord and prophet, in short the most important persons in the Twleve, unfold. Other characters do enter at times, for instance in Joel where farmers and, possibly, priests speak, and in Malachi were the nation apparently asks questions. At all times the reader is forced to follow the ebb and flow of plot, argument, characterization, tone, etc. without the benefit of *explicit* editorial help. All the aspects of the content are present, but are communicated directly from the books' main figures.

Habakkuk's first-person presentation varies somewhat from the rest of the Twelve. Here the prophet frames his discussion of Yahweh's actions in history by mixing mainly first-person narration with some hints of third-person patterns. He tells of his questioning of God in 'I' form, but then explains in 2.2 that what follows is what Yahweh replies. Chapter 3 is a psalm, or a prayer that functions as Habakkuk's final understanding of God's purposes for Israel. Though the format changes, however, the force of the text remains that of a first-person presentation. Verses like 2.2 and 3.1 thereby serve, much like the 'says Yahweh' passages, as a means for the author to direct and focus a dramatic presentation.

From this brief, introductory analysis of manner of imitation it is clear that this aspect of genre analysis, like the medium of imitation, does not reveal any serious disjuncture in the literary unity of the Twelve. Even though each book is not narrated in the same way, there is a discernible unity of how both types of narration are utilized. Hosea, Jonah, Haggai and Zechariah are very different books, yet they use the third-person discourse in very similar ways. Malachi may present a direct message through a series of questions, while Micah lets the main speakers give the arguments, but both reflect a consistent content and purpose. Therefore, as will be seen later, the narrative voice of the book of the Twelve cooperates with the medium and content of prophecy to transmit a unified presentation.

Conclusions

Several observations arise from this section on the major elements of genre. First, a basic definition of the term 'written prophecy', or at least of 'minor prophetic written literature', has emerged. Written prophecy uses prose or poetry, choosing either medium based on the type of message the prophet wishes to convey. Neither medium is used by chance or as a matter of convenience. Second, the content of written prophecy contains certain definite aspects. The prophets declare an urgent message of sin, judgment, and restoration in a unified and unique way. Some of the minor prophets have all the elements mentioned above, while others display one or more but not all. In the Twelve, those books that delineate some but not all the traits combine with other books to reveal the prophetic warnings and promises. Third, the manner of imitation, or narration, in the minor prophets displays a conscious effort to use first or third-person narration for specific purposes. Prophecies very different in content and date utilize the same type of narration in similar manners. Finally, the evident unity in the literary nature of the twelve books demonstrates the likelihood that unity may exist in other spheres as well. It is also probable that an analysis of the literature itself will provide information on which to base further research. Only when the main tenets of a genre are unveiled can other elements of a work, such as structure and plot, be explicated.

Thus, there is no reason to deny the possibility of discovering the unity of the Twelve at this point. None of the books vary from accepted notions of prophecy, whether those notions derive from the major or minor prophets. Had any or some of the Twelve diverged significantly from the basic literary form then perhaps hope for the books' unity would be lost. No such divergence exists. In fact, this chapter hints at possibilities of other common threads in the minor prophets. Further analysis is therefore in order.

Chapter 3

THE STRUCTURE OF THE TWELVE

Introduction

Now that some understanding of the literary nature of prophecy has been reached it is possible to examine the structure of the minor prophets. The parallels between the content of prophecy and the shaping of the corpus will become increasingly clear as this chapter progresses. In these books literary type and final literary form are definitely wedded.

In Chapter 1 the inability of scholars to explain the ordering of the Twelve was noted. Canonical and historical critics alike fail to find a unifying coherence in the sequence of the books. All realize, however, that, with few exceptions, the minor prophets have appeared in their present configuration. Brevard Childs offers the following survey:

> The order of the books within the section of the Latter Prophets varies considerably within the Jewish lists. The Talmudic order has the sequence: Jeremiah, Ezekiel, Isaiah, the Twelve; the French and German manuscripts the tradition: Jeremiah, Isaiah, Ezekiel, the Twelve; the Masoretic and Spanish manuscripts the order: Isaiah, Jeremiah, Ezekiel, the Twelve (cf. Ryle, Excursus C; Swete, 200). The discussions on the variation in order within the Talmud (Baba Bathra 14b-15a) indicate the latter puzzlement over the divergent traditions. The rabbinic explanations are clearly homiletical rather than historical in nature (1980: 309).

Of all the facts mentioned by Childs the most glaring is that the Twelve remain intact regardless of where they are placed.

Perhaps only the Septuagint changes the order of the minor prophets. In this tradition the first six prophecies appear in this sequence: Hosea, Amos, Micah, Joel, Obadiah and Jonah. Of course the final six books remain in their common order, while the first six vary a good bit. There is no apparent effort to mix Malachi with, for instance, Hosea and Jonah, which may indicate that, whatever purpose the first six prophecies serve, they serve it as a group.

Various explanations of why the order of books appears in its present form have been forwarded (cf. Ch. 1). Most of these notions are historical in nature. Scholars either hold that the collectors of the Twelve had some chronological scheme in mind or that the editors tried to match books according to length, catchwords, or nationality of the prophet. C.F. Keil claims:

> In the arrangement of the twelve, the chronological princi-
> ple has so far determined the order in which they occur, that
> the prophets of the pre-Assyrian and Assyrian times (Hosea
> to Nahum) are placed first, as being the earliest; then follow
> those of the Chaldean period (Habakkuk and Zephaniah);
> and lastly, the series is closed by the three prophets after the
> captivity (Haggai, Zechariah, and Malachi), arranged in the
> order in which they appeared (1869: 2).

This approach has some difficulties, as even Keil admits when he writes: 'Within the first of these three groups, however, the chronological order is not strictly preserved, but is outweighed by the nature of the contents' (1869: 2). Thus, Keil is forced to conclude that some non-historical factors play a role in the Twelve's sequence. His best explanation is that length and the regional origins of books provide clues to why the prophecies are in their canonical order. He says that

> the plan adopted in arranging the earliest of the minor
> prophets seems rather to have been the following: Hosea was
> placed at the head of the collection, as being the most com-
> prehensive, just as, in the collection of Pauline epistles, that
> to the Romans is put first on account of its wider scope. Then
> followed the prophecies which had no date given in the head-
> ing; and these were so arranged, that a prophet of the king-
> dom of Israel was always paired with one of the kingdom of
> Judah, viz. Joel with Hosea, Obadiah with Amos, Jonah
> with Micah, and Nahum the Galilean with Habakkuk the
> Levite (1869: 3).

That numerous scholars have disagreed with Keil's historical conclusions hardly needs to be said. Today even conservative scholars tend to date Amos before Hosea at least in its written form (La Sor et al. 1985: 319). Other writers are adamant in their claims that actual chronology does not decide the sequence of the minor prophets. George Adam Smith notes:

> Recent criticism, however, has made it clear that the Biblical order of 'The Twelve Prophets' is no more than a very rough approximation to the order of their real dates... Of the first six prophets the dates of Amos, Hosea, and Micah (but of the latter's book in part only) are certain. The Jews have been able to defend Hosea's priority only on fanciful grounds. Whether or not he quotes from Amos, his historical allusions are more recent. With the exception of a few fragments incorporated by later authors, the Book of Amos is thus the earliest example of prophetic literature, and we take it first (1929: I, 7).

Though this is a very old statement, Smith's opinion is not very different from that of more recent criticism. It is now a somewhat standard opinion that though Hosea's king notations may predate Amos, it is doubtful to say conclusively that Hosea was the first of the two to minister or be *written* (cf. Wolff 1977: 89; 1974: xxi). Thus, while the compiler of the Twelve may have placed Hosea first to reflect the history of Israel, to have done so may have ignored the primacy of Amos.

Hans Walter Wolff takes a somewhat modified approach to the belief that the minor prophets' structure hinges on historical criteria. He first lends some support to the notion by saying:

> To the extent that chronological criteria were decisive for the arrangement of the Twelve, they were straight-forward criteria, especially of regnal synchronisms. Such data are supplied in the superscriptions to the books of Hosea, Amos, Micah, Zephaniah, Haggai, and Zechariah; and they indeed provide a chronological framework for the collection of the Twelve (1974: 3).

In other words, Wolff seems to indicate that the dated books hold the group together by providing clearly dated chronological keys to the outline of the minor prophets. After this statement, however, he admits that such historical tapestries come unravelled when one attempts to explain why the other books are in their respective places. Wolff claims that 'a separate investigation of each of the remaining six books is required to account for its specific placement within the framework' (1974: 3). He then concludes:

> Hence, in view of the absence of chronological data in the book of Joel, those who arranged the Hebrew collection of the Twelve Prophets must have used other criteria to determine its position between Hosea and Amos (1974: 3).

At this point Wolff concedes that chronological concerns cannot uncover the motivation behind the books' configuration. Historical details are definitely not irrelevant, but they are likewise not overriding in this discussion.

Brevard Childs mentions a few other possibilities for the reasoning behind the canonical shape of those books. Agreeing with Wolff (1974: 3), Childs notes that 'catchword connections between books were operative (e.g. Amos 1.2 and Joel 3.16)' (1980: 309). Catchwords certainly exist in the Twelve, but one would be hard pressed to find enough catchwords to unite all the books. Childs also suggests: 'At other times mechanical factors such as length of the scroll played a role' (1980: 309). While it is impossible to discredit this idea, it is equally impossible to prove it. Besides, the fact that the Twelve can fit on one or two scrolls does not divulge why the *order* remains the same. Despite his interest in canonical issues, Childs does not offer any conclusions about the whole corpus. Rather, he decides the most vital aspect of the canonical shaping of the minor prophets resides in the formation of individual books (1980: 310).

From this brief survey it is clear that no consensus on the Twelve's structure exists. Those who hold to some notion of a chronological emphasis admit that the books are not in chronological order (cf. Keil 1869: 4; Wolff 1974: 3). In fact, most writers assume the prophecies are not in an accurate time sequence. Such ideas as the importance of catchwords or scroll length lack the ability to unite more than a book or two. It is fair to conclude, then, that Smith summarizes the findings of current scholarship when he states: 'But all this is only to guess, where we have no means of certain knowledge' (1929: I, 6).

As was stated in Chapter 1, this book seeks to examine the contents of the Twelve in hopes of deciding whether or not these prophecies are a unity. If there is a unified structure to the minor prophets it can only be revealed through literary analysis. Recognizing this fact, Wolff writes:

> We can see, then, that matters of content dictated Joel's position before Amos, and not some knowledge of the time the book was composed. Here we must recognize a common literary development in which considerably more recent, topically relevant material was prefaced to older writing in order to inform its interpretation... In all likelihood those who arranged the collection of the Twelve wished us to read Amos and the following prophets in the light of Joel's proclamation. For manifest in Joel is a comprehensive view of prophecy closely akin to that governing the prophetic corpus in its final, canonizing redaction (1974: 3-4).

What this 'content' is Wolff never illuminates, but his observation is surely correct. It is probable that historical research has not successfully uncovered the structure of the Twelve because that structure is governed by literary principles. The rest of this chapter seeks to discover and illuminate some of these principles. This chapter *does not* attempt to suggest the redactional process of structuring the Twelve from the acquired data. Instead, it tries to explicate the text as it is in hopes of forging a fresh perception of the canonical order of the minor prophets. If these hopes are realized, then interpreters will have new tools to use in exegeting these books.

Determining Factors in the Twelve's Structure

Every quality literary piece is the result of an author's ability to blend a number of stylistic elements. Plot must coincide with character, structure with plot and purpose, theme with structure and plot, and so forth. All these literary facets work together in specific ways to create a unique artistic whole. It is safe to say, then, that certain genres encourage certain types of structures. It is, therefore, also fairly safe to say that recognizing the unified nature of the prophetic genre within the

Twelve may provide clues to the present structure of those books.

A close analysis of the Twelve reveals some definite patterns in the positioning of the minor prophets. It appears that the books are ordered as they are so that the main points of the prophetic message will be highlighted. In fact, the Twelve are structured in a way that demonstrates the sin of Israel and the nations, the punishment of the sin, and the restoration of both from that sin. These three emphases represent the heart of the content of the prophetic genre. The Twelve's external structure therefore reflects its literary type.

Some caution must be exercised at this point. It could be argued that since each of the Twelve are prophecies, and thus contain the literary traits of prophecy, that of course sin, punishment, and restoration are evident in the Twelve. To declare such thematic devices to be major structural keys would just impose a unity on these disparate books. A related complaint could arise, which is that the whole cycle of sin through restoration occurs in many of the books, sometimes more than once. If each book does not serve only one structural function, such as sin *or* restoration, then the complexity of some of the prophecies argues against a unified structure. The first issue has some merit, but to be entirely valid it has to assume that literary works cannot serve an individual purpose while demonstrating artistic multiplicity. A work like *The Canterbury Tales* shows how flawed such thinking is, since it weaves various tales together to recount a single journey. Under such conditions other works, such as *Gulliver's Travels, Don Quixote*, etc., have no defining structure. In their case the genre determines their structure. The second argument assumes the opposite. That is, if a work is complex then it cannot fit into a discernible structure as a single explanatory unit. Again, such an argument betrays more prejudice against the idea of unity than an understanding of literature. As a literary piece, Chaucer's 'Knight's Tale' is more involved than Obadiah, yet this medieval story fits the overall scheme of the *Canterbury Tales*. Quite complicated prophecies like Amos and Micah can surely also fit into a larger context. In fact, their propensity to repeat the great themes of prophecy, much as a great symphony constantly recycles major movements, reinforces the structure of the Twelve.

Though other objections to this means of examining the minor prophets' structure could indeed surface, one immediately comes to mind. It is inevitable that someone will claim that these twelve books were written and edited by a large number of people living in different times under divergent life situations. Thus, says the argument, any structure is either incidental or contrived. Of course the answer to this observation is that centuries ago the ancient community of faith joined these works and thereafter considered them one work. This canonical action merits analysis. It must also be noted that the existence of the book in its final form warrants a literary analysis. All of the above-mentioned historical facts are of great importance, and literature is composed in a historical context, but they are incapable of discovering the tenets of the long-assumed coherence of the Twelve.

Within the Twelve the great themes of prophecy emerge. Sin, punishments and future salvation are portrayed throughout the books, but are also set forth clearly in distinct sections of the Twelve. No doubt this unity developed over a period of time. Regardless of the historical factors at work, the shape of the minor prophets includes the formation of the entire corpus and not just the individual prophecies. Ronald Clements observes:

> What we are concerned to argue here is that this process of development cannot be restricted to the separate prophetic books, so that each of them can be treated in relative isolation from the rest as a self-contained entity. Rather, we must see that ultimately the final result in the prophetic corpus of the canon formed a recognizable unity... (1977: 53).

It makes a great deal of sense to expect unity to grow out of the significant facets of literary prophecy's content. That sin, judgment and renewal are the main ideas of the message of the prophets can hardly be denied. Therefore this chapter seeks to use these ideas as a starting point for examining the Twelve's structure. Ronald Clements testifies to the logical nature of this methodology when he concludes that it is fundamental to the hermeneutical traditions of both Jews and Christians that the prophets spoke of a coming salvation for Israel. On the other hand, critical scholarship has consistently found the most challenging feature of prophecy to lie in its threats and denunciations, warning of the coming of judgment upon a godless people. The place where both aspects are brought together is to be found in the structure of the canonical collection of prophecy. The threat of doom is followed by the word of salvation, which does not evade the judgment but looks beyond it. By holding these two things together in this way, the prophetic part of the OT Canon witnesses to the wholeness of the Word of God (1977: 55).

Though Clements does not develop this thesis for the structure of the minor prophets, he does suggest that thematic patterns are a viable means of determining literary framework.

The Structure of the Twelve: Definition

Some idea of what is meant by 'structure' must be determined before the outline of the Twelve can be discussed. Since parts of the definition of structure are covered above, this section is brief. First, the use of the term structure does not mean a structuralist methodology is in force here. Rather, the common notion of structure as a unifying scheme is what is meant. 'What unifies a work?' is the question under consideration.

An analysis of a literary work's structure is vital because practically every aspect of a piece is uncovered by its framework. Edgar V. Roberts illuminates the cohesive nature of structure when he says:

> Structure is a matter of the relationship among parts that are usually described in terms of cause and effect, position in time, association, symmetry, and balance and proportion...
> Literary artists universally aim at a unified impression in their works, and because literature is a time art (it cannot be comprehended as a whole in one moment, as can a painting or a work of sculpture), the study of structure attempts to demonstrate that the idea and the resulting arrangement of parts produces a total impression (1973: 119).

A work's structure, therefore, unites its various themes, images, ideas, characters, plots, points of view and time sequences. It is the glue that holds an artistic piece together.

Good frameworks are one with the other elements of the art form. That is, they are appropriately chosen in relationship to genre, plot, etc. A well-crafted structure logically unites these components. The failure to do so betrays a lack of unity in the text that can destroy the author's communication with a reader, thereby spoiling the work's impact.

Another characteristic of a sound structure is its ability to be logical and sequential. Roberts emphasizes 'In a good work of literature, the parts are not introduced accidentally. One part demands another, sometimes by logical requirement' (1973: 120). This logical component of structure can either grow out of ideas, time, sequence, or characterization (Roberts 1973: 121). At times all three work together. Whatever the organizing principle, however, a structure is only effective if it demonstrates how the many aspects of a work move a text forward from its beginning to its conclusion.

This brief definition in no way fully defines the study of structure. Hopefully the analysis of the books themselves will fill out this description. Still, the comments are enough to show that the structure of a work is so vital to its meaning that the importance of examining the framework of the Twelve is self-evident. If the *overarching* unity of the books is not observable, then unity in more minute areas is hardly tenable. Any glaring lack of structural unity in the Twelve mars its 'unified expression' and puts this study back where it started.

The Structure of the Twelve: Outline

Since the major thematic aspects of the minor prophets and their neighbors are, as has been mentioned repeatedly, the sin of the covenant people, the purging of that sin, and the reclamation of the sinners, it is best to envision a tri-partite structure of the Twelve. Various sub-structural units will emerge, each one related to its larger heading, but three divisions will dominate. Each section will be delineated and explicated to see how, or if, these foundational ideas unfold. Though some of this structural discussion overlaps with the chapter on plot, such overlap is kept to a minimum.

In the Twelve, the conscious effort to divulge sin, punishment, and restoration proceeds in the following sequence. The first six of the prophecies examine the covenant and cosmic nature of sin. This examination is nearly encyclopaedic in its thoroughness. Following this section, the next three books capture the essence of covenantal and cosmic punishment. Hope is not absent, but it is definitely muted. Finally, the last three prophecies relate the possibility of restoration. Restoration is portrayed as past, present, and future, much as God's covenant relationship and judgment of any breach of that relationship is past, present, and future oriented. Other books mention restoration, of course, but without making that idea its main issue. In this scheme I stress the phrase 'main issue', lest arguments over the *presence* of sub-themes overwhelm the discussion. More than one motif can appear in a book (cf. Ch. 2), but one main purpose for each of the prophecies is discernible in this structure. Note the following chart:

Chart 1: The Structure of the Twelve

Hosea
Joel
Amos
Obadiah   Sin: Covenant and Cosmic
Jonah
Micah

Nahum
Habakkuk   Punishment: Covenant and Cosmic
Zephaniah

Haggai
Zechariah   Restoration: Covenant and Cosmic
Malachi

1. *Covenant and Cosmic Sin: Hosea–Micah*
These six books reflect a wide variety of interests and span a long period of time. There is no apparent historical connection between the books, nor is there a geographical link to bind

them together. What is evident, however, is that all six books, viewed together, compose a comprehensive polemic against sin. They also mention punishment and redemption too, but usually as they relate to the topic of sin. A short book-by-book analysis reveals the function of this portion of the Twelve. Because of its introductory nature, Hosea will be dealt with at greater length than some of the other books, but all twelve will receive treatment.

Hosea's own structure has been debated at some length. The discussion usually revolves around the role of chs. 1, 2 and 3 (the Gomer accounts) within the book's remaining eleven chapters. The purpose and historical accuracy of the recounting of Hosea's marital difficulties is often the focal point of discussions on the book's structure. For instance, Leon Wood posits four possible interpretations of the marriage. He states that the marriage is either an allegory, a literal union in which the prophet chooses an unchaste partner at God's command, a story of spiritual infidelity, or a literal marriage in which Gomer became unchaste later (1985: 164-66). Wood accepts the last view, and thereby believes chs. 1–3 prefigure chs. 4–14 by comparing Hosea's marriage to Yahweh's relationship to Israel. James Luther Mays takes a similar approach to the marriage, stating that it is an actual event with a kerygmatic purpose (1969: 23-24). He also sees chs. 1–3 as an introduction to the rest of the book, though he thinks chs. 4–14 'lack the clear plan of the first' (1969: 15). Few, if any, commentators, however, reflect on how the structure of the prophecy relates to the structure of the Twelve.

One other issue related to Hosea's initial three chapters is the possible theories of its formation. W.R. Harper accepts 1.2-6; 1.8ff.; 2.4-7, 10-14, 15, 19 as 'original' to Hosea's message, while 1.1, 7; 3.5; 2.4b, 6, 12, 18; 2.8-9, 16-17, 20-25 are secondary additions to the text (1905: clx). On the redaction of Hosea 1–3 H.W. Wolff postulates that

> the account from Hosea's early period (1.2-4, 6, 8f) was combined with Hosea's own written words (2.4-17; 3.1-5), which represent a second period of his preaching and probably also come out of politically quiet times. The combination of both these literary components resulted at the same time in the addition of Hosea's sayings from 733 and later (1.5; 2.1-3, 18-

25). The redactor's note in 1.2a may also belong to this process. 1.1, 7 and the additions in 3.5b originate from a Judaic
redaction; 2.10b is a gloss (1974: 12).

Though greatly interested in how the texts were compiled,
both Harper and Wolff recognize the final form of this passage
is a prelude to the remainder of Hosea. Still, there is no significant attempt to discover any wider context for Hosea's, or the
Twelve's, structure.

Hosea 1–3 serves two very important structural functions.
First, this section sets the stage for chs. 4–14, as is universally
recognized. It functions as a microcosm of the book, Yahweh's
covenant relationship with Israel, and Hosea's message. It also
links Hosea to other literary prophecies such as Isaiah,
Jeremiah, Ezekiel, Jonah, etc. through the prophet's role as a
kerygmatic symbol. Several themes that pervade Hosea are
introduced here, including prostitution, infidelity, lawsuit (ריב),
repentance and the significance of the 'last days'. Perhaps
most importantly, the notion that Yahweh forgives is suggested in this passage as well. In fact, no strong motif in the
prophecy is lacking in this clearly introductory section.

A second structural task Hosea 1–3 attempts is to serve as
an introduction to the Twelve. Chapter 1 in the Hebrew text
plainly portrays the besetting problem of sin addressed
throughout the Twelve, but especially in Hosea–Micah.
Through Hosea's children, the text explains that Israel will
receive no pity because they are not acting like God's people.
The second chapter opens with the declaration that despite
their evil ways the nation will be reunited and multiplied, but
only because they will suffer punishment from Yahweh.
Chapter 3 indicates that through the crucible of exile God will
purify the chosen people. From this base Hosea continues and
builds, as does the Twelve.

Surely the claims of other prophets are foreshadowed in
Hosea 1–3. Joel's calls to repentance, Amos' promise that
Yahweh's wrath will not 'turn back', Obadiah's promise of
restoration, Jonah's direct disobedience and Micah's summary of Israel's infidelity are prefigured. The punishment of
3.4-5 is given more definite contours in Nahum, Habakkuk,
and Zephaniah. Haggai, Zechariah,and Malachi explore the
ramifications of Hosea 1.11 and 2.2. Such correspondences are

not mere coincidences due to a similarity of subject matter. One could take Hosea 1–3, affix it to virtually any of the other eleven books and have an introduction to the prophetic genre that explains the purpose of that book.

How does Hosea 4–14 operate in the Twelve? These chapters unfold the constant disregard of the Sinai covenant by Israel, Yahweh's anger at this outrage, God's unwillingness to cast off His 'child', and the solution to the whole problem, salvation through judgment. The major theme, though, indeed the mental picture that remains in the mind of nearly every reader of the book, is the harlotry of Israel. Like Gomer, Yahweh's 'spouse' strays far from what is acceptable covenant behavior.

Hosea 4–14 demonstrates Israel's infidelity through a series of alternating speeches. Throughout these eleven chapters a dramatic sequence exists where first Yahweh then the prophet, or the prophet then Yahweh, denounce, exhort or predict. Either can serve as revelator or interpreter. This dramatic sequence is repeated in Joel, Obadiah, Micah, Nahum, Habakkuk and Zephaniah. In a way it reappears in Malachi as well. A few examples of alternating speeches will illuminate the portrayal of harlotry in Hosea.

In 4.1-15 the first set of speeches occurs. Hosea revisits the imagery of chapter two in his speech (4.1-3) by declaring that Yahweh has a charge, or dispute (רִיב), against the people of the land. He mentions five specific sins, with adultery capping the list. This sin obviously points back to Gomer. Yahweh's first speech (4.4-15) is even more specific. Here the Lord denounces priest (4.6-9), prophet (4.5), and people (4.9-14) as lovers of adultery and prostitution. Yahweh's assertion in 1.2 that the nation is 'guilty of the vilest adultery in departing from the Lord' is thereby supported. From the very start of the prophetic drama the metaphor for Israel's transgression is prostitution.

Other sections of dialogue continue the prostitution motif. The prophet mentions prostitution in 4.18; 5.7 and 9.1. Yahweh says they are all adulterers in 7.4, and bases his call to repentance on his extreme love for the chosen people (11.1-4). As the book progresses, Israel's adultery is defined as idolatry and rejection of the law. This development is seen in Hosea's speech in 9.1-9, where the prophet says the people are corrupt and destined for punishment, and in Yahweh's response in 9.10-13, which notes that Baal worship will be their downfall. Even in the hopeful conclusion to the book 'waywardness' and its remedy 'love' play a conspicuous role (14.4).

From this brief survey of Hosea its place in the structure of the Twelve begins to take shape. The first three chapters do double duty as an introduction to both the Twelve and the rest of Hosea. Chapters 4–14 set forth God's general attitude toward the sin of Israel. That is, to turn from Yahweh to Baal is idolatry certainly, but, more specifically or picturesquely, is also adultery on the level of prostitution. Hope for restoration exists in the prophecy, as does the threat of punishment, but it is the agonizing portrayal of a wife-nation playing the prostitute for Baalistic cults that permeates the book and tears at the reader's imagination. In the Twelve, then, Hosea opens the book's treatment of punishment and forgiveness. Hosea begins a six-book catalogue of how Israel has not kept faith, stayed married, to Yahweh. How this adultery has taken place becomes more specific as the other books enter the story.

Joel's contribution to the catalogue of sin is at first much more difficult to see because of its emphasis on the Day of Yahweh, a term associated with punishment. As with Hosea's stressing of restoration, one must ask if this important theme has an equally vital purpose behind it. In Joel, the Day of Yahweh will fall heavily on two parties, Israel *and* other nations that have oppressed the Lord's covenant people. Though the sin of Israel is not blatantly obvious in the book the transgression of the nations is evident. A glance at both objects of punishment helps put the positioning of Joel in the Twelve into perspective.

Unlike the recipients of Hosea's condemnation, the sin of God's people in Joel is much more subtle. Judgment is fast approaching, but is not coming because of an obvious rejection of Yahweh and a subsequent embracing of idolatry. Rather, the religion pictured in Joel has lost its vitality. The Lord and His presence are taken for granted. Richard D. Patterson comments:

> Although God had abundantly blessed the Judah of Uzziah's
> day, the people had taken God and his blessings for granted.
> Faith had degenerated into an empty formalism and their
> lives into moral decadence... The ceremonial system was
> designed to express a heart relationship with God. By their
> sin they had forfeited any right to religious ceremony (1985:
> 233).

Patterson's assessment of the book's situation is supported by
the constant call to the priests to mourn and wail (1.13), to the
people to fast (2.15), and to all in general to 'rend your heart
and not your garments' (2.13). Each of these exhortations
relates more to the inward state of the nation than to their
outward disobedience. Any repentance must therefore come
from the heart and not just from external observances. Julius
Bewer concludes; 'Fasting and sackcloth he does not reject, but
they are not enough. Repentance is a matter of the heart, and
it must be sincere and thorough-going, if it is to avail at all'
(1911: 68).

Added to the sin of the covenant nation is the new motif of
the sin of foreign countries. While Hosea focuses exclusively
on the problems of Samaria and Judah, Joel denounces the
actions of Israel's enemies. A great judgment will take place at
the time of the Day of Yahweh that will punish 'all nations'
who have scattered God's people, divided their land and taken
their children into captivity and slavery (3.1-3; 4.1-3 in
Hebrew). Because they have plundered God's people and sold
them to the Greeks, the Lord will place on them the same
catastrophes (3.4-8; 4.4-8 in Hebrew). Israel, on the other
hand, will return to their land with their fortunes restored and
their sins forgiven. Joel's emphasis of worldwide accountabil-
ity to Yahweh prefigures the first two chapters of Amos, where
the generic term 'nations' takes on definite contours as
various countries are named and condemned.

It is instructive to adopt the Masoretic text's division when
placing Joel within the framework of the Twelve. In the
Hebrew, chs. 1–3 deal with the sin and restoration of Israel,
while ch. 4 recounts the future blessing of Israel. The first
three chapters thereby buttress the claims of Hosea by adding
the dangers of inward sin to the problem of external idolatry
and adultery. Chapter 4 introduces a common theme, the sin

of non-covenant nations, and leads to Amos' fuller expansion of this notion. Joel therefore functions as a significant revelation in its own right, but also serves as a bridge between two larger prophecies.

Thematically and structurally, therefore, Joel continues the chronicling of sin in the Twelve. Again, punishment and restoration are present without taking over the book. Evident in the prophecy are calls to repentance and denunciations of specific offenses. The exclusion of the 'heathen' from future blessing supports the idea that the main focus of that section is on sin. Though relatively small and practically undatable, Joel plays a strategic structural role as completer and foreshadower of other prophecies. Without its presence, Amos' preaching against Israel's neighbors comes as a radical shift, and Hosea's book could be twisted to mean Yahweh demands external religion alone.

Amos has perhaps received more critical attention than any other minor prophet. Its date, compilation, situation and message have been examined by a host of commentators, both in commentary series and monographs. Hardly any aspect of the book remains untouched by critical analysis. This study does not pretend to add anything new to historical or linguistic discussions of Amos, but it does hope to build on some of these writings while examining Amos' structural implications.

Various approaches to Amos' structure have been put forward. Several writers posit a three-part framework that divides the book into oracles against neighboring nations and Israel (chs. 1–2), sermons on ethical sin (chs. 3–6) and visions of the end (chs. 7–9). S.R. Driver (1901: 95), Erling Hammershaimb (1970: 13) and W.R. Harper (1905: cxxx) represent this position. J.A. Motyer (1974: 7) suggests a similar scheme, though he divides the major parts of Amos into the roar of the lion (1.2-3.8), the encircling foe (3.9–6.14), and the sovereign Yahweh (7.1–9.15). James Luther Mays separates the visions and Bethel episode from the other major sections in order to explain the structure of the book by theorizing about its redaction (1969: 13). Even in this viewpoint the basic motifs of the prophecy are clear. Finally, John D.W. Watts claims the book has two basic parts. The first section represents the 'words of Amos' (chs. 1–6) that recount conditions in Samaria. The second portion, chs. 7–9, tells of a series of visions that are associated with the events of the prophet's life (1966: 14).

Though these critics may not agree on every point, they do indicate a general consensus that three major sections occur in Amos. One could divide 7.1–9.15, but that passage refers to visionary experiences in the main, so a tripartite framework remains a strong option. Watts' approach reflects a desire to separate the book into 'words' (1.1) and 'visions' (7.1), which is a good textual methodology, but conceals the strong non-Samaria content of 1.3–2.3. It is best, then, to view Amos' structure in three parts recognizing that 7.1–9.15 is a diverse section. Generally speaking 1.1–2.16 deals with world-wide sin, 3.1–6.14 with the ethical sins of Northern Israel, and 7.1–9.15 with the punishment and restoration of Judah. How this structure fits into the framework of the Twelve will become apparent as the discussion proceeds.

Because Joel's final chapter describes the sin of Israel's neighbors there is a smooth transition between Joel and Amos. There is also word play that unites the two. A most obvious example of this linguistic tendency is the likeness between Joel 3.16 (4.16 in Hebrew) and Amos 1.2. The former verse reads: 'The Lord will roar from Zion and thunder from Jerusalem; the earth and the sky will tremble', while the latter says: 'The Lord roars from Zion and thunders from Jerusalem; the pastures of the shepherds dry up, and the top of Carmel withers'. In Hebrew the similarity is even more striking, since the first two lines in both passages are identical.

Apparently Yahweh's roaring is over the sin of the nations, though it can also refer to God's action in judgment. Amos declares the sins of six nations, Syria, Philistia, Tyre, Edom, Ammon and Moab, and then condemns certain actions of Judah and Israel. Nearly all these groups have committed acts of cruelty against other nations or individuals, and Israel is so crass that she sells the poor into slavery for a pittance (2.6-7). Through this parade of nations Amos clearly portrays Yahweh as master and judge of the entire earth. The sins of the nations must be announced because all people are accountable to the Lord.

Section two in Amos (3.1–6.14) elaborates on the ethical corruption of Israel. Just as Hosea recounts the external sin of idolatry, so this part of Amos deals with such outward acts as breaking the covenant (3.2), oppressing the poor (4.1), promulgating phony worship (4.4), promoting injustice (5.12), encouraging complacency (6.1), and accumulating obscene amounts of wealth (6.4-7). Amos employs very picturesque language when portraying these transgressions. Samaria's greedy women are depicted as 'cows of Bashan' (4.1) that are sleek, well-fed, and cruel. Their punishment is as striking as their sin, for the book says they will go into exile like fish on a line (4.2). Israel is described as a person fleeing 'a lion only to meet a bear', and as one presumably safe at home but who will be bitten by a snake there (5.19). Sinners are therefore falsely confident creatures who will be taken unaware by the impending judgment of Yahweh. This portion of the prophecy thus describes the faults of Israel as plainly as the first section does the iniquities of the nations.

Internal disobedience is not absent in Amos, however, as the last segment (7.1–9.15) of Amos attests. The prophet's encounter with Amaziah in Bethel (7.10-17) demonstrates that at the very heart of Israel's problems with God is their unwillingness to hear and heed the word of the Lord. Similarly, their lack of desire for spiritual instruction is dramatized through the image of the people 'staggering', 'wandering' and 'searching' for a message from Yahweh but never able to receive this blessing (8.12). As in Joel, neglect leads to punishment. Faulty practices stem from incorrect attitudes in this prophecy as in all other Biblical accounts.

Several observations on the framework of the minor prophets arise from this brief glance at Amos. First, by including both inward and outward transgressions the book summarizes the two previous prophecies. Because Amos discusses the wrongs committed by Israel's neighbors at some length it expands Joel's hints on the subject. The general descriptions of Joel are illuminated through the giving of the names and crimes of specific countries. Though not as adamant as Hosea about spiritual infidelity, Amos still exhorts the covenant community to base its practices on a constant desire for the word of the Lord. Second, any vagueness concerning what constitutes sin disappears in Amos. Who sins, what their sins are, why they sin, how God feels about the sin and what God will do about sin are all covered in Amos. Thus, the book clarifies the Twelve's definition of sin and its consequences through its stark and vivid portrayal of sin in Israel. The question is no longer *if* people sin, rather it is *how* they sin. Third, because it is such an exhaustive catalogue of transgressions, Amos is a crescendo in the opening portion of the Twelve. Obadiah will start a new sequence on sin that culminates with Micah. For now, sin is internal and external, covenantal and cosmic, evident yet avoidable.

Amos 9.11-15 plays an interesting role in the structure of the minor prophets as the Book's means of moving from Amos to Obadiah. All scholars recognize the hopeful nature of this conclusion to the book whether they feel it is original with Amos (McComiskey 1985: 270-74) or an addition to the text (Harper 1905: xxxii). What commentators have apparently, and oddly, tended to miss is the structural function of 9.12. Here Edom is mentioned as a place Israel will possess in the last days. Most writers correctly observe that Edom is an old and stereotypical enemy (cf. Ps. 137!) but are somewhat puzzled at its appearance in this pericope. For instance, James Luther Mays comments:

> The specific reference to Edom and the text's presupposition that Edom is only a remnant fit best into a time after the fall of Jerusalem in 586, when Judean resentment rose to a shrieking crescendo, and Edom was subject to severe pressure from the south and east (cf. Obad. 10-14; Lam. 4.21f.; Ps. 137.7). It is difficult otherwise to explain the singling out of Edom for particular emphasis; and in the mid-eighth century that nation was independent and intact (1969: 164).

One reason to single out Edom at this juncture is to lead into Obadiah's denouncing of Edom. Though this possibility may be incorrect, it is certainly logical to expect the editor of the Twelve to include one of Amos' oracles on Edom, and the book itself reveals more than one was given (cf. 1.11-12), as a preface to the next book in the Twelve. Certainly Amos' promise that Israel will 'possess the remnant of Edom' parallels Obadiah's prediction that the exiles 'will possess the towns of the Negev'. Indeed the governing verb is very similar in both verses, יִירְשׁוּ in Amos 9.12 and וְיָרְשׁוּ in Obadiah 19. The purpose and context of the two passages also appear to be the same, which means the pericopae are joined by more than a catch phrase. Obadiah illuminates the concept of Edom's place in Israel's future much as Amos 1.2–2.16 completes ideas in Joel 3.1ff. (4.1ff. in Hebrew).

Obadiah's structure is a bit difficult to determine simply because the book is so short. After the inscription in v. 1 and a declaration by an envoy in v. 2, Yahweh apparently speaks through to v. 18 and the prophet delivers the last three verses. Within this scheme the Lord, with the envoy's help, announces Edom's doom (vv. 2-9), gives the reasons for that pronouncement (vv. 10-14), and states the day of Yahweh is near (vv. 15-18). The prophet closes the book with a hopeful, for Israel, look at the future (vv. 19-21). At the center of the prophecy is the sin that causes Edom's downfall. As in Amos 1.11, Edom demonstrates a lack of compassion, with this particular instance occurring when Jerusalem was destroyed. Obadiah accuses the Edomites of committing violence against David's city (v. 10), says they 'stood aloof' while the city was ransacked (v. 11), claims they despised the Jews, rejoiced over their trouble, and boasted over their fall (v. 12), states that they looted the town (v. 13), and relates how they mistreated the refugees from the fallen city (v. 14). Thus Amos' observation about Edom's lack of compassion is substantiated. Edom's sin is that of mistreating its neighbor in time of need.

It is fairly obvious that Obadiah continues the foreign-nation motif begun in Joel. As an ancient foe of the covenant people, Edom was most likely one of the countries Joel believes Yahweh has earmarked for destruction. Amos not only explicitly mentions the above-mentioned crimes of Edom, but also sees its downfall as a harbinger of the day of the Lord. In these ways Obadiah fits very well into the sin section of the Twelve. Much as Amos expands preceding ideas, so Obadiah illuminates the Edom threads of Joel and Amos. Sin is in the forefront of Obadiah as it is in the previous three books. Here, too, the iniquity of Edom seems to represent the sin of other nations as well. God takes note of what happens beyond the borders of Israel.

But what is Obadiah's structural relationship to Jonah, the book that follows it? One can hardly read Jonah without sensing a rich use of irony that permeates the work. Perhaps the most ironic twist of all is that Jonah, the Hebrew man of God, wants to treat Nineveh as Edom, Assyria and her other enemies treat Israel. Obadiah 10-14 describes Jonah's attitude perfectly. He is quite willing to stand aloof and hope for Nineveh's obliteration. Thus he is no better than an Edomite! Such unexpected equivalencies are not unknown in the Twelve, as the oracles in Amos 1.3–2.8 and Zeph. 2.4–3.5 demonstrate. Obadiah thereby foreshadows the ruthless and ungodly actions of Jonah. More sin is yet to be discovered.

Perhaps because its literary artistry has been accepted for so long, and it is narrative in form, Jonah has been examined by a number of literary critics. Edwin Good and Mona West highlight the irony in Jonah in their respective works, and in doing so locate the essence of the book's intention. Both writers correctly observe that the major concern of Jonah is to use the prophet as a symbol of the audience's exclusivistic tendencies, nationalistic pride and callous lack of compassion. The juxtaposition between what Jonah is and ought to be, what he preaches and the crowd's reaction, and what he hopes will happen to Nineveh and what actually takes place reflects the author's desire to prod Israel into new patterns of behavior. As West explains:

> The incongruities and opposition draw the audience into a dynamic encounter with the message of the book... Whether the irony was intended specifically to criticize prophetic hypocrisy, blatant nationalism, jealousy over the repentance of such great evil, or expound on the love of God, it is evident that the post-exilic audience of Israelites were not living up to the expectations that God had for a people that were to be a 'light to the nations' (1984: 240-41).

In effect, then, Jonah and all like him are as sinful as the Edomites in Obadiah. Like Edom, Jonah is more interested in watching the destruction of his enemies than in working for their salvation.

Edwin Good intensifies the notion of Israel's sin by treating the book as biting satire instead of as a straightforward parable. The force of Jonah thus moves from a didactic story to a forceful attack on unacceptable attitudes and behavior. Once more Jonah represents the people, and the satirist's ability to portray the absurdity of the prophet's deeds highlights the absurdity of the actions of the whole nation. This absurdity reaches its climax when Jonah cares more for the plant than for Nineveh. Good concludes that

> Jonah, unable to take seriously either of his confessions of Yahweh, 'the God who made the sea and the dry land' (ch. 1.9), 'a God gracious and merciful, slow to anger and great of grace, and one who repents of evil' (ch. 4.2), is the personification of that arrogant isolationism which holds the God of heaven and earth in its pocket, all the while making pious noises about his universal reign and the breadth of his compassion (1981: 53-54).

Every phase of Jonah's structure contributes to the ironic picture of Israel as presented through the life of the prophet. Basically each chapter is a section unto itself. More specifically, however, 1.1-16 recounts the call of Jonah to go to Nineveh, his subsequent disobedience to that call, and his experiences with the seamen. Next, 1.17–2.10 covers Jonah's time in the whale and how God offers him a second chance. Then 3.1-10 portrays the prophet's 'ministry' to Nineveh. Finally, 4.1-11 reveals Jonah's displeasure with Yahweh's mercy.

In the first section irony appears on two fronts. Though Jonah is a prophet and is called to a task he flees from the Lord's command. Other prophets have some difficulty accepting their divine function (e.g. Jeremiah), but Jonah is the only one who does the opposite of what he is told. Equally ironic is the fact that the sailors recognize the power and majesty of God while the 'man of God' languishes in the deep. Chapter two's major purpose is to demonstrate the temporary nature of Jonah's repentance. His actions reflect the tendency of even covenant people to turn to Yahweh in distress, only to carry out the Lord's orders half-heartedly, if at all. Just how limited Jonah's acceptance of his prophetic task is becomes evident in 3.1-10. If forced to preach he will do so, but the message will be a shadow of the great prophetic preaching found elsewhere in the canon. Indeed, the pagan king of Nineveh appears more responsible for the repentance of the city than God's messenger (3.6-10). No doubt the ugliest picture of Jonah, though, emerges in ch. 4. Here the prophet's anger flares because a plant dies but people do not. Like the Edomites who 'stood aloof' and rejoiced in the destruction of Jerusalem (Obad. 11-12) Jonah positions himself to watch God destroy Nineveh. Also, like Edom, the prophet will learn how far Yahweh's mercy extends. Israel's sin is that of hating a neighbor. Those who lack compassion always incur the wrath of a merciful Creator, as Amos 1.2ff. definitely indicates.

Micah's connection with Jonah as an adjoining book is not significant, but this sixth book in the Twelve does have a close relationship with its five predecessors as a whole. In fact, it functions as a summary of the main concerns of those prophecies while working to complete the structural section on sin. Other connections exist between Micah and Hosea–Jonah, but the few following correspondences help illuminate their interrelationship. Micah alludes to Hosea in 1.7 through the use of prostitute imagery as a means of describing Israel. Joel is brought to mind in 1.15 when a conqueror threatens the land. Throughout the book, ethical transgressions that are mentioned remind one of the excesses denounced by Amos (e.g. 2.1ff.). Micah's warning to Israel's enemies to beware of gloating over her demise mirrors Obadiah's dire predictions about Edom. Even Jonah is addressed, since 4.1-5 claims that many countries will worship the Lord, and perhaps 5.7-8 speaks to Jonah's fear of the Assyrians. Clear to the end of the book Micah stresses God's covenant with Israel (7.15), as does Hosea and Amos. The sins of foreign nations will be judged as in Joel, Amos, Obadiah and Jonah. Both inward and outward iniquities are exposed (cf. 2.1ff. and the classical passage of true worship, 6.6-8). In practically every way possible Micah analyzes and summarizes the previous five prophecies. This book is still creative and telling in its own right, however, and deserves as much scrutiny as possible.

A good bit of the scrutiny already afforded Micah revolves around its own individual structure. Several options have been forwarded which basically fall into three categories. Each proposition must seriously consider the presence of three calls 'to hear' various aspects of the word of Yahweh (1.2; 3.1; 6.1) as keys to the division of the work. Who is called to hear and what they are called to hear bears directly, of course, on the message Micah presents. Some writers simply break the book at every new appearance of שמע, and assert then that chs. 1–2,

3–5, and 6–7 contain threats of doom and promises of hope within each separate segment. John T. Willis follows this pattern, though he also charts other significant aspects of symmetry in the book such as the relationship of covenant lawsuits and oracles of hope in chs. 1–2 and 6–7 (1969: 191-97). Leslie Allen agrees with Willis' division of Micah, because he believes each segment is characterized by short or long oracles of hope or doom (1976: 257-61). The advantage of Willis and Allen's position is that the unity of the canonical form of the book is maintained through the recognition of various literary techniques.

Other interpreters break the book into three parts, but with the sections being chs. 1–3, 4–5, and 6–7. Redactional and thematic concerns lie behind this scheme. John M.P. Smith summarizes both concerns well. As for the latter issue he observes:

> The book of Micah falls naturally into three parts... They are chs. 1–3, chs. 4 and 5 and chs. 6 and 7. They are differentiated from each other by their contents, tone and point of view and to some extent by their poetic form. Chs. 1–3 contain almost exclusively denunciations of sin and proclamations of approaching punishment; chs. 4 and 5 devoted almost as exclusively to words of hope and cheer; while chs. 5 and 6 combine these two elements (1911: 8).

Smith's conclusions at this point are partially true, in that these sections do reflect the themes he mentions, but he fails to recognize the diversity of motifs inherent in the chapters. On the former matter (redaction), Smith, like Mays (1976: 21), thinks the theology of hope, stylistic differences, etc. between chs. 1–3 and 4–7 argue against a unified eighth-century work. Thus, chs. 1–3 must be the material to which the rest of the book responds. Smith's final assessment of chs. 4–7 therefore concludes:

> Nothing short of a complete reversal of current views concerning Hebrew eschatology, such as that proposed by Gressmann, could make these chapters intelligible for the age of Micah. Furthermore, as the foregoing history of criticism shows, it is impossible to regard the chapters as a unit in themselves... (1911: 12).

Smith's conclusions betray what unity exists in the text. Even if one grants Smith his historical conclusions he has not dealt adequately with the discernible progression of Micah's structure.

At this point some may agree with Ralph Smith and decide certain scholars 'try to organize the seemingly unorganizable' (1984: 8). Such resignation is unnecessary, though, if the place of Micah within Hosea–Micah is seriously considered. Since, as has been mentioned, Micah brings together the various emphases of its five predecessors, it is likely that the prophecy's structure reflects the sin of Israel and the other nations. James Luther Mays argues that Micah has two parts: chs. 1–5 and 6–7. In this arrangement the first two commands to hear are directed towards foreign nations and the final one to Israel (1976: 2-12). Micah's first summons comes to the 'peoples' and the 'earth', and 5.15 predicts the wrath of God on the 'nations', so Mays' idea has merit. The summons of ch. 3, then, is basically a call to hear the verdict of the indictment begun in 1.2. Therefore, 6.1-2 signals a conflict between God and Israel alone. The nations must hear Yahweh's complaints against the covenant people so they will know why God judges them. Further, the nations must learn to come to Yahweh if they are to survive (4.1-4), and must also learn how futile it is to stand against Israel (4.11-13). As for Israel, they must confess their inward and outward uncleanness (6.9-7.6) if they are to be forgiven (7.18-20).

With consummate accuracy, then, Micah summarizes the רִיב begun in Hos. 4.1 and concluded in Mic. 6.2ff. Israel breaks the Sinai covenant, prostitutes themselves (1.7), acts unjustly (2.1ff.), eschews real spirituality (2.6), harbors worthless priests and prophets (4.11) and is therefore bound for destruction. Though the nations will sweep down upon Israel, like in Joel and Obadiah, they too are under the judgment of God because of their misdeeds (5.10-15). As in Jonah, Yahweh has mercy on every country on earth (4.1-4). By shaping the book into two major parts, the author allows covenant and cosmic sin to emerge in all its ugliness. Even the hopeful conclusion to Micah (7.18-20) is based on a confession of sin and plea for pardon. Like Hosea–Jonah, Micah stresses that God does forgive, but the main point is that specific sins must be removed.

Through this summary, the Twelve argues for the need of repentance. Israel and the nations may remain in their individual and collective sinful states, but to do so is to ignore the graphic description of their faults found in Hosea–Micah.

This brief look at the first six minor prophets in no way exhausts the ways the books mount their case against iniquity. Indeed more interrelationships are noted in the chapter on plot. Still, some foundational assessments arise. Hosea attacks the spiritual infidelity of the covenant people. Joel repeats that theme, then inaugurates the discussion of the sins of all people. Amos, of course, summarizes these notions, and adds much detail about outward transgression. Obadiah, drawing on Amos 9.12, continues to reveal how foreign nations displease Yahweh and at the same time leads into Jonah by denouncing heartless neighbors. Jonah highlights the inward-outward sin of nationalistic spiritual prejudice. Micah provides, like Amos, a summary of other books, and includes keys to repentance and faith. As a group these books are a cohesive unit. They work as a structural whole with a common goal of presenting a devastating picture of sin and its consequences. At this point the wisdom of placing the books in their canonical order is apparent. If the remaining six books fulfill a distinct purpose as well as Hosea–Micah, then the Twelve as a whole is a powerful unit indeed.

2. *Nahum–Zephaniah: Covenant and Cosmic Punishment*

It is clear that, though Hosea–Micah mentions the possibility of punishment and restoration, no ultimate fulfillment of this threat/promise exists in these books. There is no complete catharsis for the covenant or foreign people. Sin must be punished. Joy must follow. In fact, there can be no restoration except as it rises out of the ashes of judgment. How that punishment occurs is the theme of the next three minor prophets. Nahum portrays the punishment of Nineveh, which represents the judgment of all foreign countries. Habakkuk chronicles the chastisement of Jerusalem through the prophet's search for the meaning of the Babylonian crisis. Finally, Zephaniah, much like Micah, sums up the punishment motif by demonstrating how Israel and its neighbors will suffer through the day of Yahweh. Because of judgment, though, all people have the opportunity to 'call on the name of the Lord and serve him shoulder to shoulder' (Zeph. 3.9). So Zephaniah prefigures the restoration emphasis in Haggai–Malachi.

Nahum presents in cold, stark language the fate of any nation that refuses to repent of the sin explained in the first half of the Twelve. Nineveh, the object of Yahweh's affection in Jonah, is now the target of divine wrath. Written sometime between the fall of Thebes in 663 BC (3.8-10) and the fall of Nineveh itself in 612 BC, this prophecy sets the standard for picturesque predictions of doom. C. Hassell Bullock illuminates the powerful effect of the book when he declares that

> if there was any doubt that the Lord would take vengeance upon Nineveh, the evil capital of Assyria, Nahum with his graphic word pictures of her fall would remove it out of mind. The sight of warriors dressed in red, flashing steel, madly racing chariots, frantic Assyrian soldiers hurrying to the wall, galloping horses, piles of corpses, combined with the sounds of women moaning like doves, leaves the audience with the feeling of having tuned in on the devastation. The scenes with all their visual horror, painted with the colorful hues of Nahum's vocabulary, give an immediacy to divine judgment that mere threats and promises cannot give. The threat of judgment is present in the book (1.8, 14; 3.5-6), but the reality of judgment is the thing that Nahum seeks to bring to his audience (1986).

Commentators observe that the structure serves the dual function of revealing the nature of judgment and the character of Yahweh. Certainly these notions are two sides of the same motif. S.R. Driver states that ch. 1 describes the personality of God as kind and wrathful at the same time (1.7-8), ch. 2 portrays the defeat of Nineveh, and ch. 3 tells why such woe comes to the city (1906: 11-12). John M.P. Smith basically agrees with Driver's reasons for a tripartite structure (1911: 267). Bullock focuses on the Lord's character, saying Nahum shows God as avenger and savior (1.2-8), as judge (1.9–2.2), and bringer of woe (2.3–3.19) (1986: 221-22). None of these positions are particularly faulty, though Bullock's scheme makes the final section too long. Driver's assessment captures the intent of the book, if the revelation of Yahweh's character is fit into this structure, and so it is followed below.

Because Yahweh is a 'jealous' God, He will punish those who owe Him allegiance. Previous mercy has been offered Nineveh (cf. Jonah), but now no mercy remains. Though not easily angered, the Lord will not leave the guilty unpunished (1.5). Who are the guilty? Those who plot against the Lord by doing evil (1.9, 11). Nineveh is such a place. Chapter 1 ominously threatens Nineveh that the Lord says: 'I will prepare your grave, for you are vile' (1.14). Judah will survive for a time because of the downfall of Nineveh, but this grace is more a result of God's anger at the Assyrians than any great pleasure in the covenant people.

In ch. 2 the threats of the previous section are actualized in a series of three vivid scenes. Verses 3 and 4 describe the coming of Assyria's enemies, with the latter verse adding almost mythic qualities to the invaders, since their chariots 'look like flaming torches' and 'dart about like lightning'. The Assyrian forces, on the other hand, are pitiful in comparison. Even their best troops stumble as they go to war (2.5). Their attempts to secure the city and the palace end in disaster (2.5-6). Why? Because such is God's plan for the city (2.7). All that is left is the moaning of the people over the city's demise (2.7) and an ebbing away of the place that resembles water going out of a pool. Now that scenes depicting the might of Nineveh's foes and the weakness of Nineveh itself have been presented, the prophet mocks the plight of the Assyrians in 2.11-12. Though formerly a lion's den, the lion will be left desolate without prey (2.13). All who show contempt for Yahweh eventually become contemptible themselves.

Whenever judgment falls God has a concrete reason for why that punishment is necessary. In Nineveh's case, it comes because it is a 'city of blood, full of lies, full of plunder, never without victims' (3.1). To earn such an approbation is to truly plot agains the Lord (1.9, 11), since God is creator and sustainer of the whole earth. The final section of Nahum offers the motivation behind Nineveh's downfall while at the same time taunting the city for its helplessness. Her fortresses are like figs that drop easily into the mouths of hungry eaters (3.13), her soldiers are mere women (3.13), and her leaders are like locusts that fly away when the day gets too hot (3.17). Nineveh falls, but instead of mourning this event encourages rejoicing. All nations recognize the cruelty of Assyria, and once more the emphasis of Amos, Obadiah, and Jonah on neighborliness resurfaces. Edward Dalglish claims this chapter is a malediction, 'in which the spoken word, implied or uttered in the name of the deity, was impregnated with power to secure its fulfillment' (1972: 242). If so, the curse certainly found its fulfillment in the eventual crushing of Nineveh.

Nahum's short prophecy demonstrates the validity of the promises of judgment in Hosea–Micah. Nineveh is the first in the Twelve to learn that punishment follows sin. Because of the assurances afforded Judah in ch. 1, however, one is left to wonder if Yahweh will judge the covenant people as well. Does sin have covenant, as well as cosmic, consequences? Habakkuk answers that question. The section opened by Nahum plays an extremely vital role, since without judgment the prophets' complaints about sin are quite toothless, and without chastisement there can be no meaningful or final restoration.

Habakkuk is a significant theological treatise because of its interest in why God acts. The questions the prophet poses to the Lord are deep and telling. Due at least in part to this theological depth, Habakkuk's place in the structure of the Twelve is pivotal. Placed in the center of the punishment section, this book completes God's most dreaded threats. Even Israel must suffer if the nation will not fulfill its covenant obligations. Though the Lord agonizes over 'giving the people up' (Hos. 11.8) in the sin section, He is now able to do so in order to get them back later. Thus, Habakkuk is the culmination of Hosea–Nahum. God will judge. It is the beginning of hope as well, since the Lord tends to redeem those He punishes. Habakkuk must ask and answer difficult questions, then, if it is to perform it canonical purpose.

Most scholars agree that the structure of Habakkuk is based on the prophet's questions to God (1.2-4 and 1.12–2.1), Yahweh's answers to those queries (1.5-11 and 2.2-20), and the prophet's prayer, or psalm, that concludes the book (3.1-19). Some discussions of unity and redaction do exist, but such considerations are not major issues in Habakkuk studies. The questions raised by the prophet tie the book to predictions of judgment in Hosea–Micah, to the certainty of God's punishment of non-covenant states described in Nahum, and to the inevitable chastisement of Jerusalem featured in Zephaniah. Habakkuk's prayer exemplifies the prophetic belief that Yahweh can judge all peoples because the Lord is sovereign over all creation.

Habakkuk's initial complaint is against his own people. Through a series of four questions, the prophet basically demands to know why the Lord allows the wicked to prosper. Related to this desire to know why such outrages are allowed is his determination to find out how long these iniquities will remain unpunished. Both are good, canonical questions as well. How long Yahweh waits before moving against sin and why Yahweh waits must be answered if the earlier parts of the Twelve are to remain viable warnings. God's answer comes as a surprise to the prophet. Yahweh will act soon, but this action will come in the form of an invasion by the Babylonians, a nation whose deeds sound very much like those committed by the Assyrians and described in Nahum. Thus, the wicked punish the wicked. Such a notion is amazing indeed and will lead to a second question. Before moving on, however, one must realize the significance of the punishment of Judah. Just as the preceding prophets predict, the covenant people will receive God's wrath. How long will God spare Israel? No longer than it takes to send the Babylonians against Jerusalem.

The second complaint (1.12–2.1) relates to 1.5-11 in that the prophet realizes that if Babylon punishes Israel then the wicked still prosper. Therefore, he wonders if Yahweh will allow Babylon 'to keep on emptying his net, destroying nations without mercy?' (1.17). Surely this problem relates to the threats agains the foreign nations contained in Joel, Amos, Obadiah, Jonah and Micah. Their evil cannot pass unnoticed either. Yahweh's response draws together various sins and condemns them all. Righteousness characterizes the people of faith, but arrogance, greed, oppression, murder, cruelty, idolatry, violence and shame mark the life of Babylon. When Babylon experiences Yahweh's judgment all her wickedness is reversed against her. Those extorted, plundered, exposed, and oppressed will rise against Babylon, so the victimizer becomes the victimized. From God's reply it is evident that no wicked nation, covenant or cosmic, will escape divine wrath. Within this second response, too, the Lord declares that all punishment results as part of His plan to fill the earth with the knowledge of Himself (2.14). All that happens will answer the prophet's query; 'O Lord, are you not from everlasting?'— which really addresses Yahweh's sovereignty. Because God is righteous *and* sovereign, no sin can go unpunished lest God's glory be diminished and name sink in esteem.

The prayer recorded in 3.1-19 celebrates the satisfactory answers Yahweh offers to Habakkuk's complaints. The Lord's righteousness and power are no longer challenged, and the prophet has learned the lesson of 2.4, as is evident in 3.19. At all points God has proved faithful. Regardless of how bleak the national situation becomes, Habakkuk promises to watch, wait, and hope for Yahweh to act (3.16-18). As 1.5 promises, the prophet is amazed at God's answer (3.16), but this dismay is preferable to a growing distrust in the sovereign God.

If Nahum left any doubts about the punishment of the foreign nations, Habakkuk relieves them. Even mighty Babylon, successor to Assyria as the major threat to Israel's security, has sinned and thereby come under God's wrath and judgment. The book also mentions the threat of punishment looming over the covenant people. They can, and will, suffer for their sins. Such ideas are startling to say the least, particularly in this section of the Twelve, since the focus so far has been on Assyria, a foreign country. Habakkuk's structure of complaint against Israel then complaint against Babylon perfectly illustrates the major components of the punishment motif. In this way it fits the middle section of the Twelve's sin–punishment–restoration framework. In fact, its hard answers to hard questions makes its place that much more valuable in the punishment segment.

Zephaniah gathers the major elements of Nahum–Zephaniah in much the same way Amos and Micah summarize the emphases on sin in their section. As in Hosea, Joel, Amos, Micah and Habakkuk, Judah will suffer for its sin, so also in this book it will suffer through the day of the Lord. As in Joel, Amos, Obadiah, Jonah, Micah, Nahum and Habakkuk, so also in Zephaniah the nations outside Israel will be punished for their iniquities, again through Yahweh's day. The sins of the covenant nation are recounted very clearly as in Hosea, Amos, etc., and a list of foreign countries bound for chastisement is included that is not unlike the one in Amos. Despite the summary nature of the prophecy the book still displays creative structural characteristics of its own.

In order to bring together the various strands of the punishment material, Zephaniah utilizes the familiar prophetic image of the day of the Lord. Cosmic punishment is at the forefront as the book begins, since the whole earth will be swept away in the wake of God's anger (1.2-3). This cosmic devastation becomes more detailed as the book progresses. Judah is a specific target of the day, as is Philistia (2.4-7), Moab and Ammon (2.8-11), Cush (2.12) and Assyria (2.13-15). At the end of the time of judgment a remnant from many nations will worship Yahweh (3.9), and Judah will experience restoration (3.14-20). Very systematically the structure of the prophecy reveals these implications of covenant and cosmic punishment.

Various writers have observed the presence of three major parts of Zephaniah. According to S.R. Driver these parts are impending doom (1.1-18), repentance (2.1–3.7) and future restoration (3.8-20) (1891: 341-42). Probably sections one and three accurately portray Zephaniah's intentions in those passages, though Driver's emphasis on repentance in a section heavily weighted with denunciations of both Israel and the heathen seems overdone. The three divisions as located by Childs are threats against Judah (1.2–2.3), threats against nations (2.4–3.8), and hope to both (3.9-20) (1980: 458). These ideas are closer to the purpose of Zephaniah than Driver's, but Childs fails to note the importance of the alternating of speakers to the structure of the prophecy. Like many of the other minor prophets, Zephaniah constantly shifts between orations of the prophet and those of Yahweh. Three cycles of speeches occur in the book, with 1.2–1.17 describing a coming day of judgment, 1.18–3.5 telling the effects of that judgment and 3.6-20 setting forth the restoration that comes as a result of the judgment. Thus, three major divisions do exist in the prophecy, and they are fashioned by a series of provocative speeches.

The first significant section of Zephaniah consists of five speeches, three by Yahweh and two by the prophet, which describe the general nature of the Day of the Lord. The first two speeches set forth the idea of catastrophic judgment and provide a name for that punishemnt. The third and fourth state, like the book of Habakkuk, that Judah will suffer through the day of the Lord, and again explain the nature of Yahweh's judgment. The Lord finishes the initial portion of the prophecy by flatly stating that the sin of the people will result in condemnation.

Once a general notion of judgment is presented, the book's second major division reveals who will suffer with Judah in the terrible punishment (1.18-3.5). Zephaniah gives the opening speech in this section, claiming that the 'shameful nation', Judah (2.1), will be joined in judgment by Philistia. Yahweh responds by adding Moab and Ammon to the list (2.8-10). The prophet agrees that God should destroy all idols in 2.11, only to be followed by Yahweh's condemnation of Cush (2.12). Finally, the prophet blasts Assyria and finishes his sober statements as he began them—with a denunciation of Judah (3.1-5). Even a casual perusal of this part of Zephaniah reminds one of Amos' parade of nations, and the oblique references to punishment in that book are given as specific threats here. Therefore Zephaniah summarizes punishment by dramatizing the logical results of sin.

Section three of Zephaniah plays a strategic structural role in the Twelve. It provides the climax for the punishment division of the minor prophets, as one might expect, but it also introduces the Twelve's structural emphasis on restoration. In the midst of sure doom and devastation, Yahweh's first speech offers *hope* through the Day of Yahweh (3.6-13). A remnant will be saved that will be joined by nations purified by judgment. This development is foreshadowed in 2.3, 7, and 9. The prophet exults in this resolution (3.14-17), and is followed by the Lord's promises to the remnant (3.18-20). At this point an incredible change has occurred: God's judgment is the means of restoration. Only through punishment can restoration emerge. Thus, 3.8-9 provides the knowledge that after Yahweh's day there will be blessings for the remnant. Just how those blessings will materialize is the focus of Haggai–Malachi.

It is, therefore, fairly clear that Nahum, Habakkuk and Zephaniah all chronicle the certainty of God's punishment of iniquity. Whether one nation or many, individual or group, great or small, all will fall prey to the fearful judgment of God. Lest this wrath seem overwhelming, however, these books teach that 'the just shall live by faith' (Hab. 2.4), that God is still sovereign (Hab. 3.17-19), that Yahweh is punishing justly (Nah. 1.3), and that a remnant can survive that dreadful time (Zeph. 3.6-20). But sin does have direct and telling consequences. Assyria, Israel, and all the surrounding nations are under Yahweh's control. Though the punishment seems harsh, yet it is just.

3. *Haggai–Malachi: Hope for Restoration*
If the book of the Twelve ended with Zephaniah, it would be an incomplete portrayal of the major prophetic ideas. Though Zephaniah includes a hopeful future, how that future unfolds would remain a mystery. Haggai, Zechariah, and Malachi offer a consistent pattern for how restoration will take place. While earlier books have hints of God's plans for Israel, these prophecies divulge specific fulfillments of those promises, both in the historical life situation of the covenant people and through still further predictions for the future.

Since Haggai and Zechariah probably ministered about the same time (c. 520 BC; cf. Ezra 5.1; 6.14), scholars have often discussed their messages together. Various links exist between Zechariah and Malachi as well, not least of which is the presence of the recurring phrase 'a burden of the word of Yahweh' (משא דבר יהוה) in Zech. 9.1; 12.1, and Mal. 1.1. Very few commentators, however, have examined how the *three* books are related. An exception to this tendency is Ronald W. Pierce, who asserts that Haggai–Malachi has five 'literary connectors' that unite the three books. These five connectors include the historical framework of Haggai/Zechariah 1–8, the literary and thematic unity of Zechariah 1–14 (the series of night visions), the oracle titles of Zechariah 9, 12 and Malachi 1, the interrogative element in the Haggai–Malachi corpus, and the narrative genre of the three books (1984: 277-85). Pierce also believes there is a definite thematic unity in the prophecies. In a summary of his approach Pierce says that

> through a style of rhetorical questions, the messages of the prophets of the return are closely related to each other. The author begins with the inquiries of Haggai's sermons (1.4; 2.3, 11-12), moves to the curious prophet of the night visions, Zechariah (chaps. 1–6), who preaches his sermons with a style much like that of his contemporary (cf. Zech. 7.5-7; 8.6), then concludes his work with the six sermons of YHWH's mysterious 'messenger', in which the audience asks the questions and the prophet responds (Mal. 1.2, 6-7; 2.10, 14, 17; 3.7, 13). The question/answer schema is broken periodically by several brief interludes (Hag. 1.12-15; 2.20-23; Zech. 6.9-15; Mal. 4.4-5) and one major oracular section (Zechariah 9–14) (1984: 401).

In Pierce's scheme even 'the major interruption, Zechariah 9–14, holds an important key to the central thrust of the work as a whole' (1984: 401), since this section leads into Malachi by showing how the post-exilic community fails to meet Yahweh's expectations.

Certainly, the stylistic analyses Pierce presents are sound in their conclusions. There are indeed a number of literary traits that bind the books together. Pierce's conclusions on the tone of these prophecies are also interesting. He decides that the writers present a negative picture of the post-exilic nation (1984: 411). Joyce Baldwin disagrees to a certain extent with this interpretation, as do other writers, by deciding that Haggai–Malachi is cautiously optimistic about Israel's future restoration (1972: 13-24). Such discussions raise the important questions of whether the books really stress restoration and if so what kind of restoration is meant.

There is no doubt that each of the last three minor prophets intends to call for and predict the restoration of various aspects of Israel's life. Haggai speaks of the new temple as a symbol of restored worship. In this way the prophecy gives an historical event to match predictions like Ezekiel 40–48. Zechariah declares that Jerusalem and indeed the whole covenant people will be restored as 'holy to Yahweh' (14.20-21). Malachi is definitely a sober book, but it also stresses restoration in that it demonstrates what the covenant people must do to bring about a new order. This final book of the Twelve also explains that, as Zechariah emphasizes, a Messianic figure will help the restoration take place. Why the tone of these books is a bit dark will be discussed in Chapter 4, but here it will be stressed that this tone does not alter the basic restoration motif in the section's structure.

Most scholars divide Haggai into four sections, since the book consists of the collection of four dated prophecies that are in chronological order. Joyce Baldwin states: 'From the precise dates given in the text we discover that Haggai preached the sermons recorded in his book within the space of fifteen weeks during the second year of Darius 1 (521-486 BC)' (1972: 29). Each of the four message introduces a new subject, thus providing a smooth transition from one topic to the next.

Haggai's first sermon (1.1-15) challenges the post-exilic community to build a new temple. Each of the first three 'words' explore this theme. The prophet first argues that, quite simply, the temple ought to be built. Because the people have built their own homes and allowed Yahweh's house to remain a ruin they are under the wrath of God. Haggai declares:

> You have planted much, but have harvested little. You eat,
> but never have enough. You drink, but never have your fill.
> You put on clothes, but are not warm. You earn wages, only
> to put them in a purse with holes in it (1.6).

These problems will disappear only when God's temple is constructed ' "so that I may take pleasure in it and be honored", says the Lord' (1.7). Amazingly, the people heed Haggai's sermon and begin work on the temple a scant twenty three days after the oracle is delivered (1.15). Therefore, the building's physical restoration is a reality.

Spiritual restoration of the temple is the theme of the prophet's second dated message (2.1-9). Here Yahweh states that although the new house of worship is less impressive than its predecessor (2.3), He is still keeping all promises to Israel (2.5), is still present among the people (2.4-5), and will make the 'glory of this present house... greater than the glory of the former house' (2.9). This last declaration is quite startling indeed if one merely looks at the physical dimensions of the sanctuary. What will make the new temple greater is the fact that God's glory will be in the place (2.7), which will draw all nations to the area of worship (2.6-9). Through the restoration of Yahweh's presence both Israel and the surrounding nations can come to the Lord.

Sermon three (2.10-19) states that a cursed, defiled Israel will once more be blessed now that the temple has been restored. In 2.10-14 the prophet shows that Israel is impure by questioning the priests about how inanimate objects become ceremonially unclean. Because Israel, an unclean people, has 'touched' the land, it too has become defiled and thereby has ceased to yield a normal crop. Now that the house of Yahweh is built, though, all will be well.

Finally, the fourth message (2.20-23) concludes the book with a prophecy about Zerubbabel, the governor of Judah. Apparently the restoration of the temple brought on messianic hopes that Haggai felt would find some fulfillment in Zerubbabel. It is impossible from a modern standpoint to know exactly what the prophet intended to convey about his governor. Perhaps, as Joyce Baldwin suggests, 'as time passed, and Zerubbabel was not honoured as had been expected, the Messianic hopes were transferred to his descendants' (1972: 54). Whatever the original intention of this oracle, its function in the book of Haggai as a whole is that of one more example of the benefits of the temple's restoration. As a leader in the rebuilding project Zerubbabel is blessed by Yahweh. Great events will quite naturally follow the return of God's glory to the temple.

Though a somewhat simple book, Haggai does an excellent job of beginning the restoration emphasis of the last part of the Twelve. David L. Petersen sums up some of the facets of Haggai's structural concerns when he writes:

1. It memorializes a major cultural achievement, the rebuilding of the temple. From its perspective, Haggai's words provided the impetus whereby reconstruction was carried on.
2. The book highlights the role of Haggai as he assisted the people in dealing with the restoration of the temple

compound—in initiating reconstruction, facilitating the official restoration of the sacrificial cultus.
3. The book provides for the prospect of future weal. Judah is now obeying a prophet's words. Since, according at least to deuteronomistic history, disobedience of a prophet's words resulted in destruction, obedience to Haggai's words should yield prosperity.
4. The temple compound, now in operation, and the cultus, recently reinstituted, deserve the support of the people (1984: 36).

Perhaps Petersen's third point is the most important one for this study. Because restoration has begun, spiritual renewal can follow. What else needs to be restored is the subject of the final two books of the minor prophets.

Zechariah is a very complex and demanding book. Its unusual visions, messianic images and critical problems make it a great challenge to interpreters. Due to this complexity, scholars have come to some widely divergent conclusions about the structure, nature, and purpose of the book. Despite all these differences of opinion, however, practically every commentator on Zechariah feels the prophecy stresses restoration of some kind. Some writers stress the restoration of the temple, some of Jerusalem, and some of the cosmos (e.g. Petersen 1984: 195-96), but all do focus on a renewal motif.

Part of the problem scholars have deciding on Zechariah's structure and purpose is due to disagreement on its date and authorship. A majority of Old Testament scholars believe chs. 1–8 and 9–14 are two very different works penned by two or more authors working many years apart. Many conservative scholars (C. Hassell Bullock 1986; Kenneth Barker 1985, etc.) argue that the book is a unity, and therefore it comes from the hand of Zechariah himself. More and more scholars today, though, claim that regardless of the prophecy's origin it *functions* as a unified literary construction. This idea is the most profitable way for all parties to approach Zechariah's structure and purpose, since the final form of the text is capable of conveying the book's message.

Though Zechariah mentions various people, places, and institutions that need cleansing and restoration the renewal of

Jerusalem is the key to all other instances of restoration. If the city of God is what it is meant to be, then the people, the nation, the heathen, as well as the universe can become pleasing to Yahweh. Certainly, temple restoration is vital to Zechariah's purpose, but the prophet's vision is much greater than any individual person or institution. Even Jerusalem itself is a symbol of renewal that extends far beyond its own walls. As John D.W. Watts observes:

> The theme of the book is the kingdom of God. This theme is presented in many variations interwoven with other themes. Jerusalem's relation to the kingdom is a thread which runs through the whole book. The Lord's intention to reestablish his dwelling there is the reason for building the Temple. God's coming and dwelling in Jerusalem are signs of her election. She is the centerpiece of the drama of 'that day'. When all else falls under the Lord's final judgment, Jerusalem will stand exalted and confirmed (1972: 311).

David L. Petersen's *Haggai and Zechariah 1–8* supports this view of Jerusalem's centrality in Zechariah. Petersen claims that Jerusalem's physical reconstruction is a harbinger of more utopian hopes for the future. Thus,

> Zechariah's visions stand somewhere between purely mundane concerns and a utopian vision of renewal. The visions are not concrete in the way in which Haggai concentrates on agricultural yield (Hag. 2.14-19) and on the preservation of capital (Hag. 1.6), and they are not concrete in the way in which Ezek. 40–48 provides detailed measurements for the restored temple compound. Nor are Zechariah's visions utopian as are the expectations for wealth in Hag. 2.6-7 or as is Ezekiel's vision of a society without religious error (Ezek. 43.7). Zechariah's visions stand somewhere between utopian social vision and concrete physical and social detail (1984: 113).

By being 'in between' reality and utopia, Zechariah can both challenge and encourage its audience. The physical restoration of Jerusalem thereby promises to lead to a spiritual renewal of everything connected with Yahweh's dwelling place.

Jerusalem's renewal, with all its accompanying benefits, is clearly portrayed through the structure of Zechariah. Joyce

Baldwin, following P. Lamarche, has shown that the entire prophecy displays a chiastic framework (1972: 74-81, 85-86). Other writers follow a simpler pattern. Despite the soundness of Baldwin's work, it is not necessary to trace the full complexity of the book's framework to demonstrate Zechariah's main emphases. The section 1–8 breaks into three distinct parts: an introduction to the book (1.1-6); visions (1.7–6.15); and messages related to the visions (7.1-8.23). Chapters 9–14 can be divided into two parts: the intervention and rejection of Yahweh and the shepherd (9.1–11.17) and the final victory of the Lord (12.1–14.21) (cf. Baldwin 1972: 85-86). Jerusalem plays a prominent role in each section.

Zech. 1.1-6 paves the way for the prophet's dated visions (1.7-6.15) by rehearsing the past unfaithfulness of Israel. These six verses serve as a warning to the present group that, just as Yahweh punished their forefathers' sins, so will He judge their iniquities (1.5-6). The only hope for the post-exilic community is repentance and contrition (1.6). Once this change of heart and lifestyle occurs God will move to help the nation.

A series of eight visions is utilized to show how the Lord responds to repentance. It is impossible to scrutinize each vision here, but even a brief analysis of these texts reveals how vital the restoration of Jerusalem is to Zechariah's message. The very first vision raises the issue of why God withholds mercy from Zion (1.12). Yahweh's response is that He is still 'very jealous for Jerusalem' (1.14), that He 'will return to Jerusalem with mercy' and rebuild His house (1.16), and that He 'will again comfort Zion and choose Jerusalem' (1.17). The third vision finds 'a man' measuring Jerusalem who is told that Jerusalem will be an unwalled city whose protector is Yahweh (2.1-9). Once more the Lord promises to choose Zion (2.12). Vision four deals with the cleansing of the priesthood, but bases this cleansing on the fact that Jerusalem has been chosen by the Lord (3.3). None of the other visions mention Jerusalem by name, but the temple is discussed (4.9; 6.12) and the prophet says people will come from many nations to rebuild the house of worship (6.15). Thus, from the establishment of Jerusalem will come such by-products as the cleans-

ing of the priesthood, the return of the exiles, and the rebuilding of the temple.

Chapter 7 opens a new section in an old fashion. The
prophet declares, as he does in 1.1-6, that the people have
failed to keep their covenant with God in the past. Yahweh's
only recourse was to punish them by scattering them among
the nations (7.14). Again, what is the Lord's remedy?
Zechariah reports:

> This is what the Lord Almighty says: 'I am very jealous for
> Zion; I am burning with jealousy for her'. This is what the
> Lord says: 'I will return to Zion and dwell in Jerusalem.
> Then Jerusalem will be called the City of Truth, and the
> mountain of the Lord Almighty will be called The Holy
> Mountain' (8.2-3).

As a result of God's presence there will be peace in Jerusalem
(8.4-5), the exiles will return 'to live in Jerusalem' as God's
people (8.7-8), the temple will be rebuilt (8.9), the land will be
fruitful (8.12), the people will become righteous (8.14-19) and
the Jews will bless all nations (8.20-23). All these wonders arise
from the Lord's decision to choose and restore Jerusalem.

Section four continues the Jerusalem-restoration motif by
reverting to an idea that is prevalent in the earlier sections of
the Twelve: Israel's enemies will meet sure and certain doom
because they have oppressed God's people (9.8). All the old foes
are mentioned, Syria, Tyre, Sidon, Philistia, etc., so the person
who reads the Twelve as a book is not surprised at this point by
any unusual or new emphases. What is surprising is that,
instead of including Israel in the list of sinners as is customary
in the Twelve, Zechariah immediately predicts the restoration
of Jerusalem. This restoration results from the advent of a
messianic king who rides into the city on a donkey (9.9).
Peace, return from exile, and vindication before enemies are
again promised to the covenant people (9.10-13). Because the
Lord will be present in Zion, the nation will be protected (9.14-
17) and the people will be restored. Chapter 10 expands the
predicted restoration beyond Jerusalem to include all of Judah
and even Ephraim (10.6-7). Nothing can halt God's program
of restoration, for even wicked 'shepherds', or leaders, will be
foiled in their attempts to lead Israel astray (11.17). Once

more all restoration begins with Jerusalem and moves outward.

If anything, Jerusalem's role in the restoration process is heightened in the fifth and final section of Zechariah (12.1–14.16). Chapters 12 and 14 are especially glowing in their appraisal of the city's future fortunes. Though besieged by all nations (12.3), God 'will make Jerusalem an immovable rock for all the nations'. How can the city survive against such odds? The prophet declares: 'The people of Jerusalem are strong, because the Lord Almighty is their God' (12.5). So strong are Zion's inhabitants that the weakest of them will be like David (12.8). After chapter thirteen notes that the Lord will cleanse the citizens of Jerusalem to make them God's people (13.1, 9), Zechariah's closing word is that the city of David will stand forever. Other parts of the land may be dry as the desert, but Jerusalem will flourish (14.10-11). All nations will worship Yahweh there (14.16-19), as Micah and Zephaniah have already promised, and every element of Zion will belong to the Lord. No comment could summarize the significance and extent of Jerusalem's renewal any better than Zechariah's concluding statement:

> On that day 'Holy To The Lord' will be inscribed on the bells of the horses, and the cooking pots in the Lord's house will be like the sacred bowls in front of the altar. Every pot in Jerusalem and Judah will be holy to the Lord Almighty, and all who come to sacrifice will take some of the pots and cook in them. And on that day there will no longer be a Canaanite in the house of the Lord Almighty (14.20-21).

Another significant by-product of the restoration of Jerusalem is that other countries will turn to the Lord. Though they go to Jerusalem at least in part because they have been defeated in battle by Israel, they are going to truly worship Yahweh (14.16). Egypt is singled out as a representative of Israel's enemies, which shows that, regardless of how bitter the hatred between the covenant people and their foes has been, they will be reconciled and serve God together (cf. Zeph. 3.8-9). Through this pericope, Zechariah shows that just as sin and punishment occur on a cosmic level so restoration will also take place on a world-wide scale. Such inclusivism is not a primary concern in Haggai or Malachi, but Zechariah's comments reveal a continuity of such concerns evident in all three segments of the Twelve.

Several structural bases pertaining both to the Twelve as a whole and the final segment of the group are covered by Zechariah. First, its emphasis on the final restoration of Jerusalem answers concerns raised in Joel, Amos, Micah, Habakkuk, and Zephaniah. The chosen city will have a place in God's plans for the universe. Therefore, Zechariah provides a restorative corollary to earlier messages of condemnation and punishment. Second, the book presents step two in Yahweh's scheme of restoring the covenant nation to its intended position of prominence. Haggai focuses on the temple, and Zechariah, while exhibiting multiple concerns, centers on Jerusalem, but they both look forward to a time when punishment will not only cease but will lead to new glory. Finally, by serving as a bridge between Haggai and Malachi, the prophecy helps span the issues raised by the post-exilic community. The dated visions akin to Haggai and the 'burdens' comparable to Malachi demonstrate that the literary form of the book stands 'in between' (cf. Petersen 1984) other works in much the same way its message links the mundane and the utopian.

Coming after Zechariah and at the end of the minor prophets, Malachi at first appears to be enigmatic, or even disappointing. After all, Zechariah finishes with a resounding promise of revival and restoration, and the previous eleven books have built the expectation of a great message of restoration. Why then does Malachi present so many barriers to restoration? Why are so many sins chronicled? Does the prophecy deal with restoration at all?

A few scholars are negative about the value and originality of Malachi's work. Joyce Baldwin, though not herself in this camp, summarizes this attitude by observing:

> It has become usual to disparage Malachi and belittle his message by saying that the creative period of prophecy had passed, and that he was more like a scribe or a casuist than a prophet, interested merely in the details of the ritual and in applying the letter of the law. Men like Amos, Isaiah, and Jeremiah, by contrast, belonged to the first rank of prophets (1972: 215-16).

Other writers, however, see the book as a unique packaging of old and established concepts. John M.P. Smith says:

> The very vigour of our prophet's faith shows that his religion does not lie upon the surface of his soul and that it cannot be satisfied with externalities, but is of the very essence of his life and can be content with nothing less than the presence of God. In this respect he is a true successor of the great prophets (1911: 11).

There is some truth in both viewpoints. Malachi does insist on correct worship. He does claim that adherence to ancient traditions is necessary for a proper relationship with Yahweh. On the other hand, he argues that ritual adherence only results from a heart-felt faith in God (3.16). It is, therefore, incorrect to say that the book is derivative and surface-oriented, thereby relegating it to some lower echelon of the prophetic writings. Malachi attempts to reveal the cost of restoration and the barriers to that renewal. To do so he utilizes some fairly unusual techniques—all of which are very effective. Thus, though Malachi may not be exactly what one would expect to follow Zechariah's hopeful conclusions, the prophecy nevertheless is a sober and fitting end to the Twelve.

Malachi is a difficult book to outline because it consists of a series of questions asked by the Lord and the nation. It is possible to divide the text into seven parts (Driver 1906: 286-87), eight parts (Baldwin 1972: 219), two parts (Bullock 1986: 343), or three parts (John M.P. Smith 1911: 3). Probably the most coherent way to approach the structure is to treat five of the six disputation passages together and give the prophecy a three-stage framework. In this scheme, section one declares Yahweh's covenant love for Israel (1.1-5), section two features five disputes that show how God's love has been rejected (1.6–3.15), and section three demonstrates that restoration comes through repentance, the day of the Lord, and the coming of 'the prophet Elijah' (3.16–4.6; 3.16-24 in Hebrew). There is a clear progression from the covenant to restoration in Malachi, and the question-answer format of the main portion reveals these themes in a creative and thought-provoking fashion.

Part one of Malachi sounds much like other pericopae in the minor prophets. God declares His love much as in Hosea. A new literary device, however immediately follows the Lord's statement in 1.2, for a disappointed, discouraged, post-exilic Israel flatly asks, 'How have you loved us?' Yahweh defends the claim to love Israel by comparing the chosen nation to Edom. Though a brother to Jacob, Esau's descendants are 'hated' by God and consigned to a wasteland. Israel, on the other hand, though punished will rise again. Before this restoration can take place, though, some obvious sins must be removed, so Malachi asks five more questions of the people. The prophet's first question establishes the relationship between Yahweh and Israel so further exchanges can show present problems in that relationship.

At least five disputes dot the second segment in Malachi's structure. Each of these disputes are characterized by questions and counter-questions. Building on the statements about God's love in 1.1-5, the first controversy revolves around Yahweh's assertions that Israel has dishonored her 'father' by despising His name (1.6-11), that the nation profanes true worship of the father (1.12-14), and that the priests have not lived up to their calling (2.1-9). Each instance proves how Israel has taken God's love for granted. The next dispute shows that the people of Israel break faith with one another by proliferating divorce in their country (2.10-16). In short, they do not properly love one another. As in the earlier discussions the nation acts as if it does not know why God is angry (2.14), but Yahweh accepts no excuses. Ideas very similar to those found in Habakkuk are featured in the third controversy (2.17–3.5). God is weary of hearing the people claim that it is the evildoer who prospers. He states that a 'messenger' will come who will usher in the day of the Lord. Because this day is coming, the next issue raised through the question-answer motif is repentance, since a turning from sin is the nation's only hope for survival (3.6-12). Finally, the nation reverts back to the theodicy issue in 3.13-15. One more time Yahweh's character is called into question.

Can such a nation be restored? Malachi's final section gives a three-pronged answer to that question (3.16–4.6; 3.16-24 in Hebrew). Israel can be restored if those who fear the Lord look to Him (3.16-18). It can be restored when God sends a prophetic figure before that day who will reconcile the people to themselves and to the Lord (4.4-6; 3.22-24 in Hebrew). Quite obviously, Malachi's expectation is that the possible renewal will become a reality. Lest the nation think restoration will come easily, the writer has dwelt on how the people themselves must be restored. A restored Jerusalem and a restored temple are not God's ultimate goal unless these places are inhabited and used by a holy people. All the blessings of the Mosaic covenant are available if only the nation will obey the author of that covenant. Malachi *does* stress the hope of restoration, albeit in a very down-to-earth fashion. His method of doing so demonstrates how the lofty predictions of Zechariah can become reality through the nation's basic, everyday commitment to a covenant-love relationship to God.

Two vital structural gaps are filled by Malachi. First, the prophecy effectively summarizes major segments of the Twelve. The emphasis on love and divorce remind the reader of Hosea. The admonitions of the priests echo Joel and Zechariah. The stressing of Yahweh's day of punishment links the book with Amos, Zephaniah, etc. Malachi's conclusion ties together the Haggai–Zechariah–Malachi corpus by claiming that all facets of restoration will indeed take place. Secondly, Malachi concludes the restoration section of the Twelve by showing that temple construction (Haggai) and the restoration of Jerusalem (Zechariah) only have significance if the people themselves turn to God, appreciate their covenant heritage, and observe correct temple practices. Still, the restoration will come.

The last three books in the Twelve therefore work together in a very coherent way to consummate the images of hope that appear in the first nine prophecies. Rather than interpreting these prophecies as mere echoes of earlier, greater prophets, one should view them as the final piece of a larger structural whole. They systematically answer questions about who will be restored, what will be restored, and how both will be restored. To remove these works from the Twelve would impoverish both the literary and historical significance of the prophetic message. Without Haggai-Malachi the *other* books become shadows of what they are when completed by these post-exilic writings.

Conclusion

Though not without certain difficulties, it is plausible to argue that the minor prophets are joined by a discernible structural unity. This unity is based on the major characteristics of the prophetic genre itself. Hosea–Micah does focus on various types of sin, as scholars have recognized for centuries. Even a tiny book like Obadiah gains added significance when it is understood as one part of a larger whole.

Nahum–Zephaniah explains the logical consequences of sin. The fact that both Israel and its neighbors are singled out for judgment makes more sense when these books are interpreted as canonical responses to their predecessors. Restoration in all its many facets is clearly the major idea in Haggai–Malachi. This great theme becomes even more significant when the reader becomes aware that the renewal process is a centuries-long, twelve-book effort that is both covenantal and cosmic in scope.

Of course it is impossible to declare with ultimate authority that the last compiler of the Twelve purposely shaped the corpus as discussed in this chapter. It is possible, though, to say that in their final canonical form these twelve diverse prophecies mesh together as a unit that unfolds the basic tenets of prophecy much more effectively than any single book of the group could alone. In so doing they also present a history of Yahweh's dealings with Israel. It is possible, therefore, to refute statements like that of Gerhard von Rad:

> Like the historical tradition, the prophetic corpus lies before us in what are, to some extent, very shapeless collections of traditional material, arranged with almost no regard for content or chronological order, and apparently quite unaware of the laws with which we are familiar in the development of European literature (1965: 33).

In short, the Twelve is a generic and structural unity. Other literary aspects of the Book need exploration, but at this point unity can be defended from these two very vital artistic categories.

Chapter 4

PLOT AND THE TWELVE

Plot: A Working Definition

Now that some understanding of the genre and structure of the minor prophets has been achieved, it is necessary to examine related literary aspects of the Twelve to test further the possibility that the books are a unified construction. One of the most basic of all artistic aspects is plot. As was noted in Chapter 3, plot is very closely aligned with structure, since both are related to how a work holds together and functions as a unit. Structure reveals plot and plot determines structure. Still, the two terms have several mutually exclusive duties in literary criticism and thus deserve separate treatment. There will of necessity be some overlap between the discussion of structure and the analysis of plot, but hopefully this overlap will aid the perception of newly introduced ideas rather than merely repeat what has already been said.

Scholars define plot in a number of ways. Some view it as a structural device, some as a means of introducing and developing characters, some as simply a pattern of events, and some as a means of ordering the emotions of the reader. With so many possible meanings for 'plot' it is prudent to once more go back to Aristotle for a working definition upon which a larger outline of the term can be constructed. Aristotle believed that a plot should include some very specific elements if it is to be effective. First of all, it must reveal a definite progression of events that take place due to causal necessity:

> Now, according to our definition, Tragedy is an imitation of an action that is complete, and whole and of a certain magnitude. A whole is that which has a beginning, a middle, and an end. A beginning is that which does not itself follow

anything by causal necessity, but after which something
naturally is or comes to be. An end, on the contrary, is that
which itself naturally follows some other thing, either by
necessity, or as a rule, but has nothing following it. A middle
is that which follows something as some other thing follows
it. A well-constructed plot, therefore, must neither begin nor
end at haphazard, but conform to these principles (1974: ch.
7, 37-38).

Note that the events that compose the beginning, middle and
end take place as a natural process based on 'what is possible
according to the law of probability or necessity' (1974: ch. 7,
39). So plot is, at its most basic level, a unified sequence of logi-
cally-caused happenings.

Aristotle also elaborates on how a beginning, middle, and end
are formed. He argues that

every tragedy falls into two parts, Complication and Unraveling or Denouement. Incidents extraneous to the action are
frequently combined with a portion of the action proper, to
form the Complication; the rest is the Unraveling. By the
Complication I mean all that extends from the beginning of
the action and the part which marks the turning-point to
good or bad fortune. The Unraveling is that which extends
from the beginning of the change to the end (1974: ch. 18, 47).

In Aristotle's mind every well-formed plot has its three major
sequential segments formed by a distinct problem or conflict
that must be resolved. Without this quality, plot could become
no more than an insignificant account of something that has
taken place. Importance and impact are given a story through
these aspects of plot, and without these elements, as Holman
warns, 'plot does not exist' (1972: 398). Holman takes Aristotle's emphasis on complication and unraveling and demonstrates that these two ideas are normally revealed by an
author introducing the action, presenting the story's conflict,
bringing the conflict to a crisis point, using falling action to
begin to provide a solution to the conflict, and by finally providing the conclusion, denouement, to the major problem (1972:
398). All these facets are implicit in Aristotle's comments.

Because there can be many types of conflicts in a story, there
are several kinds of plots evident in literature. For instance, a
story may be comic, tragic, ironic, etc. Aristotle contended that

what makes a plot comic or tragic is based on the manner in which an author chooses to imitate life:

> Since the objects of imitation are men in action, and these men must be either of a higher or a lower type (for moral character mainly answers to these divisions, goodness and badness being the distinguishing marks of moral differences), it follows that we must represent men either as better than in real life, or as worse, or as they are (1974: ch. 2, 32).

To portray people better than they are recreates a tragic plot, and to picture them as worse than they are produces a comic plot (1974: ch. 2, 33). Tragedy takes a character who is superior in quality to other human beings and changes that protagonist's fortunes from good to bad, and does so effectively enough to inspire terror and pity into the reader (1974: ch. 14, 42-43). Comedy, on the other hand, portrays a main character who often has less innate ability than normal people but still, despite opposition, triumphs. Since the conclusion is more 'pleasant' to the audience, there is little or no regret at the end of the story (1974: ch. 5, 35).

In his *Anatomy of Criticism*, Northrop Frye charts the differences between comic and tragic plots quite clearly. Frye demonstrates that the action in tragedy consists of the righting of some imbalance in nature caused by the hero's disturbing the correct distance between deity and man, nature and miracle, or law and obedience (1967: 209). For example, Prometheus steals fire from the gods, thus lessening their mystique, but thereby aiding mankind. His punishment regains the gods' rule over the earth. The wedding of Oedipus and his mother is against nature, so his blinding somehow allows law to prevail. Thus Frye concludes:

> The righting of the balance is what the Greeks called *nemesis*: again, the agent or instrument of *nemesis* may be human vengeance, ghostly vengeance, divine vengeance, divine justice, accident, fate or the logic of events, but the essential thing is that *nemesis* happens, and happens impersonally, unaffected... by the moral quality of human motivation involved (1967: 209).

So tragedy's main function is to restore cosmic order regardless of whether the means chosen seems just or not. In fact, if the reader senses frustration, sadness, or outrage then the tragedy is a success. Because tragedy's plot takes the hero from glory to defeat, Frye characterizes this action as an inverted U. Though the protagonist ascends to great heights he will come crashing to the depths (1967: 207).

Comic action is a perfect contrast to tragedy. Frye notes: 'The obstacles to the hero's desire... form the action of the comedy, and the overcoming of them the comic resolution' (1967: 164). Whereas obstacles overwhelm the hero in tragedy, in comedy the protagonist conquers everyone and everything that blocks the path to his object of desire. Besides the granting of the hero's fondest wish, comedy converts the opponents of the hero and includes them in the society of the hero and his followers (1967: 164-67). Such inclusion appears in Aristophanes, Shakespeare, Shaw, etc. and indeed in all comedy. Rather than an inverted U, then, comedic action is best portrayed by a U. The main character or characters may slide to the bottom of the author's scale of fortunes, but will inexorably rise once more to the top.

One other element of plot Aristotle mentions is that plot and characterization must work together if a story is to reach its fullest potential. Surely by now this tenet is quite evident, but the notion still bears repeating. Despite his recognition of the importance of characterization in plot, Aristotle believed that the piece's story line takes precedence over its characters. He explains:

> The plot, then, is the first principle, and, as it were, the soul of a tragedy: Character holds the second place. A similar fact is seen in painting. The most beautiful colors, laid on confusedly, will not give as much pleasure as the chalk outline of a portrait. Thus Tragedy is the imitation of an action, and of the agents, mainly with a view to the action (1974: ch. 6, 37).

Aristotle did not assert that characters are unimportant, indeed they are second only to plot, rather he believed that characters only take shape as they are fitted into a definite type of plot. Critics have always been divided on whether plot or characterization is more necessary to a literary work. After all, neither exists very well without the other. How this discussion affects the study of the minor prophets will be discussed below.

Before summarizing the various parts of this definition of plot, it is vital to emphasize that the connection of these strands is based on what the author of a literary piece intends his work to accomplish. Or, put another way, each writer chooses what materials will make the best plot for his purposes. Many events, ideas, and emotions are available to an author, but, as Hugh Holman explains:

> The demands of *plot* stipulate that the author *select* from this welter of event and reflection those items which have a certain unity, which point to a certain end, which have a common interrelationship, which represent not more than two or three threads of interest and activity. *Plot* brings order out of life; it selects only one or two emotions out of a dozen, one or two conflicts out of hundreds, only two or three people out of thousands, and a half-dozen episodes from possible millions. In this sense it focuses life (1972: 398).

This statement applies to the minor prophets just as it does to other writings. Certainly only some of what the prophets did and said is in the Twelve, so what is included in that unit was chosen and shaped out of a larger body of material for a specific reason.

From this brief survey it is possible to offer a working definition of 'plot'. Plot is a selected sequence of logically caused events that present a conflict and its resolution by utilizing certain established literary devices (introduction, complication, crisis, denouement, etc.). Further, it is character-oriented, normally reflects a comic or tragic perspective, and must have an important message to proclaim. Though other aspects of plot may exist, these characteristics are the heart of the term's meaning.

Plot and the Twelve

What remains to be decided is whether the Twelve can be said to have a plot. That the Book has a recognizable genre and structure argues in favor of a positive answer to this question, but is not conclusive, since a lyric poem may have a structure without having a full-blown plot. Still, the complexity of its structure and sub-structures points to the reality of a well-defined plot in the Twelve. The obvious way that the prophecies join together to announce sin, punishment, and restoration reveals that the final form of the Twelve has a unified and purposeful arrangement. This section of Chapter 4 will use the working definition of plot outlined above to develop a strategy for analyzing the plot of the Twelve. After that strategy is completed, the next part of the chapter will examine the plot of the minor prophets itself.

By now it is hardly necessary to argue that the minor prophets are shaped as a sequence of purposeful events. This fact has already been established in Chapter 3. A powerful picture of Israel and its neighbors' sin, its consequences, and its eradication is painted in the Twelve. The fact that books having little historical or regional affinity are placed next to one another leads to this conclusion, as do the main themes of the books themselves. How this purposeful sequence works will be demonstrated in the next section of the chapter, but should require no further elaboration at this point. What does need to be said, however, is that the Twelve's plot movement is not as obvious as that of narrative. There is some straightforward narrative in the minor prophets (e.g. Amos 7.10-17 and Jonah), but it is subsumed under a larger framework that is not as easy to recognize. The Twelve, indeed all the latter prophets, compose a uniform message by putting their concerns into a specific order. Their plot sequence is still very selective, very purposeful, very sequential, and very effective. Therefore, when one views plot as more than a product of prose narrative, its importance for the Twelve becomes evident.

Various characters are vital to the plot of the minor prophets. Though these characters and their characterization are covered in Chapter 5, it is necessary to introduce them now. Of course the major figure in these books is Yahweh, the creator, sustainer, covenant maker, judge, and restorer of all peoples, cities, and nations. God's dealings with Israel and even the foreign nations shape the Twelve's concept of sin, punishment, and renewal. Israel is a second persona in the Twelve. Most of the time Israel is a rebellious figure who is nearly pitiful in its destructive pride. Whether covenant breaker, oppressor, candidate for judgment or doubter of God's love, Israel normally acts in a negative fashion. On the other hand, though, from Israel comes the remnant, the group of faithful covenant-keepers from whom God will form the people of the restoration. There is, thus, both a positive Israel character and a negative Israel figure. The former is ultimately the Israel of the glorious renewal mentioned in Zechariah, while the latter is the fallen Israel of the sin and judgment delineated in Hosea–Zephaniah. Other chief characters in the minor prophets are the heathen nations outside Israel. Though less significant than Israel, this persona, or group of personae, stand against Israel, are used by God to punish Israel, and are judged and redeemed alongside and through Israel. In short, these countries serve as Israel's foil.

Last, but certainly not least in significance among the characters are the prophets themselves. Some of the minor prophets are relatively well-drawn, fully developed characters, such as Jonah and Hosea. Others, however, like Joel, Obadiah, Zephaniah, etc. are almost invisible in their own books. So unnecessary is Malachi's personal background to that book's message that numerous scholars feel the name is an oblique reference to some 'messenger' of the Lord. Still, real individuals have forged these books and shaped their creative messages, and at times their personalities are evident in their works. Just as importantly, the role of a prophet is often discussed in the corpus, even in prophecies where historical data on the individual prophet is scarce. Part of the conflict in the Twelve exists in the lives of the prophets, for they must represent both God and the people, denounce sin and plead for mercy, ask questions and be men of faith, as well as reveal God's will and at the same time interpret it for the people. The prophets struggle to discover their identity much as the other non-divine characters attempt to find their place in God's order of existence.

Conflict and resolution in the Twelve are closely related to the Book's sequence of events and development of characters. Sin, punishment, and restoration occur because of the activities of the major figures, and all these aspects are fuelled by a chief conflict. At its most basic level the Twelve's conflict revolves around Yahweh's attempt to forge Israel into a faithful nation. This goal can only be achieved if Israel will keep its covenant with its Lord. Yahweh uses every possible means to get Israel to keep her covenant promises and eventually has this goal for the chosen nation completed. A secondary, but vitally important, goal is to redeem all the peoples of the world. Since Yahweh is the creator of the universe, this desire is quite natural. God's power will be evident to all when Israel and its neighbors worship their creator as sovereign God. It could be argued, therefore, that the conflict in the minor prophets is the rebellion of the whole world against God. Perhaps, but Israel is the focal point of the prophets' preaching, so it is best to concentrate on that group as the key to the restoration of the universe.

As in other types of literature, the Twelve's plot follows a definite pattern of introduction, complication, crisis, falling action and resolution. These stages correspond with the Book's structure and unfold its conflict. Hosea and Joel introduce the problem that exists between the Lord and creation. Israel has broken the covenant with God, which Hosea presents as a clear case of spiritual prostitution. Joel mentions Israel's sin, but furthers the discussion by noting that all nations must answer to God for what they have done. Amos, Obadiah, Jonah, and Micah provide the complication of the conflict Hosea and Joel introduce. Amos names specific sins that constitute spiritual prostitution in the chosen people, plus he lists why God is displeased with Israel's neighbors. Obadiah and Jonah elaborate on the sin of hating one's neighbor, which breaks the most fundamental of God's laws (cf. Lev. 19.18), while Micah summarizes the main points of his five predecessors. These six books boldly declare that God's dispute with Israel comes, not because of a single transgression, but because of a long-term, deep-seated rejection of Yahweh's person and covenant.

Nahum and the first part of Habakkuk continue to complicate God's relationship to Israel and the 'heathen' countries. Assyria, a significant country, will be destroyed because of its ruthless treatment of other lands, according to Nahum, which makes the reader wonder if Yahweh will redeem any foreign nations. Equally important is Habakkuk's fear that Babylon's conquering of Judah signals the end of the Lord's concern for the covenant people. This fear initiates a struggle of faith for the prophet too. Because of these twin tensions, the prophet's crisis of faith and the uncertain future of all nations, covenant or otherwise, Habakkuk marks the apex of the conflict between the Lord and the world. If no further word comes, the final decision of God is to totally devastate the universe.

Zephaniah begins the process of falling action and resolution, but only after showing how complete God's judgment will be. Though the 'day of the Lord' will 'sweep away' everything on earth (1.1-6), God will preserve a remnant of Israel and convert the nations because of, and through, divine wrath. Thus, the tension produced by Hosea–Habakkuk is somewhat relieved. Zephaniah's promise of a restoration to come, though not yet a fully developed concept, hints at the Twelve's denouement, which is finalized in Haggai–Zechariah.

Final restoration of Israel, and through her the rest of the earth, does not come easily. The temple, long neglected, must be rebuilt, Jerusalem must be purified, and the people of God must shake off their lethargy so that they will show covenant love to their Lord. Each stage of this process contributes to the denouement. God will only restore Israel when that nation cherishes proper worship, and will only restore the other countries through the renewal of the covenant people. When Malachi concludes with the idea that Israel will respond to a prophet akin to Elijah, however, the process of restoration is complete. Temple, city and worshippers are all in a proper relationship to Yahweh, thereby leading to the reviving of the relationship of God and other peoples. Despite the difficulty of the formulation of the denouement, Yahweh has accomplished the major goal in the Twelve. Israel and all creation have been reconciled to the divine plan for them.

What kind of plot does the book of the Twelve exhibit? Is it tragic, comic, both, or neither? When answering these questions it is important to keep the ultimate goal of the Book in mind. Quite clearly the final purpose of the Twelve's plot is to present the restoration outlined above. This assertion, though, is contrary to the conclusions of many writers. Ronald Clements notes:

> We have already pointed out that it is fundamental to the
> hermeneutical traditions of both Jews and Christians that
> the prophets spoke of a coming salvation for Israel. On the
> other hand, critical scholarship has consistently found the
> most challenging feature of prophecy to lie in its threats and
> denunciations, warning of the coming of judgment upon a
> godless people. The place where both aspects are brought
> together is to be found in the structure of the canonical col-
> lection of prophecy. The threat of doom is followed by the
> word of salvation, which does not evade the judgment, but
> looks beyond it. By holding these two things together in this
> way, the prophetic part of the OT canon witnesses to the
> wholeness of the Word of God (1977: 55).

Much of the concern exhibited over the doom oracles derives
from a properly perceived importance of the prophets' ethical
exhortations. Oppression, materialism, idolatry and righteousness are universally applicable subjects and surely need
careful consideration. It is possible, though, to maintain a sense
of the magnitude of these issues without losing sight of the fact
that the overwhelming conclusion of the prophetic corpus is
that God will save all who repent. Surely Clements is correct to
stress that an *interpreter* can only 'bear witness to the wholeness of the Word of God' by recognizing that the ultimate goal
of prophecy is salvation. Any study of the Twelve's plot therefore, must, keep in mind the whole message of the Book, but at
the same time must emphasize that the direction the body is
headed is toward restoration.

Many Old Testament literary scholars now designate
prophecy's plot as either 'comic' or 'comedy' because of its
hopeful conclusions. In *The Great Code: The Bible and Literature*, Northrop Frye divides the scriptures into seven phases:
creation, revolution, law, wisdom, prophecy, gospel, and
apocalyptic, and concludes the prophets felt that the human
race was in a state of rebellion against God, but that this
situation was not permanent. Frye summarizes:

> the prophet sees man in a state of alienation caused by his
> own distractions, at the bottom of a U-shaped curve... It pos-
> tulates an original state of relative happiness, and looks for-
> ward to an eventual restoration of this state, to, at least, a
> 'saving' remnant (1982: 128-29).

Though the present is bleak, the future is bright. Frye continues 'The prophet's present moment is an alienated prodigal son, a moment that has broken away from its own identity in the past but may return to that identity in the future' (1982: 129). Due to his holding to the U-shaped nature of prophecy Frye evidently thinks prophecy's plot line is basically comic.

Other writers have examined whether prophecy is either 'comic' in the modal sense that its functional tenets reveal comic tendencies without being generic comedy, or even comedy in the generic sense. Quite notable among these efforts are the essays produced in *Semeia 32: Tragedy and Comedy in the Bible*. In general, the writers in this volume find that comparing prophecy to comedy illuminates the biblical materials a great deal, so much so, in fact, that they say prophecy is comic in nature. They are not prepared to claim, however, that the prophets wrote comedies. Thus, they distinguish between mode and genre, which reflects sound literary analysis.

For instance, Edwin Good notes various correspondences between prophecy and classical comedy in his study of Daniel. Good thinks the 'stories (chs. 1–6) show an overall comic plot line, and each of them presents both a comedy in miniature and moments of humor' (1985: 41), but wisely adds that it is more problematic to refer to chs. 7–12 as comic (1985: 41). Writing about Hosea, Martin J. Buss states that

> the poetic forms of tragedy and comedy contribute to the prophecy of Hosea by representing the quality of actual and potential forms of existence. A tragic mood expresses sympathy with the downfall of a nation. Comic elements, in a distancing mode, make fun of the people's foolishness and, in an integrative form, express joy in a new relation with God. An ironic tension holds together positive and negative impulses. Resolution is to come in the realization of love as the fulfillment (end) of human life and divine purposes (1984: 71).

What Buss describes is the U-shaped plot Frye outlines. Unless there is some problem, some tension and some interaction with tragic motifs, a comic plot degenerates into shallow humor. These aspects of the best in comic plots are supremely evident in the Twelve's portrayal of Israel's relationship with Yahweh. Both Good's and Buss's articles reveal the fact that examining the comic elements in prophecy may aid an understanding of the message of individual books and the prophetic corpus as a whole.

Despite the enthusiasm for attributing comic tendencies to prophecy, some critics in the *Semeia* volume provide needed cautions to the interpretation of prophetic plot. Norman Gottwald observes that the prophetic books are not the same type of literature as the classical Greek comedies. Furthermore, he feels that

> what makes the application of tragic and comic categories to prophecy at all possible is that the prophetic writings are a kind of occasion-oriented commentary on an implied narrative. This implied narrative is the ever-moving point of juncture between Israel's remembered past viewed as an arena of the judging and saving work of God and the specific events unfolding within the immediate milieu of any particular prophet (1984: 83).

Certainly Gottwald's assessments at this point are correct. His most vital contribution is his realization that there is an underlying 'implied narrative' moving throughout the prophets that summarizes Yahweh's dealings with Israel. David Gunn adds the caution that not all the canonical prophets, or indeed even all the classical comedians, utilize a perfect U-shaped plot (1984: 119). Gunn also shows that any given author may combine the various aspects of comedy in any way that best suits the needs of his work, so absolute definitions of 'comedy' or 'comic' are non-existent even though general principles of the terms can be located. Perhaps Yair Zakovitch provides the most important caution of all when he exhorts all interpreters to refrain from imposing non-Biblical concepts on the scripture (1984: 109). Rather than 'comic' or 'tragic', Zakovitch prefers to call the prophets 'optimistic' and 'pessimistic'. This preference is significant because Zakovitch is using those words in a tonal, or modal, sense. It *is* impossible to call every individual prophetic book a full-fledged comedy, but it *is also possible* to say the prophets have a comic outlook.

To this point tragedy has not been mentioned as a potential unifying mode for prophetic plot. There are several reasons for this omission, most of which are apparent by now. First of all, most scholars admit that, though doom oracles are a major factor in the prophets, the most obvious trend in those books is to predict a positive future for Israel and all other peoples. Second, the characters in the prophets do not reflect tragic traits. Not even the prophets themselves are superior in kind to other human beings, nor is Yahweh ultimately unjust or frustrated in His purposes for the world. Third, there is no sudden rise and crushing defeat of Israel. Ultimately, Israel and her neighbors triumph through the grace of the Lord. Thus, the overall tenor of the Twelve is not tragic. There are moments of defeat and disappointment, but these events make the universe's ultimate restoration that much more poignant.

It is thereby necessary to conclude that the Twelve, based on its story line, characters, and purpose, is comic. This assessment means that the Book is comic in mode, but belongs to the genre of prophecy. As was stated in chapter two, a work may belong to one genre and be characterized by another. The minor prophets are a practical example of this principle. It is also true that prophecy employs comic principles for its own selective purposes. By so doing the Twelve incorporates a U-shaped implied narrative that explains how the prophets proclaimed what could be in the light of what had been.

The Plot of the Twelve

In the minor prophets the various stages of plot (introduction, complication, etc.) coincide with Frye's notion of a U-shaped comic framework. The fortunes of Israel and the rest of creation begin to plunge downward in Hosea and Joel, fall even further in Amos–Micah, reach their nadir in Habakkuk, begin to inch upward towards the end of Zephaniah, climb sharply in Haggai and Zechariah, and complete their ascent with Malachi. This U-shaped progression is illustrated in chart number two. Using the aspects of plot set forth earlier in this chapter it is possible to divide the Twelve into the following parts: introduction to the plot's major problem (Hosea and Joel); complication of the plot's chief problem (Amos–Micah); crisis point of the plot (Nahum and Habakkuk); climax and falling action (Zephaniah); denouement, or resolution, of the plot's problem (Haggai–Malachi). Malachi both completes the

Book's resolution and provides a concluding admonition to the chosen people. These aspects of the Twelve's plot are developed in the remainder of the chapter.

Chart 2: The Twelve's Comic Plot

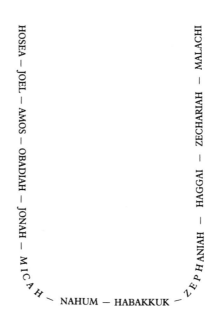

Introduction	=	Hosea–Joel
Complication	=	Amos–Micah
Crisis	=	Nahum–Habakkuk
Falling Action	=	Zephaniah
Resolution	=	Haggai–Malachi

1. *Introduction to the Downward Trek: Hosea and Joel*

Hosea wastes no time in beginning the arduous descent of Israel into the jaws of the Day of the Lord. In the second verse of the book Yahweh commands the prophet to take an adulterous wife 'because the land is guilty of the vilest adultery in departing from the Lord'. To illustrate the adultery of the nation further, the son born to Gomer and Hosea is named

'Not My People', since Israel has shown herself to be an illegitimate, rebellious child. Such an obvious reference to the doubtful parentage of the nation and the human child demonstrates the gravity of how extensively Yahweh's covenant with Israel has been violated. Subsequent references to harlotry in Hosea's family reinforce the Lord's initial declarations of Israel's unfaithfulness. In 2.2-23 Hosea tells his children to rebuke their mother for her adulterous activities, since these deeds have disgraced both husband (2.2) and children (2.4). Though Gomer seems unrepentant (2.5), the prophet conceives a plan to recapture his wife that includes depriving her of her physical needs (2.8-9), access to her lovers (2.11-13) and the opportunity to attend idolatrous, thus lewd, celebrations (2.11-13). Of course God's plans for the restoration of Israel parallel these steps. The Lord promises to lure Israel back to the desert so that the Exodus–Sinai relationship may be renewed (2.15). Thus, Israel will once more be 'married' to God (2.16), turn away from idols (2.17), renew the covenant previously offered (2.18-20), and have the land restored (2.21-23). Chapter 3 serves as an epilogue to the whole process.

Harlotry continues to work as a symbol of Israel's broken relationship with Yahweh throughout much of Hosea. Chapter 4 uses this motif to introduce a fuller explanation of God's complaint against the people. Some form of the term 'to commit prostitution' (זנה) appears seven times in 4.10-18, and passages like 4.1 speak of faithlessness and other ideas related to the breaking of a covenant. Two aspects of the prostitution theme are prominent in 4.10-18. At first, spiritual adultery is in the forefront of the indictment. Hosea claims that Israel has deserted the Lord (4.10) due to 'a spirit of prostitution' (4.12). After this opening criticism, however, prostitution assumes concrete moral and ethical connotations in 4.14-18. Here the nation is accused of physical adultery (4.13-14). The two concepts are joined when the prophet reveals that Israeli men sleep with temple prostitutes of the Baal cult. Obviously such actions contradict the promises Israel made at Sinai, thereby consigning the nation to the curses associated with disobedience found in Deuteronomy 28 (cf. Deut. 28.16-19 and Hos. 4.10).

Israel's descent into sin continues to be described in terms
related to adultery in 5.3-4, 6.10, and 9.1. The first passage
refers back to 4.12. Israel's problem is that it harbors a 'spirit
of prostitution' that will inevitably lead to destruction. A
related image in 5.7 completes God's charges against the people by claiming their actions make them 'illegitimate children'
born out of unfaithfulness. All that can happen after such sin is
that God will, and must, punish their actions (5.14-15). After
the prophet exhorts the nation to repent in 6.1-3, Yahweh
repeats the accusation that they have broken the covenant,
are thus unfaithful, and deserve the title of prostitute (6.4-10).
Even though there is no explicit mention of harlotry in chs. 7–
8, there are references to adultery (7.4) and to Ephraim selling
herself to lovers (8.9). No better summation of the consequences of Israel's deeds could be offered than that found in
8.7: 'They sow the wind and reap the whirlwind'. Finally, 9.1
denies Israel the privilege of enjoying prosperity, because their
prostitution will lead to exile (9.3). Chapters 9–10 grow out of
this final reference to prostitution. Faithlessness on Israel's
part leaves God with no option, so they will no longer enjoy the
benefits of divine love (9.15; 10.12-15).

In Hosea, alongside the imagery of prostitution, adultery,
etc. is the prophet's constant emphasis on the covenant. When
the former metaphor basically concludes after chs. 9–10, the
latter emphasis takes over and completes the prophecy.
Undoubtedly the tone of the last four chapters is set by Hos.
11.1-7, which repeats the love Yahweh has shown to Israel
and how blatantly that love was spurned. Israel is called God's
'son', but has proved to be a son who runs from the father
(11.2), worships foreign gods (11.2), fails to recognize his own
benefactor (11.3), and who thus will face his father's punishment (11.5-7). This love and sonship summarizes the basis for,
and content of, the covenant between the Lord and the nation.
James Luther Mays comments:

> In the oracle Yahweh surveys the entire life story of Israel
> as the son of God; and, as the story unfolds, the history of
> Israel becomes an astonishing witness to the very life of
> Yahweh himself. Verses 1-4 tell of Israel's past, weaving
> together the saving acts of Yahweh and the sin of his people
> ... Verses 5-7 sketch the present plight of the people who

have left their God. They are on the verge of being swallowed up by the great powers of history, shattered by the ravages of invasion, and yet clinging to another god who cannot save them (1969: 151).

Verses 8-11 provide a final word on the straying of God's 'son' by noting that His love compels God to redeem Israel.

Hosea 11.1-11 serves at least two plot functions. First, it continues the downward slide of the nation towards judgment. The people have broken their promises to the Lord and must suffer the consequences of their actions. Second, the hope offered in 11.8-11 foreshadows a future upsurge of Israel's fortunes that is most discernible in Haggai–Malachi, but is also present in Hos. 14.4-9. Coupled with the sexual infidelity imagery in chs. 1–10, the denunciations against covenant breaking in chs. 11–14 present in outline the sin problem developed by the first six minor prophets. Because Hosea ends on a potentially hopeful note, however, the reader can envision that better times may be ahead for the covenant people.

Breaking the covenant is described in both concrete and abstract terms in Hosea 11–14. On the one hand, the nation acts like a rebellious child (11.2), a frightened child (11.10), a type of their 'father' Jacob (12.2-6, 12-14), and a foolish child (13.13). On the other hand, specific sins are mentioned such as dishonesty in business (12.7), pride (12.8), idolatry (13.2), and ingratitude (13.6). The specific accusations are somewhat undeveloped, so, as in the first ten chapters, Israel's apostasy is couched mostly in symbolic terms. Thus, despite the fact that there is a switch from metaphors of marital infidelity to those of covenant breaking, there is a consistency in Hosea's main mode of communicating his message. More detailed descriptions of Israel's faults must come in other prophecies. This book prefers to use arresting word-pictures to proclaim its message. Besides relating to one another by manner of presentation, it is also evident that adultery and covenant breaking are intersecting themes. To commit adultery means a special covenant has been broken, and to break the covenant is to commit spiritual adultery.

Clearly Hosea's prophecy claims that Israel has fallen from an exalted position as the special people of God, even as a 'son' to a group that faces inevitable judgment. Their sins present

such an affront to God's covenant standards that the prophet
calls the people 'prostitutes' and 'wayward children', thereby
shaming and embarrassing them. Hope for the future may
exist, as passages from 1.10 to 14.8 attest, but only as the result
of a repentance that does not seem to be forthcoming. In fact
Norman Henry Snaith argues: 'Exile awaits Israel, and all
chance of avoiding this has gone. Whatever message of hope
there is in the genuine writings of Hosea, there is no hope of
avoiding this national disaster' (1953: 45). Hope can only lie
beyond a coming catastrophe, as 3.4-5 demonstrates, and this
catastrophe is the focal point of Joel 1–2.

Joel's prophecy begins with a call to hear an important message. What message? Following Hosea's concluding verse,
which encourages the wise and discerning individuals in
Israel to walk in God's ways instead of stumbling like the
wicked, Joel explains what happens when prophetic warnings
are ignored. The message, then, is that the threats mentioned
in Hosea will become concrete events if Israel fails to repent.
Like Hosea, Joel's prophecy explains what is wrong with the
covenant people and what will happen to them because of
their sin. Also like Hosea, Joel is somewhat oblique in presenting its imagery. Instead of listing numerous specific crimes
against Yahweh, a very general approach to sin and punishment guides the book. Therefore, Joel stands with Hosea as a
presenter of the basic plot conflict in the Twelve, but allows
later works to develop the more complicated aspects of that
conflict. Nearly every commentator on Joel attests to the general nature of Joel's work, especially when attempting to date
the prophecy. J. Hardee Kennedy's comments on Joel's date
and word pictures typify most modern scholarship:

> The book of Joel cannot be dated with certainty. Internal evi-
> dences alone are available, and these are too obscure to fur-
> nish a definite answer. As a result, the opinions of inter-
> preters are sharply divergent. Two primary dates have been
> proposed, one very early and the other quite late, the first
> during the reign of King Joash in Judah (ca. 837 BC) and the
> second in postexilic times (ca. 400 BC) (1972: 64).

Such a variety of ideas can be attributed at least in part to the
metaphorical nature of Joel. Whether early or late, this book

makes a significant contribution to the Twelve's emphasis on the plunging morality of God's creatures.

After the call to 'hear' and 'tell' in 1.2-3, Joel proceeds to unfold a first governing metaphor. Verses 4, 6 and 7 recount an invasion of the land, first by swarms of locusts and then by a powerful nation. Both invaders devastate the land, leaving fields ruined (1.10), vines stripped (1.11), trees barren (1.12), and the people mourning (1.12). Scholars differ over whether the invasion is past or present, literal or figurative, nature-induced or military in origin. It is probably best to interpret the locust plague as a literal event that caused the prophet to declare that an even more catastrophic event—the coming of a foreign army—would occur if the nation continued in its iniquity. As Leslie C. Allen explains:

> Amos and later prophets had spoken of the Day of Yahweh as Yahweh's intervention in signal catastrophe against his enemies. Joel sees in the locusts the dawn of this very day. Zephaniah had urged the people to repent and perchance avert from themselves the wrath about to be poured out upon Israel and other nations (1.14–2.3). Joel repeats his call, to which his horrified hearers respond. To interpret the Day of Yahweh and similar eschatalogical motifs as merely poetic and hyperbolic metaphors is to do Joel an injustice. They represent rather a conviction that the end is at hand, heralded in this unprecedented destruction caused by the locusts, which threatened the very survival of the community (1976: 30).

So, despite Joel's comparison of an army to a swarm of locusts, the intent of the image is to use a common event to announce a predictable consequence of the people's actions. Locust and army are deliberately left undivided so the one will constantly bear witness to the other.

Several facets of the Day of Yahweh are exhibited in Joel 1. First of all, it is described as an event that leaves the land fruitless and barren, as was mentioned above. Because of the thoroughness of the locusts, there can be no harvest and, thus, no sacrifice offered in the temple (1.9-12). Cattle will suffer (1.18), and even what was stored prior to the Day cannot last (1.17). Because of the totality of the destruction 'the joy of mankind is withered away' (1.12). A second aspect of the Day of the Lord in the first chapter is that the devastation comes as a judgment of the Lord on the people for something they have done (1.15). If studied in isolation, there seems to be no specific reason for this severe punishment, but, if read canonically as the natural result of Hosea's warnings, the judgment makes sense. What unfolds relates to the whole sweep of Israel's history instead of just to Joel's time period. Finally, chapter one indicates the necessary reaction of the covenant nation to the Day of Yahweh. Mourning, fasting, and repentance are the only attitudes that can help them (1.8-14).

Chapter 2 (2 and 3 in Hebrew) completes the picture of the dreaded time of judgment. In vv. 1-11 a general description of the Day is offered, in 2.18-27 God's response to Israel's repentance is featured, and in 2.28-32 the future fortunes of a renewed nation is the theme. Each successive image helps put the coming punishment in its proper perspective.

Fittingly, the initial portrayal of the Day of Yahweh makes the invasion of a foreign army sound like the coming of a huge swarm of locusts. When the dreaded enemy comes its ranks are so numerous that their movements darken the sky (2.2). Like a locust swarm they consume the land (2.3), and they cover walls, cities, and houses (2.7-9). In short, this enemy will be everywhere. Regardless of the human leader of the forces it is ultimately Yahweh who heads the punishing army (2.11), for Israel's sins are a rejection of the Lord. Such images convey doom of monumental proportions and are therefore intended to shock the audience into an awareness of the consequences of their actions. Leslie C. Allen aptly comments that

> the whole passage is suffused with tones that heighten the locust plague to a macabre religious pitch. The armory of eschatological prophecy is ransacked in order that, under a barrage of its themes, the religiously insensitive community may be compelled to react aright to the seriousness of the present situation and its critical significance in terms of their relation to Yahweh (1976: 67).

How the coming devastation can be avoided dominates 2.12-17. Since Yahweh's nature includes mercy, Israel may possibly change the future. Even though destruction seems inevitable, God says 'even now', at the very brink of judgment, if the people will repent with all their might, rend their hearts and return to their Lord, 'He may turn and have pity' (2.12-14). Every segment of society must join in the repentance. Elders, children, brides, bridegrooms, priests, etc. must all gather for national mourning before any chance of respite becomes possible. Standing as it does between 2.1-11 and 2.18-32, this pericope creates a tension between what is and what may be. Will justified severity or humble repentance prevail?

Joel's answer relieves the tension. If the people change, 'then the Lord will be jealous for his land and take pity on his people' (2.18). Yahweh's pledge of restoration here reminds one of Hosea's promises in 2.21-23. Both passages say the Lord will remove shame from the sinner, restore grain, new wine, and oil to the penitent, and restore the covenant relationship between Israel and God. Further, Joel 2.28-32 (3.1-5 in Hebrew) predicts that Yahweh's Spirit will fall on the whole nation causing Israel to become a nation of prophets. It is not entirely clear whether all these benefits come before or after the day of punishment, since 2.31-32 (3.4-5 in Hebrew) calls on all people to come to the Lord for salvation. Regardless of the timetable, if one is to escape God's wrath, one has to turn humbly to God and trust in divine mercy. At this point Joel holds before Israel the possibility that judgment can be averted, but this opportunity is conditional, since the same nation condemned in ch. 1 must repent in ch. 2. The people must decide if they will accept Yahweh's offer, and a positive answer to that offer is not a foregone conclusion.

In its concluding chapter, Joel inserts a new plot element into the discussion of Israel's descent into sin that completes the introduction of the major problem of the Twelve. It is not only Israel that has sinned against the Lord. Indeed all countries have failed to act as God desires. Joel claims that the most basic of all transgressions the nations commit is a mistreatment of Israel. They have scattered the covenant people, taken their land, treated them miserably, and sold them into slavery (3.2-6; 4.2-6 in Hebrew). For these and other crimes the Day of Yahweh will fall with vehemence on Israel's neighbors, much as chapter one warns that the covenant people will experience God's wrath. On the other hand, when the Lord punishes Tyre, Sidon, Philistia, etc. Israel's fortunes will be restored through forgiveness (3.21). Egypt and Edom will be desolate

wastelands, but Judah and Jerusalem 'will be inhabited forever' (3.19-20; 4.19-20 in Hebrew). It is important to note,
however, that these promises appear to be fulfilled only after a
period of exile, so whatever hope the prophet envisions grows
out of a confidence in the purging power of God's day of judgment.

Hosea and Joel present the problem of the Twelve's plot in a
simple, yet densely textured, way. Israel's sin is plainly portrayed as prostitution, faithlessness, covenant breaking and
dead formalism. Yet the specifics of such iniquities are not
elaborated in great detail. Likewise, the sins of the nations are
boiled down to inhumane treatment of Israel. Further explanation must come later. At the same time both books make use
of metaphors that intersect one another, first literal, then
figurative, and then impossible to separate. These images are
effective simply because they can operate on various levels.
Even with this flexible imagery, though, Hosea and Joel paint a
simple and stark picture of Israel's sin: the covenant people
have left their God and must suffer punishment. Somehow the
nations will share this condemnation.

One objection may remain to viewing Hosea and Joel as the
beginning of the universe's descent into judgment, which is
the fact that promises of hope exists in both prophecies. The
answer to this objection is that, though both books describe a
better future for Israel, neither thinks that future will arrive
unless judgment comes first. After all, Hos. 11.11 and Joel 3.2
state that God's mercy follows punishment (cf. also Hos. 3.4-5).
The magnitude of the sins of Israel and the surrounding
countries grows when the reader realizes that these books
present the awfulness of what will be, or has been, in the light
of what could have been (or will be). At no time does either
prophet write that the people will avoid wrath.

So the basic problem of the Twelve's plot is in place. It is also
true that its solution is introduced. If all nations will repent
they can avoid the ravages of the Day of Yahweh and the plot
can receive an early resolution. Since it is evident that no such
repentance is in view, the reader can only expect a continuation of the slide into the bottom of the U-shaped plot.

2. *Complication of the Plot's Problem: Amos–Micah*

Just how far from repentance all nations are becomes very apparent as the next four books unfold. Though the probability of a hopeful conclusion is quite low in Hosea and Joel, the odds of such a resolution reduce even further in this section. Amos, Obadiah, and Jonah stress particular sins, while Micah summarizes the arguments contained in the whole sin section.

No single minor prophet lists the sins of all peoples with any more detail than Amos. In fact, Amos seems almost encyclopaedic in scope as he enumerates Israel's breach of the Sinai covenant and the nations' breach of the universal covenant of the human race. He is just as adamant about the inevitability of judgment. Snaith's comments on both aspects of Amos's oracles correctly assess the prophet's message:

> Again and again Amos thunders in judgment against immoral and inhuman practices, mostly on the part of the wealthy ruling classes... God will begin at the altar, for that is where the rottenness begins, and He will strike through the whole land (8.14). No one will escape, wherever he may hide, though they dig down to hell, climb up to heaven, hide in the thick undergrowth of the Ridge of Carmel, sink themselves in the depths of the sea, or even get taken into exile to a land far away (1953: 47).

From Amos' perspective sin seems hopelessly ingrained into the fabric of the whole Middle East.

As was noted in Chapter 3, Amos 1.2 and Joel 3.16 are strikingly similar in the Hebrew text. In Joel the roaring and thundering of the Lord signals the onslaught of judgment, so when Amos repeats the phraseology it is done to alert the reader that the new book wants to repeat and explicate that judgment. Amos also begins where Joel stopped—with the sins of other countries—but, whereas Joel mentions only one sin of this group, Amos will enumerate many such faults. The plot function of this opening section (1.2–2.16) is to demonstrate the enormity of the sin problem in Israel and its neighbors, and, thus, to complicate any resolution of the conflict between Yahweh and creation.

Until it turns to Judah and Samaria the book's chief complaint against the nations is that they callously abuse one another. Joel's accusation that they mistreat Israel is bad enough, and not really unexpected, but Amos shows they even have no pity for one another. This cruelty creates what Hammershaimb calls 'breaches of a universally valid moral law' (1970: 22). In other words, the fact that Damascus 'threshes' Gilead (1.3), Gaza sells whole cities into slavery (1.6), Tyre also sells human beings (1.9), Edom totally lacks compassion (1.11), Ammon rips open pregnant women (1.13), and Moab desecrates the remains of the dead (2.1) violates every aspect of human decency. Though not the covenant people, these groups must answer to the merciful God who created them. Because they lack mercy themselves God will judge them mercilessly, a point the individual punishments attest. It is significant to realize, as James Luther Mays points out, that the main function of 1.3–2.16 is to place all nations on an equal footing under the judgment of God. Mays comments:

> Finally, there is the problem of the norms by which the nations are indicted. On what grounds are they accused of offences against Yahweh? In the sequence Amos ranges Israel alongside the nations, *and* the nations alongside Israel. Both relations are significant. Israel is put in the general category of sinful kingdoms (9.8) subject to Yahweh's wrath. They are as vulnerable as the rest to punishment (3.2). And the nations are spoken of with a formal structure that is appropriate for Israel. They are subject to Yahweh's norms, can be indicted by him for misconduct, and their punishment justified in terms of a system of responsibility to him (1969: 27).

Cosmic sin is shown by Amos to be much worse than Joel had previously intimated. Righteousness does not exist in these countries, and judgment will come against them. Quite significantly, Amos offers no hope for any change in the nations' behavior and no hope that they will be forgiven by Yahweh. No upturn in the descending story line appears at this point.

Further complicating any possibility of reconciliation between God and the world is the immorality of the covenant people. Beginning with 2.4, the prophet builds an airtight case against Judah and Samaria that precludes any opportunity of escaping the day of the Lord. The first two denunciations serve as introductions to the remaining accusations in the book.

Amos says Judah has rejected God's law and committed idolatry (2.4-5), and that Samaria oppresses the poor, loves sexual immorality, and also commits idolatry (2.6-8). God's election of Israel and subsequent care for the people mentioned in 2.9-11 includes both parts of the nation, so the punishment described in 2.12-16 applies to both as well. The prophet expands his analysis of the status of Israel in the rest of the book, but already he stresses the improbability of any repentance on their part and thus any mercy on Yahweh's part.

Despite the urgency of the first message, the nation apparently refused to heed Amos's warning, perhaps because the people felt God would not reject the chosen country, so more oracles are presented to convince them of their sin. Chapter 3 presents logical arguments designed to waken the nation from its spiritual stupor. Driver summarizes Amos' arguments by writing:

> Amos begins by rudely shaking the Israelites from their security. The Israelites argued that the fact of Jehovah's having chosen the nation was a guarantee of its safety; but the prophet replies, You mistake the conditions of His choice; for that very reason He will punish you for your iniquities (3.1-2). Nor does the prophet say this without a real power constraining him; can any effect in nature take place without a sufficient cause? (3.3-8). Let the heathen themselves testify if *justice* rules in Samaria! (3.9f.). Ere long, Jehovah will visit Israel: its pride and luxury will be brought to a sudden end, its palaces will be spoiled, and its altars thrown down (3.11-15) (1901: 155-56).

After 3.15 the book's introductory matters are finished. The prophet has dealt with the presence of sin in the nations mentioned and has also answered basic disputes with his position. Now that the people have no excuse, Amos will uncover their transgressions one at a time, in stark detail, and proclaim the consequences of those sins.

Three strands of thought interact in Amos that unify the prophet's message of cosmic sin and punishment. First, as all commentators note, Amos chronicles the iniquity of Israel, though this strand is not as prominent as the other two. Various faults are mentioned, including oppression (4.1-3; 5.11-12), injustice and bribery (5.7-10, 12), inordinate luxury (4.1-3;

6.1-7), and empty worship (4.4-5). Second, and closely linked
with the first emphasis, the prophet exhorts the covenant
people to repent. The initial plea for change comes in 4.6-11,
where Yahweh recounts the many efforts made to show the
nation its mistakes (4.6). Because Israel has ignored these
lesser judgments, a more comprehensive punishment will
result. In 5.4-6 and 5.14-15 Amos counsels the people to 'seek
the Lord and live' and to 'seek good, not evil' so that mercy
may become possible, and as a last resort the prophet boldly
proclaims that Yahweh desires justice and righteousness
more than sacrifice (5.21-26).

That Amos expects no real repentance on Israel's part is
practically self-evident in 7.1-9.10, for in this section the
prophet lays out the reality of a coming judgment that fits the
transgressions of the covenant people. Like Joel, Amos thinks
the day of Yahweh could come by locust or fire (7.1-6), though
he indicates Israel may be spared those calamities, as a famine
consisting of no word from God (8.11-14), as an invasion of a
foreign army (7.17), or as exile (9.4), but it certainly will come
as darkness and inescapable doom (5.18-20). There is now no
escape from exile for Israel. Even the hopeful echos in 9.11-15
arise out of the ashes of exile. For Amos, all hope of averting
disaster has totally disappeared.

After completing Amos the reader of the Twelve should
sense the depth of covenant and cosmic sin and its natural
consequences. The rays of hope in Hosea, Joel, and Amos in no
way alleviate the conviction expressed in these books that
doom inevitably waits. But the minor prophets have not
finished. Judgment cannot be avoided, but more reasons for
that wrath must be offered before it happens.

Throughout Hosea, Joel, and Amos there is an almost
dizzying fall by Israel from the blessings to the curses of the
covenant. It is particularly the style of Amos to bombard the
reader's senses with images of sin and damnation in order to
create the idea that Israel's descent has been swift and irrevo-
cable. Thus, the conflict of the Twelve's plot seems similarly
insoluble. Obadiah, as a very short book, provides a pause in
this trend by dealing with a single subject and its ramifications.
Even as a slight break in the speed of the plunge into the U-
shape, Obadiah still contributes to the complication of any rec-

onciliation between God, the elect nation and the world as a whole.

Obadiah returns to Joel's and Amos' concern over the fate of the Gentile countries, with Edom serving as the example of God's will on the matter. Basically Obadiah elaborates Joel's comments on how Israel's neighbors oppressed the chosen people and how those actions will cause Edom's destruction. This emphasis justifies the prophets' condemnation of Edom, and at the same time explains the fairness and irony of passages like Amos 9.12 that predict Israel will possess Edom's land. According to Obadiah, surely the fact that Edom rejoiced in Jerusalem's fall (v. 12), looted the town (v. 13), killed its refugees (v. 14), and sold the survivors into slavery (v. 14) qualifies that country for judgment. Just as Israel will face the Day of Yahweh because of its unrighteousness, so will Edom or any other foreign country suffer God's wrath for similar offenses. Obadiah warns, 'The day of Yahweh comes near against all nations. For according to what you have done it will be done to you. Your actions will be returned on your head' (v. 15).

On another level, however, Obadiah dispels any hope of real change in the future of nations. One reason for this conclusion is that Edom has no compassion for other people. Verses 10-14 picture a nation that enjoys the destruction of a neighbor. As in Amos 1.3–2.3, such attitudes are denounced. Israel's attitude towards its neighbors emerges in Jonah.

The hatred Edom feels for Israel darkens further any hope that the world's nations can be reconciled to one another and to the Lord. In fact, Edom would gladly see Israel burn on the Day of Yahweh, so it is safe to say that all of creation still heads for destruction. Obadiah's comments once more put foreign groups on the same level as Israel, since Amos and Obadiah together place all nations out of God's favor. In slowing the condemnation of Israel, though, this brief prophecy raises the question of whether Israel is more merciful to its enemies. If the covenant people are to escape punishment, they must surely display more righteousness than the so-called heathen.

Jonah crushes any notion of Israel's superiority over even the Edomites in a very systematic fashion. Jonah symbolizes the hatred Israel harbors for an enemy, for though God's mercy extends to even a wicked place like Nineveh Israel cannot feel pity for a people who are sinners like themselves. First of all, Jonah rejects God's command to try to get Nineveh to repent of its many evil practices by taking passage on a ship to Tarshish (1.3). Next, Yahweh must force the fugitive prophet to preach to Nineveh by putting him in the stomach of a great fish. Then the prophet only half-heartedly preaches, though he gets a better response than most of the canonical prophets. Finally, and undoubtedly worst of all, Jonah longs to see Nineveh crushed by the Lord and becomes depressed when that destruction does not occur. Indeed, he feels more distress over the demise of a shade-giving plant than over the death of a city. Yahweh's classic answer to Jonah's prejudice concludes the book: 'Should I not be concerned about that great city?' (4.11). The point of the book is, as Julius Bewer believes, that

> all men are God's creatures. He is the God of all and just as full of love and care for heathen as for the Jews and just as ready to pardon them, if they abandon their sins and resort to Him. Should we not share His love and his purposes? (1912: 64).

Because of Jonah-like attitudes, Israel demonstrates as much hatred for Assyria as Edom displays for Jerusalem. In fact, Ninevites can be seen as more righteous than the covenant people here, since they at least repent when they hear God's word.

Speaking of the early part of the book, Peter Craigie astutely captures the essence of Jonah's plot:

> Jonah's flight from God is one of perpetual descent. Having gone down to the port of Joppa, and there having gone down into a ship, he now goes down beneath the deck (verse 5), hoping to rest after this trying experience! But though the fleeing prophet thinks he has found some respite at last, there is no peace for the ship in which he has set sail (1984: 219).

Neither does Jonah find rest on a hill overlooking Nineveh. Jonah's descent parallels the slide by Israel and the nations away from Yahweh's favor chronicled in the earlier books of the Twelve. Like Jonah, Israel ran from God (Hosea), failed to learn the lessons attached to punishment (Amos 4.7-13) and, like Edom, hated their neighbors (Obadiah).

All the questions asked about the nations in Obadiah can be asked of Israel in Jonah. Like the Edomites, Israel, represented by Jonah, generates much hatred for its enemies. Like the Edomites who 'stood aloof' while Jerusalem perished, Jonah withdraws eastward to view the death of Nineveh. There exists no more hint of kindness in the covenant people than is evident in the Gentile countries. As did Obadiah, Jonah slows the descent of the plot long enough to allow the reader to consider Israel's sin of exclusivism and cruelty, but once understood Jonah's message marks a new low point in the Twelve's story line. God's creation has little hope of restoration to a proper relationship with its creator if all nations are unrighteous, unkind and unconcerned. Only drastic measures have any chance of reversing this depressing set of circumstances.

Micah completes the Twelve's sin section and, thus, introduces some final complications in the comic plot. As was surveyed in Chapter 3, scholars rarely agree on Micah's structure, so it is not surprising that Micah's own plot and its place in the Twelve are not easy to define. Though other valid approaches to Micah certainly exist, the book clearly inextricably links themes of sin, punishment, and restoration. Accusations intersect with calls to repentance, threats of punishment, and hints of restoration. Once more, any restoration can only transpire after a time of severe judgment which the prophet feels will inevitably happen. This makes their squandering of the *knowledge* of restoration part of the world's punishment. Why this judgment will fall constitutes Micah's major theme, so again it is sin and how sin complicates any possibility of reconciliation that dominates Micah.

Chapter 1 opens with what at this point in the plot seems to be a logical conclusion. Micah announces the Lord is coming to judge the world because of Judah and Samaria's sins, and that this event will be a cause of great grief in many lands. Sins committed include idolatry (1.7) and prostitution (1.7), both of which always receive condemnation from the prophets. After the mutual hatred detailed in Obadiah and Jonah, the reader could not, or at least should not, be surprised at what Micah declares.

The depth of Israel's depravity increases with revelations of new sins like coveting and defrauding (2.1-2), false prophecy (2.6-11), acceptance of bribes (3.11), fortune telling (3.11), and taking Yahweh's presence for granted (3.11). In the first three chapters Micah uses an Amos-like approach to convey his message. Even as Amos introduced his book by uncovering one sin after another done by one country after another, so Micah pours out his indignation at Israel's sin in rapid-fire fashion. After the focused presentations of Obadiah and Jonah this method of presentation bombards the reader with a renewed sense of why judgment must sweep down on Israel.

Source and redaction critics have often posited that Mic. 4.1 comes from a different author or tradition than chs. 1–3 because the earlier passage speaks of judgment and chs. 4–5 mention the hope of restoration, among other reasons. James Luther Mays represents this viewpoint when he writes about 4.1-4:

> The prophecy could hardly have been spoken by Micah. The vocabulary and style of 4.1-4 have no parallels in oracles which can be assigned to him with confidence. The message has no place in the mission of Micah as defined by these oracles and his own vocation (3.8), and it is clearly a direct contradiction of 3.12, the prophecy for which he was remembered a century after it was uttered. The subject of YHWH and the nations is a feature of the final formulation of chs. 1–5, and it is most probable that the saying came into the book in this stage of its development... (1976: 95).

Such historical distinctions may be quite unnecessary, especially if the prophetic tradition that judgment is redemptive is taken into account. After all, the Exodus tradition taught that conquest came only after the 40 years of wilderness punishment. When Hosea speaks of wooing Gomer-Israel he claims that she must first be taken to the desert. Joel also thinks the Day of Yahweh falls on the nations so Israel can be redeemed. Therefore, that restoration naturally follows, and is a part of, judgment seems self-evident.

Even writers who reject the probable historical unity of Micah tend to point out its theological and thematic coherence. Mays says:

> The theological integrity of the prophecy lies in its unity. The text as a whole portrays the way in which the appearance of YHWH's reign on earth will inaugurate an imperial peace that transforms the conditions of life for nations and individuals (1976: 93).

Hans W. Wolff agrees that chs. 4–5 probably belong to a redactional period rather than to Micah's time, but also finds that these chapters carry on the message of chs. 1–3. He notes that

> the process of editorial compilation was concerned not only with presenting Micah's original oracles but, beyond that, also with providing prophecy's full range of witness concerning Zion and a guide for Israel and the nations as they travel on their path through history to their goal (1978: 86).

Regardless of the historical or redactional setting, then, most authors admit the basic unity of the book's attempt to chart the fate of Israel and the nations.

One approach to the ongoing plot of Micah 1–5 is to note how Micah serves as a prophet of a coming millennial age in Jerusalem. Delbert Hillers charts the tendency of many cultures to long for future utopias, and lists five elements in Micah 4–5 that share the characteristics found in those cultures (1984: 6-7). According to Hillers, Micah teaches that revitalization will come when there is a 'removal of foreign elements' (1984: 6). Mic. 5.10-15 mirrors this idea, since it mentions numerous foreign objects that must disappear from Israel before restoration can occur. Hillers says 'A second common "millenial" theme is that of the time of troubles' (1984: 6). A glorious future will only result when the chosen people have their sins purged through tribulation (cf. 5.3). Next, Hillers notes that a 'reversal of social classes' is a feature of national revival (1984: 6). The oppressed must receive justice for God's reign to be complete. Fourth, 'the idea of a righteous, peaceable ruler is a common feature... and is of course present in Micah' (1984: 7). Mic. 5.2 presents the notion that a very special king will come from Bethlehem who can shep-

herd the flock, make the people secure, and glorify God (5.4).
Finally, Micah refers to the new era itself in glowing terms
(1984: 7). Israel is depicted as a blessing from God to the world
and also as enjoying vindication over all its enemies (5.7-9).

Hillers correctly assesses the prophet's remarks about
Israel, but fails to discuss the fate of the other countries. Micah
normally describes the nations as doomed to oppose Israel but
to fail to overcome her (5.7-9). Still, Micah predicts many
nations will turn to Yahweh, thereby causing all warfare to
cease (4.1-4). So there remains hope for all the people of
earth—both Jew and Gentile—to return to Yahweh's favor.

Hope therefore springs from chs. 4–5. Micah's two concluding chapters, however, cloud that possibility, though the
chance does not disappear altogether. One more time the Lord
sets forth a complaint, a ריב, against Israel. Chapter 6 recounts
Yahweh's past exertions on their behalf (6.1-5), gives the
essence of true faith (6.6-8), and describes the fate of those who
are dishonest, violent, and materialistic (6.9-16). No wonder
the prophet mourns in 7.1-6, hoping for some grace in 7.7.
Micah is confident Yahweh will keep all covenant promises
and that Israel will prosper again (7.7-17), but concludes that
sin still stands in the way of Israel's future blessings (7.18-20).
At the end Micah remains ambiguous about Israel's fate.
Certainly God's original plan for the elect nation will come to
pass. Just as certainly, though, restoration will only come
when sin has been eradicated, and the prophet definitely feels
only the Day of Yahweh can effect that change.

Starting with Hosea, the Twelve portrays the descent of
Israel into a U-shape at whose bottom lies judgment. Hosea
and Joel speak in general terms of a judgment to come against
all nations, and speak in fairly oblique ways about the sins that
cause that punishment. Amos, on the other hand, is blunt
about the iniquity of Israel and its neighbors and their much-
deserved chastisement. In some very explicit passages the
prophet outlines both sin and judgment. Obadiah and Jonah
continue the downward trend, with the former work stressing
a specific transgression of the Gentiles and the latter doing the
same for Israel. These books show that these groups' hatred
for one another precludes their helping one another return to
Yahweh. Micah summarizes the arguments of his predeces-

sors while adding the particularly sad fact that restoration could be glorious if the people would repent. All six books believe there will be no repentance unless judgment forces the countries to change. A more pessimistic outlook for the *immediate* future of the nations could hardly be imagined.

If Holman's definition of 'complication' as the 'part of a dramatic or narrative plot in which the entanglement of affairs caused by the conflict of opposing forces is developed' (1972: 115) is acceptable, then surely Amos–Micah serves as the complication of the problem introduced in Hosea and Joel. Because of all the problems associated with the creation's return to a proper relationship with Yahweh, Frye is correct in assessing the plot's progress as 'at the bottom of a U-shaped curve' (1982: 128). Only judgment can take the nations lower, though the prophets indicate that even judgment may be preferable to continuing in sin, because punishment can produce a redemptive effect. With the world in rebellion against God, the reader waits to see if there is any solution to this great conflict.

3. *Crisis Point of the Twelve: Nahum and Habakkuk*
Outside of commentary series few scholars choose to analyze Nahum. More work with Habakkuk, probably because of its emphasis on theodicy, but even then the output remains relatively small. Part of the reason Nahum receives little treatment is that the prophecy exhibits one theme, the destruction of Nineveh. As important as Nineveh was to the ancient world the subject hardly invites massive critical exploration. Most of the writing on Nahum focuses on the possibility that it houses an acrostic poem, on its redaction, and on its various forms (Childs 1980: 441-42). Its role and position in the Twelve, however, have been overlooked. Somewhat like Obadiah, Nahum assumes added meaning when its literary function emerges, for as Obadiah responds to Amos and Jonah, so Nahum responds to Jonah, Joel, Amos, Obadiah, and Micah.

Because of its singular message of Nineveh's destruction, Nahum signals the end of God's patience with the universe. Chapter one stresses the notion that Yahweh does not crush Nineveh out of any personal vindictiveness, rather the 'Lord is slow to anger' (1.3), 'good' (1.7), and 'a refuge in times of trouble' (1.7). Punishment comes instead because Nineveh 'plots evil against the Lord' (1.11). Though the Lord has a special love for friends, yet God will 'pursue His foes into darkness' (1.8). In Nahum the 'foes' are represented by Assyria, a Gentile country of great influence. If this great nation can fall, is any nation safe from the power of God's wrath?

After his apologetic for Yahweh's actions, Nahum declares that Nineveh is a city doomed to be 'pillaged, plundered, stripped' (2.10). The city's foes are powerful (2.3-4), while Nineveh's best soldiers stumble so badly in battle that 'the river gates are thrown open and the palace collapses' (2.6). How can this catastrophe occur? Very simply the prophet notes, '"I am against you", declares the Lord Almighty' (2.13). Again, if Assyria's might cannot fend off God's punishment, there is no hope for militarily weaker countries like Edom, Ammon, Moab, and Philistia to survive either.

Finally, chapter three ties the book's preceding themes together. God's punishment falls because Nineveh is a city of blood, lies, plunder, and oppression (3.1), a city that enslaves others (3.4), and a city of enormous cruelty (3.19). All who hear of the city's just judgment rejoice (3.19), which indicates the wickedness of the place more than the faulty attitudes of its enemies. Nineveh has had opportunities to repent (cf. Jonah), but has squandered such chances, and obviously no more chances are available.

When viewed as the natural result of the sins of the nations chronicled in Joel, Amos, Obadiah, Jonah, and Micah, the harsh words of Nahum against Assyria take on added significance. The prophecy becomes more than a reprise of the attitudes of Obad. 10-14 and Jon. 4.5-9. It is unnecessary, then, to adopt the position held by John M.P. Smith that

> instead of grieving over the sin of Judah and striving with might and main to warn her of the error of her ways that she herself might turn and live, Nahum was apparently content to lead her in a jubilant celebration of the approaching death of Assyria (1911: 281).

Further, Smith writes:

> In Nahum, a representative of the old, narrow and shallow
> prophetism finds its place in the Canon of Scripture. His
> point of view is essentially one with that of... the so-called
> 'false prophets' in general. For such prophets, the relation
> between Yahweh and his people Israel was indissoluble
> (1911: 281).

Other commentators are more charitable, of course (cf. R.
Smith 1984: 68), but Smith has a point if Nahum is interpreted
alone. If analyzed as part of the mainstream of written
prophecy, though, the book fits both the history of God's dealings with Israel and with the world as a whole. Israel's rise
and fall normally runs opposite to those of more powerful
nations, and Nahum's predictions fit that pattern. Viewed this
way, John Watts says, Nahum 'is a sign of the victory of God
and the basis for hope that his power and justice will ultimately conquer all evil' (1975: 120).

Nahum announces the extreme crisis of the Twelve's plot.
Judgment no longer looms beyond the horizon. It has come,
and no country or city, regardless of how powerful, can escape
God's wrath. Had Nahum denounced a lesser nation perhaps
Assyria could hope to continue its sin in peace, but, because the
judgment cycle begins with a mighty people, the totality of the
day of Yahweh becomes obvious. At this juncture of the Twelve
only shades of hope for Judah remain (Nah. 1.15; 2.2). All else
either lies prostrate before God or expects to do so shortly.

Habakkuk heightens the tension brought about by Nahum.
The prophet's first complaint (1.2-4) states that various levels
of evil exist in Judah. Included in the sins are violence (1.2),
injustice (1.3), destruction (1.3), strife (1.3) and conflict (1.3).
Due to these problems 'the law is paralyzed, and justice never
prevails. The wicked hem in the righteous, so that justice is
perverted' (1.4). Habakkuk's puzzling over 'how long' (1.2)
God will refrain from punishing Israel is by now also the question of both the reader and those nations already punished.
After all, the earlier parts of the Twelve explore the transgressions of the covenant people in much more detail than the
iniquities of the Gentiles. Since no mention of real repentance
appears in Hosea-Nahum it is reasonable to surmise that
punishment must reach Israel and reach it soon.

Yahweh answers the prophet in an amazing fashion (1.5). Babylon, a nation of supreme power (1.10-11), has been elected to chastise Israel (1.5-11). Though the chosen people, Israel must now face the consequences of a repeated refusal to repent and return to the Lord. So the unthinkable will come to pass: even Israel will suffer punishment. Coupled with Nahum's statements about Assyria this pronouncement brings the Twelve's plot almost as far down as it can go.

Because of the unusual nature of Yahweh's answer, Habakkuk voices a second grievance in 1.12–2.1. If Babylon chastises Israel, the prophet argues, then the wicked merely punish the wicked, and God is open to charges of tolerating evil and saying nothing, while the wicked devour the righteous (1.13). Yahweh promises to plunder the plunderer (2.8) and bring woe on whoever 'builds a city with bloodshed and establishes a town by crime' (2.12). Thus, both Israel and Babylon will be judged. In effect, therefore, all the earth stands condemned by God. As usual, judgment has a redemptive mission, as David Garland notes:

> In v. 14 Habakkuk is prophesying the inauguration of the universal kingdom of Yahweh upon the earth. The coming of this kingdom will be preceded by the destruction of those nations with the guilt of the Chaldeans, Assyrians, etc. Then there will be no more violence and cruelty in the world (1972: 261).

Only through judgment can this renewal take place.

In many respects Hab. 2.12-14 provides the climax of Hosea-Habakkuk. First, 2.12 proclaims the fate of all who attempt to abuse others (cf. Amos 1.3–2.3) to achieve their own wicked goals, which summarizes the concerns of Hosea, Amos, etc. Second, 2.13 demonstrates the sovereignty of God over the whole process of sin, punishment, and restoration described in the Twelve. Despite all the nations have done to rebel against Yahweh, their rebellion amounts to a mere useless exhaustion of energy. God can and will punish those who exalt themselves against their Lord. Third, 2.14 explains the purpose and end result of all Yahweh's work in creation. What is sin but the rejection of the knowledge of God (cf. Hos. 4.6)? Punishment derives from a struggle against God's reign, and restoration remains the ultimate result of all Yahweh's efforts. Renewal is as inevitable a result of punishment as punishment is of sin. Here the whole message of the Twelve hangs in the balance. Judgment is being poured out, the nations fall exhausted, the prophet bows in awe (Hab. 2.20), and Yahweh reigns. What happens next hangs on the Lord's command.

Evidently Yahweh's answer satisfies Habakkuk, since the prophet closes his book with a hymn of praise that extols the virtues of the Lord. God's power (3.2), glory (3.3), splendor (3.4), wrath (3.8), mercy (3.13), and grace (3.19) are celebrated. It is important to note Habakkuk's situation when he sang this psalm. Before any redemption or restoration takes place the prophet embodies his own observation that 'the righteous will live by his faith' (2.4), for at the end of the book Habakkuk waits patiently for a 'day of calamity to come on the nation invading us' (3.16) that has not yet arrived. Basically Habakkuk represents the reader here. Judgment has begun and the followers of Yahweh must wait to see the results of God's wrath. The reader has been taken to the depths of the U-shaped plot. More punishment may happen, but will 'only' be more of the same destruction of Israel and the nations described in Nahum and Habakkuk. At the same time, some hope has been foreshadowed in Hab. 2.12-14 and 3.16-19, which indicates the plot is still unfinished.

4. *Climax and Falling Action: Zephaniah*
At the conclusion of Habakkuk the reader, like the prophet, is waiting for Yahweh's redemption (3.16-19). Zephaniah's method of ending this suspense is to first dispel any possible doubts about the thoroughness of God's judgment. Once more the Day of Yahweh enters the scene as a metaphor of punishment, and 1.2-18 describes the complete devastation of not only Judah and its neighbors, but of all the earth. Page Kelley aptly summarizes this approaching judgment:

> The fury of that day will be focused on those who have sinned against the Lord. Their destruction will be both horrible and inescapable. It will be so horrible that their blood will be poured out as if it had not more value than dust and their

> flesh as if it were as cheap as dung. It will be so inescapable
> that neither silver nor gold will avail to deliver sinners from
> the wrath of the Lord. All the earth will be consumed and all
> the inhabitants of the earth will come to an end (1984: 95).

Zephaniah's own understanding of the Day of the Lord unfolds through a series of vivid images. The first image is that the world will be 'swept' like a floor cleaned by a broom (1.2-3). All living things are to be destroyed in this scouring of the world, so a picture of emptiness is projected. John Watts thinks 1.2-3 parallels 'Noah's flood even in the choice of words (cf. Gen. 6.8)' and that 'Zephaniah's new word from God seems intended to replace the promise of Gen. 8.21' (1975: 156). Michael De Roche disagrees with Watts, concluding that

> the crux of Zephaniah's oracle, however, is that he reverses
> the order of these beings from that in the creation account.
> Thus, Zephaniah is not simply announcing judgment on
> mankind, nor is he only disqualifying Yahweh's promise of
> Gen. 8.21. Zephaniah is proclaiming man's loss of dominion
> over the earth, and more importantly, the *reversal of cre-*
> *ation* (1980: 106).

Either interpretation makes sense, for Noah's flood judged the earth and produced a reversal of creation. What Zephaniah intends is for the audience to understand that all that has been will be no more.

Beyond this initial image Zephaniah includes descriptions of desolation that specifically include nations that have disobeyed Yahweh. In this way the general destruction displayed in ch.1 takes a more structured shape. Chapter 2 names various countries that are destined for punishment, most of whom are familiar figures to the Twelve's readers. Note the prophet's description of these places:

1. Judah (1.13): houses destroyed and emptied, vine-yards left uncultivated.
2. Philistia (2.4-7): abandoned, in ruins, empty, a place for grazing flocks.
3. Moab and Ammon (2.9): like Sodom and Gomorrah, a place of weeds and salt pits, a wasteland forever.
4. Cush (2.12): slain.

5. Assyria (2.13-15): utterly desolate, dry as a desert, a
    pasture for livestock, a haunt for roosting owls, a place
    where calls echo, rubble abounds, and beams are laid
    bare, a ruin, a home for wild animals, a place of scorn.
6. Nations in general (3.6): demolished, deserted, no
    traffic, totally empty.

As a summary book, Zephaniah lists the many sinful groups,
whether powerful or weak, in order to show that the nations
will be as desolate as nature on the day of Yahweh.

Besides the nations mentioned, Zephaniah claims that individuals also face condemnation. Whether religious officials
(1.4), royalty (1.8) or common citizen who mistakes God's
mercy for indifference (1.12-13), none who sins can escape the
Lord's wrath. Particularly offensive to Yahweh is syncretism,
which in this instance results from mixing the worship of God
with that of pagan gods (1.5) and from accepting foreign cus-
toms in Judah's court (1.8). Their worship has become as foreign as their clothing. Such lack of concern about God's standards for proper worship leads to the belief that Yahweh is a
powerless deity. Men of Jerusalem commonly say: 'The Lord
will do nothing, either good or bad' (1.12). Zephaniah describes
such thinking as being 'like wine left on its dregs', which
George Adam Smith notes 'became a proverb for sloth, indifference, and the muddy mind' (1929: 51). Along with nature
and the nations, then, individuals must be added to the list of
objects of destruction. Therefore, as 1.2-3 threatens, *all creation* will be swept away.

This gloomy picture is not the only theme, however, inherent in the Day of the Lord. Through judgment emerges the
grace and mercy of Yahweh. Several images contribute to an
opposite portrayal of God's work. An initial metaphor portrays
the remnant of Judah lying down like sheep in the wasteland
that was once Philistia (2.7). Before this pastoral image Yahweh only cares about Judah's destruction, but now is their
shepherd who creates a haven for His 'sheep'. Another image
is the purifying of the nations' lips (3.9) so they can call on the
Lord properly. In a miraculous turn of events the Gentiles are
allowed access to God. Until this point only 2.11 indicates that
Yahweh cares for Judah's enemies, yet now they receive

mercy. One more significant passage reveals this new theme of grace. In 3.14-17 the prophet encourages Judah to exult because God is 'with' the people once more (3.15). Yahweh joins the people's singing in 3.17 and soothes them by expressing love. Though Zephaniah certainly pictures the Day of Yahweh as a time of extreme devastation, from the destruction unfolds a theme of forgiveness (cf. 3.8-9).

Interspersed between the judgment and mercy notions lies the key to worldwide restoration. God leaves open the possibility that a select remnant can survive the Day of the Lord (2.3). If these people are humble and righteous—significantly different than the rest of the nation (cf. 1.4-13)—they may be spared. Indeed, God promises to care for them and 'restore their fortunes' (2.7). Closely aligned to the 2.7 passage is 2.9, where the remnant is not only spared, but allowed to plunder enemy territory. To fully prepare the remnant to rule, though, Yahweh will remove the proud from the midst of the remnant (3.11), and then leave only the meek and humble (3.12). In conjunction with these actions, the Lord will 'rescue', 'gather', 'bring home' and 'honor' Judah (3.19-20). This final act completes the restoration of God's people. The possibility of a redeemed remnant has become a completed picture of a new and powerful people. Once judgment is fully expended in 3.8 it becomes an avenue for God to demonstrate mercy through the lives of the cleansed people.

Equally merciful is Zephaniah's attitude toward the Gentiles. They too will share in creation's renewal, which is one of the by-products of the coming judgment. When their cities and gods are destroyed they learn to serve God (2.11). When wrath is spent, the Lord will purify the foreign groups so they can serve their creator (3.9). While the nations are not promised as much as the remnant, the fact that they can come to Yahweh at all is an incredible promise. Idolaters and enemies of Israel are made as acceptable as the covenant people. There could be no greater kindness extended by a Hebrew prophet than these predictions.

Various plot functions emerge in Zephaniah. First, though the prophecy hints at restoration in 2.3, 7, and 11, most of 1.1–3.8a describes the systematic annihilation of a sinful world. Creation is totally reversed, thus fulfilling threats made in all the previous books in the Twelve. The full fury of Yahweh's Day pours forth in Zephaniah. A second plot aspect is that, just as Hab. 2.12-14 declares God will fill the earth with the knowledge of the Lord, Zeph. 3.8-9 teaches that many nations will serve Yahweh, thereby restoring all creation. Ironically, judgment provides the needed renewal, since it cleanses the world of sin. Third, Zephaniah includes the nations in God's future blessings, which completes ideas like Mic. 4.1-4 and abolishes the hatred of Obadiah and Jonah at the same time. Fourth, the prophecy makes a remnant of righteous Israelis the key to all restorative works. Though small, this group will lead the world to worship the Lord in humility and truth. By stressing these elements, Zephaniah can provide a bridge between the sin, punishment, and restoration sections of the Twelve.

Quite evidently, therefore, Zephaniah serves as a pivotal book. It embodies both the climax and the falling action of the Twelve's story line. Put another way, it completes the bottom of the U-shaped and begins the journey upwards. From 1.1–3.8 the prophecy confirms all the horrible expectations of judgment in Hosea–Micah and completes the carnage begun in Nahum and Habakkuk. But from 3.8-20 Zephaniah introduces the reader to the possibilities of restoration outlined in Haggai–Malachi. Just as Zephaniah expects, it is a small group that gathered to start the restoration process, and, just as he thought, some of the glories of the future wait for consummation. Still, the importance of Zephaniah as a plot-shaper in the Twelve can hardly be over-estimated.

5. Resolution (Denouement) of the Plot: Haggai, Zechariah, and Malachi

After the complication of a plot there must be some 'unravelling' of that problem (cf. Aristotle 1974: chs. 18, 47). As Holman notes, there must be some solution, explanation, or outcome for the plot to be effective (1972: 150). In the prophetic genre it is most likely that restoration will eventually follow sin and punishment. Haggai begins this process of lifting Israel, and all creation with her, back to a position of favor with Yahweh. He does so very inauspiciously, since the prophet attempts the task with a group that has returned from exile dispirited and in no mood to build a temple. In fact, survival may be their main goal (cf. 1.5-6). From these humble beginnings Israel responds in a significant way to the word of Yahweh that comes through the prophet.

Four visions are given to Haggai, with the first three stressing certain aspects of the rebuilding of the temple. Written between 520 and 516 BC, Haggai comes after the exile, and, thus, after the destruction of the temple. Haggai's main goal is to have a new temple in place so the nation can prosper again (2.10-19). Pieter Verhoef observes that the rebuilding of the temple was important because the edifice represented the dwelling of God among the people, divine self-disclosure to them, and God's covenant with Israel (1987: 34-35). God was not thought to be confined to the temple area nor bound to dwell among the people unless they obeyed the covenant, but the temple did provide a tangible symbol of the proper relationship between Israel and the Lord. Therefore, the construction of a temple by the returned remnant would constitute a first major step towards resolving the differences between Yahweh and Israel. God took the initiative by bringing the people back, as Zeph. 3.20 promises, so now the people must do their part to become the kind of remnant described in Zeph. 3.13.

Haggai reports that God's people react very swiftly to the call to build a new temple. After Haggai's sermon in 1.2-11, which declares that all the problems of the settlers revolve around their unwillingness to take as much care for God's house as they do for their own, Zerubbabel and Joshua lead Israel to work on the temple project (1.12-15). Apparently, the whole populace accepted the prophet's message. As David Petersen says:

> With their lamentable condition, as interpreted in vs. 2-11, the people react in such a way as to demonstrate that they know the cause of their problems, of the lack of fertility and prosperity. They fear Yahweh as the agent responsible for their plight. Haggai's speeches in vs. 2-11 had been effective. This reaction of fear is that of the overall populace—the people. It is interesting that the narrator focuses on the people and not on high officials at this point in the interchange.

Perhaps this shift in audience occurs because the author recognizes who must actually do the work of temple construction. It is not just the officials who must work (1984: 56).

This immediate response to Haggai's preaching is a marked reversal of the almost universal disobedience of Israel in Hosea–Zephaniah. A new era has dawned when Israel does what Yahweh and the prophets ask instead of rejecting such messages. Other positive signs appear in this work as well, for the acceptance of Haggai's words shows that the nation realizes its dependence on Yahweh, and the rebuilding of the temple indicates Israel has become willing, probably because of the punishment it has suffered, to take definite action to repair its broken relationship with the Lord.

Each of Haggai's last three oracles offers encouragement to the faithful remnant. In 2.1-9 the prophet recognizes the new temple cannot compare to Solomon's (2.2-3), so he reassures the people that God's presence abides with them and precludes any reason for fear. Further, Haggai makes the astounding claim, '"The glory of this present house will be greater than the glory of the former house", says the Lord Almighty' (2.9). Why? Because it will be a place of peace as opposed to the war surrounding the old house of worship (2.9). If this first word was not enough, Haggai adds in 2.10-19 that, though the exiles had been sinful and the land thus blighted, Yahweh will bless them because of their new-found obedience. Obedience will thereby restore their physical fortunes. A last promise is given to Zerubbabel, who led the construction work. Because of his faithfulness, God will use him in a special, though undesignated, way.

However modest, the fresh start between Yahweh and Israel exhibited in Haggai is quite encouraging. Judgment has done its work, and a new generation seems headed in the right direction. With a physical sign of Israel's covenant with Yahweh in place, other areas of restoration can be addressed. As these issues are taken up in Zechariah and Malachi, the task is attempted with a new sense of hope brought on by the knowledge that the plot line has taken a decisive turn for the better. Restoration is under way.

From first chapter to last Zechariah attempts to extend the boundaries of Israel's restoration. At the heart of this book's plot is an inexorable rise of Jerusalem to new heights of glory, which in turn will cause the temple, the priesthood, the people, the nation, and the Gentiles to rise as well. Zechariah's first vision wonders how long mercy will be withheld from Jerusalem (1.12), while the final oracle declares that every part of the city is 'holy to the Lord' (14.21). How far Jerusalem ascends mirrors the restorative process in the Twelve and, therefore, also mirrors its plot.

Before any renewal develops in Zechariah, the prophet explains the history of the covenant people (1.1-6). In the past, Israel habitually rejected Yahweh's commands (1.4). Because of this sin, the Lord 'overtook' previous generations. Now, however, the people have wisely 'repented and said, "The Lord Almighty has done to us what our ways and practices deserve, just as he determined to do"' (1.6). Like the people in Haggai, Zechariah's audience accepts their guilt and turns to the Lord for forgiveness. In this way they open themselves to the grace of God.

Zechariah's visions in 1.7–6.15 demonstrate how quickly the restoration process moves when Israel admits its sin. The first vision provides an introduction to its successors. After an angel wonders how long Jerusalem will remain out of God's favor (1.12), the Lord gives an answer in three stages. First, Yahweh states that He is 'jealous for Jerusalem and Zion' (1.14), but angry with less repentant countries (1.15). Second, God promises to return to Jerusalem with mercy, which will be evidenced by the rebuilding of the temple (1.16). Third, and perhaps most important, Yahweh 'will again comfort Zion and choose Jerusalem' (1.17). With this special blessing assured, the nation will prosper again (1.17). Already there is a wide gap between Israel's fortunes in 1.1-5 and in this vision. The rest of the book describes Israel's rise along these three lines.

At the heart of the renewal discussed by Zechariah lies the renaissance of Jerusalem. Every one of the stages set forth in 1.7-17 includes a promise for Zion. Just as the restoration of the temple symbolized the new relationship between God and Israel in Haggai, so a newly-established Jerusalem represents the same kind of reconciliation in Zechariah. Yahweh's care for the city serves as a pledge of care for Israel as a whole.

After a brief vision that promises an end to the oppression of Jerusalem (1.18-21), the prophecy envisions a measuring of Jerusalem that means the city will exist without walls because Yahweh will be its protection (2.4-5). Exiles will return (2.6-9), causing the city to rejoice (2.10). Foreign countries will also become God's people (2.11), and the Lord will thus once again 'choose' Jerusalem (cf. 1.17; 2.12). Beyond the actual city itself, the prophet notes that the priesthood must be cleansed (3.1-10) and the temple rebuilt (4.1-14). When these tasks have been accomplished Zechariah notes that God will cleanse the land of sin (5.1-11) and deliver the land from the threats of its enemies (6.1-8). Chapter 6 closes with a second assurance that the temple and the priesthood will be restored. Practically every aspect of restoration has been mentioned by the end of ch. 6, including spiritual, physical, and national concerns. The remainder of the books reaffirm this renewal until the theme becomes a great crescendo of God's mercy. Again, Jerusalem stands in the center of God's plan for the nation, since temple, priesthood, and national awareness originate there.

Three more sections remain in Zechariah, and each one reinforces the themes already discussed. The first section (7.1–8.23) gives a reprise of the blessings offered in ch. 1. Like 1.1-5, ch. 7 reminds the people of their unsavory past, but ch. 8 echoes 1.12-17 by repeating God's pledges to bless Jerusalem (8.1-6), gather the people (8.7-8), build the temple 8.9-11), provide food for Israel (8.12-13), forgive the people (8.14-19), and include the nations in the salvation of the current people (8.20-23). Whatever doubts the reader may harbor about the permanency of Israel's new-found favor should be erased by now. The covenant nation will recover.

Not even Israel's traditional foes can halt the Lord's program of blessing the people. The first part of chs. 9–11 declares that Damascus, Tyre, Sidon, Gaza, and Ekron will all be cut off, but Yahweh says: 'I will defend my house against marauding forces. Never again will an oppressor overrun my people, for now I am keeping watch' (9.8). Anyone left in these foreign countries will serve the Lord. Joyce Baldwin comments:

> The first section of this second part of the book establishes from the start two important facts: the Lord's victory is certain, and He intends to bring back to Himself peoples long

alienated from Him. These truths underlie all that follows
and culminate in the universal worship of the King, the Lord
of hosts, in 14.16-19 (1972: 162).

These goals reach fruition because a savior will come to
Jerusalem on a donkey (9.9-13), and because the Lord will
appear to aid the people (9.14-17). At this point God guarantees the restoration of Israel by promising direct intervention
in the nation's affairs.

Chapters 10–11 continue the emphasis of ch. 9. In a new
Exodus, God will bring Israel out of Assyrian and Egyptian
bondage (10.6-12). Once there, their care will be improved due
to the removal of all bad 'shepherds', or leaders (11.4-17). So
9.1–11.17 seeks to remove any obstacles in the path of
renewal. Whether domestic or foreign enemies, Yahweh
manages to defeat any threat to the safety of the remnant, the
temple, or Jerusalem. Central to these victories is the appearance of the messianic ruler in 9.9, who will rule the world in
peace and who stands in stark contrast to the pathetic shepherds depicted in 11.4-17.

As a rousing conclusion to the chronicling of Jerusalem's
renewal, the book's final section pictures a glorious and secure
future for the city. Gentile nations may advance against the
city, but the Israelis, each one now as mighty as David (12.8),
fend off the invaders. The reason for this power is that God
chooses to 'make Jerusalem an immovable rock for all the
nations' (12.3) by fighting for them (12.9). In ch. 13 cleansing
from sin emerges as the foundation for all blessings from the
Lord, and ch. 14 caps the book by revealing that the final
restoration of Jerusalem will occur when the Lord dwells in
Zion (14.5). When that event takes place, full reconciliation
between Israel and Yahweh becomes possible. In other words,
the conflict explained in Hosea–Micah will be resolved when
Yahweh dwells among the people, and they acknowledge Him
as king. All creation is included in the reconciliation, since
even the attackers of Jerusalem 'will go up year after year to
worship the King, the Lord Almighty, and to celebrate the
Feast of Tabernacles' (14.16). Because of this healed relationship between God and all creation, every pot, bowl and utensil
in Jerusalem will be 'holy to the Lord' (14.20-21).

This brief look at Zechariah's very dense and intricate prophecy in no way fully reveals the book's artistry, but it at least points out some of Zechariah's contributions to the restoration section of the Twelve's plot. Without doubt the book relentlessly promotes the belief that Jerusalem will finally be all God wants it to be, which will lead to the rejuvenation of the religious institutions in Israel and the people themselves. Thus, Zechariah moves the story line back up almost to the top of the U-shape. Practically every obstacle to Israel's reconciliation with God has been surmounted. Foreign threats, poor leadership, lack of a major city, and the need for a temple are all removed. All that could possibly remain to stifle renewal would be the people's attitude. Some progress in that area has been made, for the people admit their transgressions in 1.5, but what remains to be seen is how an ongoing practice of holy living can be effected. Zechariah claims the future is secure. One more book will help decide if the positive plot elements evident in Haggai and Zechariah can continue.

As was stated in Chapter 3, after the glowing future Zechariah predicts for Israel, Malachi does not seem very optimistic about the nation's chances for restoration. With closer scrutiny, however, it becomes clear that, just as Haggai and Zechariah view the rebuilding of the temple and Jerusalem as signs of reconciliation between Israel and Yahweh, so Malachi believes the final proof of that reconciliation is a daily righteousness on the part of the people. Temple and city are vital physical evidence of Israel's repentance, but holiness embodies the inner reality of contrition.

Malachi confronts the covenant people with God's love for them (1.2-5), exposes their sin (1.6–3.15) and leads them to repentance (3.16–4.6; 3.16-24 in Hebrew). In the first two sections Malachi uses a series of questions to reveal how blatantly the people have defiled the temple and Jerusalem. Without their repentance the whole restoration process may be in jeopardy. This problem creates a final point of tension in the plot of the Twelve that must be resolved before the reader can feel totally confident that the story line has followed a comic pattern.

Once the prophet declares the covenant love Yahweh holds for Israel (1.2-5), he turns to the root of Israel's sin. Ironically, the problem stems from the lack of spiritual leadership given the nation by the priests of the new temple. Since they ask how they have despised and defiled the Lord (1.6-7), Malachi declares that the priests have offered blind and lame animals as sacrifices (1.8-9), kindled 'useless fires' on the altar (1.10), and despised the ministry itself (1.12-13). Because of their unfaithfulness, they are under a curse from God (2.2). Though they have a high office, the priests have failed to be good 'messengers' of the Lord (2.7-9). Robert Alden captures the seriousness of the priesthood's sin when he says that

> instead of turning men into 'the way', the priests did the opposite; they turned men from it. Such irresponsibility violated the covenant of Levi. Sins of omission were compounded with sins of commission. Malachi made it clear that God could tolerate the situation no longer. To have an ill-prepared minister, an incompetent pastor, a hireling for a shepherd was bad enough; much worse was it to have a deceiver, a schemer, a wolf in sheep's clothing for a leader (1985: 715).

Due to the priests' unwillingness to teach the truth, Israel has sunk into sins of unfaithfulness against one another, including marrying foreign women and seeking easy divorces (2.10-16). Such practices amount to the defiling of Jerusalem, the place Zechariah promised would be holy to the Lord (cf. 2.11 and Zech. 14.20-21).

Not everything is blamed on the priests, though, because in 2.17-3.15 Malachi holds the people responsible for their own actions. They weary God by asking why justice is absent and rob the Lord by withholding their tithes and offerings. Further, they speak harshly against Yahweh, because they say it is unprofitable to serve God. Though they deny each charge (2.17; 3.8, 13) the prophet documents and justifies each of the Lord's claims. As for the question about when God's justice will appear, the Lord replies the Day of the Lord is coming to set all matters straight (3.1), but that their sins will cause them to fall on 'that day' (3.2-5). Though, as Bruce Malchow points out, it is difficult to identify with total accuracy the 'messenger' who will lead the judging and cleansing of the people at that time, it is possible to say that this messenger will stand in stark contrast with the poor messengers mentioned in 2.7. Malchow theorizes that Malachi envisions a Levite here, claiming that

> the likelihood of this interpretation increases when one considers the function of the messenger of the covenant. According to vv. 3-4, he will purify the Levites so that they will offer right sacrifices in the future. It is consistent that the purifier of the Levites should himself arise from that group (1984: 254).

If so, Malachi returns to the priesthood motif, and this time argues that only a special messenger of God can save the remnant from Yahweh's wrath. At any rate, Malachi emphasizes the inability of Israel to survive true justice at this point in time, though the presence of the priestly messenger suggests the country's situation is not hopeless.

Despite the existence of other national sins, among them robbing God (3.6-12) and questioning Yahweh's goodness (3.13-15), Malachi finds hope for the future. This positive attitude derives, as it does in Habakkuk, Zephaniah, etc., from the emergence of a believing remnant that seeks the Lord. Like Haggai's receptive audience, these individuals accept the prophet's message, fear the Lord, and share in God's blessings (3.16-18). These faithful ones will endure the day of wrath and destroy the wicked (4.1-4; 3.19-22 in Hebrew). To help create the remnant, Yahweh will send 'the prophet Elijah' to turn the hearts of the people to the Lord (4.5-6; 3.23-24 in Hebrew). Elijah's appearance fits other restoration passages, which state that only an envoy from Yahweh can lead the nation in the proper direction. Haggai's word about Zerubbabel (2.20-23), Zechariah's prediction of the savior on a donkey (9.9), and Malachi's earlier promise of a purifier of the Levites (3.1-4) all join with Mal. 4.5-6 (3.23-24 in Hebrew) in this motif. The essence of these predictions is that the individuals serve as pledges of Yahweh's determination to restore every aspect of Israel's life. Prophet, priest, and people will all share in the coming renewal. All barriers will be surmounted.

Does Malachi think Israel will be restored? Though one may need to give a cautious answer, that answer must be in the affirmative. In fact, since Malachi fully realizes the problems of the community of his day and still holds to restoration, his belief in a bright future is very significant indeed. The people will be restored, along with the priesthood and the temple worship, by a holy priest to come. A great prophetic figure will help mend the faithlessness the prophet condemns and reconcile Yahweh and the covenant people. Malachi is realistic, but he is not pessimistic. In fact, this prophet balances the best of the prophetic traditions, for he despises ethical sin, announces the Day of the Lord, and envisions the new day to come. By so doing, Malachi does not only end the Twelve on an optimistic note, he also summarizes the Twelve as a whole.

Very definitely, then, Haggai–Malachi concludes the U-shape of the Twelve's plot. Beginning with the glimpse of hope present in Zeph. 3.6-20, these prophecies chronicle the renewal of the temple, Jerusalem, the priesthood, and the people. The books include other nations in the restoration as well (cf. Zech. 14.16-19; Mal. 1.11; etc), which means renewal, like sin and punishment, has both covenant and cosmic dimensions. Israel and its neighbors can renew the relationship broken by sin. Every complication raised in Hosea–Micah and every element of punishment threatened in Nahum–Zephaniah is eradicated in Haggai–Malachi. Thus, these final three prophecies resolve the problems raised in the earlier books by systematically answering the difficulties entailed in these works.

Conclusion

From the data gathered above it is possible to conclude that the Twelve does indeed exhibit an organized plot. This plot is based primarily on the history of God's dealings with Israel, beginning with their choice as the covenant people, continuing through their rebellion against God, the punishment of their sin, and their cleansing from that sin. Alongside the history of Israel runs an account of Yahweh's relationship with the Gentiles. While it is not the *primary* focus of the Hebrew prophets, how the Lord works with the other nations reveals the scope of God's sovereignty and explains in part certain aspects of Israel's history. The writers in the Twelve shape the book to follow this cosmic history, though they stress the theological nature of that history. Sin, punishment, and restoration, therefore, emerge as the plot's major components, with each idea logically following its predecessor. Thus, to borrow a phrase from Hayden White, the Twelve has a 'plot',

> if by 'plot' we mean a structure of relationships by which the events contained in the account are endowed with a meaning by being identified as parts of an integrated whole (9).

It is also possible to argue that the prophetic story line is comic in mode. Though not a comedy generically, the Twelve displays many comic features. A comic mode employs the traits of comedy to forge a positive outlook for a work. Northrop Frye lists various elements that occur in most comedy. They include:

1. The identification of the comic hero and the object of his desire;
2. The coming of obstacles or enemies to thwart the hero's goals;
3. The triumph of the hero over the obstacles and enemies;
4. The displaying of compassion for the hero's enemies;
5. The including of enemies in the hero's victory (1967: 43-49).

Certainly, in these traits one recognizes a U-shaped plot in which the story line sinks to tremendous depths before it is resolved amiably. In the Twelve, the relationship between Israel and the Lord, and, thus, the fortunes of the nation, deteriorates so badly that only the Day of Yahweh and some special messengers from Yahweh can salvage it. Still, the task is accomplished. Restoration does emerge, and the comic ending prevails over its tragic counterpart.

To call the Twelve's plot 'comic' in no way implies that there are no deep problems in the text, nor that these difficulties are not serious threats to the possibility of restoration. Quite the contrary is true, since without the likelihood of tragedy comedy becomes very pointless. Unless some tragedy is eventually warded off, any comedy is reduced to farce. Likewise, a comic plot must fend off challenges from its tragic counterpart. Unless the very end of Israel, and indeed all creation, is possible in the Twelve, restoration would be meaningless. As Walter Kerr explains:

> To contemplate any true ending for a comedy is to contemplate death. Only death will end the joke. Man can not ever be free of the matter that impedes, annoys, and limits him until he is in fact severed from that matter, until his consciousness is cut free of the machinery that clogs it (1967: 171).

To say, then,that the Twelve has a comic plot is not to say that it is funny, farcical, or stilted. It rather means that the authors wrestle with the problems of sin and judgment, but do not find them to be the ultimate victors over the human race.

Finally, it is correct to say that the Twelve's plot displays the unity of the corpus. Tightly linked with the genre and structure of the minor prophets, the plot of the Twelve delineates the story of Israel's relationship with Yahweh in a detailed fashion. From Hosea to Malachi, each individual prophecy contributes something to the ongoing attempt to demonstrate to the reader what God has done and will do with creation and why these things are so. Though with the diversity expected in such a project, the final form of the Twelve presents a plot that works with the book's structure to produce a unified prophecy. Therefore the minor prophets can be viewed as the *Book* of the Twelve at this stage of our analysis.

Chapter 5

THE TWELVE'S USE OF CHARACTERS

Introduction

Characterization is a vital, but often-neglected, aspect of literature. Despite the fact that characters amplify plot, structure, themes, and indeed all parts of an artistic piece, scholars are sometimes hesitant to spend time analyzing the intricacies of a work's major figures. Perhaps it is believed character traits will emerge from the study of a plot, but, while some aspects of characterization do grow out of studying the plot, the discussion of what and why an event takes place does not always explain the personalities and motivations of those who create events. Or, some may argue that the examination of characters often degenerates into a subjective enterprise. Again, some truth resides in this concern. Probably the best way to avoid this trap is to develop character studies only within the context of a piece's genre, plot, theme, and narration. In this way any tendency to make a person whatever one chooses may be checked. Finally, the fact that much modern literature subsumes characterization under experience tends to discourage analysis of individual literary figures.

In biblical criticism the same neglect of characterization exists in many quarters. Commentaries on prophetic books often prefer to attempt to explain the work of the prophets by charting their historical situation, message, career, etc., while leaving matters of characterization untouched. An example of this tendency is J.H. Thompson's otherwise excellent work, *The Book of Jeremiah*, in which the author uses 136 pages to introduce the book, but very little of which (perhaps pp. 94-106) describes the prophet himself. Likewise, Robert P. Carroll's recent, comprehensive treatment of Jeremiah deals very briefly with characters, mainly because Carroll strives to reconstruct what he believes is an accurate historical picture of Jeremiah. This picture, Carroll says, has been clouded by a number of non-historical issues. He concludes:

> Hence the figure of Jeremiah which is discerned in the text must not be confused with a hypothesized real person but must be interpreted as the production of the various levels of tradition making up the text. This figure will, on examination, turn out to be a very complex amalgam of social, political, and theological elements which, though lacking consistency or coherence, reflects the hermeneutically rich strands which constitute the book of Jeremiah (1986: 64).

Though only two samples of prophetic studies, Thompson and Carroll, particularly because of the quality of their books, certainly represent the mainstream of critical thought. If such attitudes prevail in the study of Jeremiah, a book that may contain more information on an individual writing prophet than any other in the canon, it is not difficult to assume correctly that the analysis of characterization plays an even smaller role in the minor prophets, where biographical information is often sparse indeed.

Beyond the various historical concerns, other factors have contributed to a lack of interest in characterization in prophetic books. One such factor is that a number of popular works on the prophets, such as Cohon's *The Prophets* and Paterson's *The Goodly Fellowship of the Prophets* emphasize characterization, which has seemingly relegated that area of inquiry to non-critical, or less-critical, studies. Other attempts to understand the prophets' personalities appear very subjective, especially those that have tried to psychoanalyze the prophets. It is quite futile to try to explain the actions of biblical characters in psychological terms if for no other reason than the lack of clinical data. More explanations may exist for the lack of interest in prophetic characterization, but, between the concern to reconstruct the figures with historical exactitude and the desire to avoid simplistic and subjective conclusions on the subject, the notion of linking characterization to the interpretation of the prophetic canon has suffered.

Since the characters in a literary work are so closely intertwined with its plot and structure, it is necessary to arrive at some means of analyzing the characters in the Twelve. Even Old Testament theology, which must delineate God's nature, often fails to show how Yahweh's character interacts with other figures in the text. Coupled with the hesitancy of scholars to discuss the prophets' characterization mentioned earlier, it is safe to conclude that whatever methodology is adopted must rise from literary circles. The rest of the chapter seeks to provide a means of analyzing the major personae in the Twelve by defining 'characterization', listing ways to reveal characters' personal traits, noting various types of characters in literature, and briefly showing how certain genres require specific kinds of characters to work best. After this introductory task has been completed, the most vital characters in the minor prophets will be discussed. Through this inquiry how well (if at all) the plot and characters of the Twelve mesh will become apparent. If the two work together, then the unity of the Twelve becomes an increasingly defensible idea, but, if not, certain conclusions about the genre, structure, and plot already outlined in this study must be reassessed.

The Discipline of Characterization

Crucial to the whole process of understanding characterization in literature is the fundamental tenet that any interpretation of a character must come from the text itself. Part of the reason historical-critical scholars have a hard time analyzing characters apparently stems from their feeling that the canonical text does not present an accurate picture of its main figures. What is important here is to delineate the characters as the text reveals them. In short, today's interpreter must treat the personae as they appear in the Old Testament if any exegetical progress is to be attained. One must trust the text to know best how to tie together its message and characters, lest the background of a piece take precedence over the piece itself. Hopefully, this formalistic principle will guide the study below.

1. *Definition of 'Characterization'*
Before characterization can be defined there must be some idea of how to define a 'character' in literature. An author

creates a *character* to be realistic and to fit the plot. Edgar V. Roberts suggests that

> we may define *character* in literature as the author's creation, through the medium of words, of a personality who takes on actions, thoughts, expressions, and attitudes unique and appropriate to that personality and consistent with it. Character might be thought of as a reasonable facsimile of a human being, with all the qualities and vagaries of a human being (1973: 45).

Most writers strive to make characters as 'reasonable a facsimile' as possible, and to do so must develop characters according to some definite criteria. Along these lines, Aristotle notes four aspects of effective characters:

> First, and most important, it must be good. Now any speech or action that manifests moral purpose of any kind will be expressive of character: the character will be good if the purpose is good... The second thing to aim at is propriety... Thirdly, character must be true to life: for this is a distinct thing from goodness and propriety, as here described... The fourth point is consistency: for though the subject of the imitation, who suggested the type, be inconsistent, still he must be consistently inconsistent (1974: ch. 15, 44).

To bring together Roberts' and Aristotle's definitions of character, a character must exhibit all the traits of personality in a purposeful, realistic, appropriate, and consistent way. If any of these aspects is missing, a character loses plausibility and, thus, credibility, which dooms the figure in the reader's eyes.

Characterization, on the other hand, is the manner in which a character is presented. Characterization includes the presentation of the many facets of the character. Roberts correctly believes that characterization 'is the sum total of typical qualities and propensities in any given individual that are controlled by that individual's drives, aims, ideals, morals, and conscience' (1973: 44). Thus, a character is a person in a story, and the characterization of that person reveals his true nature. Of course, the author chooses how and what to divulge about a character, so characterization, like all parts of a literary work, is a selective process. Very briefly, then, 'characterization' is the manner in which an author presents purposeful, realistic, appropriate and consistent characters.

2. *Ways to Understand Characterization*

How characters are created often depends on the type of narration an author selects. For instance, in lyric, epic and prose narrative, the writer has the luxury of telling the reader directly about the nature of a character, revealing character through the words of another character, or letting a character show his own nature by his words and deeds. Since the first option is not normally open to a dramatist, characterization in plays depends on the writer's ability to make a character vivid through speeches and actions alone. Since Chapter 6 deals with point of view, the implications of narration as it relates to characterization will not be explored here, but it is necessary to note at this point that characters are often revealed in those basic ways. The reader must either gather information about a character from the narrator, the character himself (either through acts or deeds), or from another character in the text. Differing types of narration will offer varying kinds of ways to explore personae, but these sources are the reader's main avenues to knowing characters.

From these sources a large amount of data on a character can be gathered. Robie Macauley and George Lanning observe that characters become known through

> Physical appearance. Movements, gestures, mannerisms, habits. Behaviour toward others. Speech. Attitude toward self. Attitude of others toward the character. Physical surroundings. Past. Fringe techniques such as names and figures of speech (1964: 63).

Some or all of these aspects of characterization may appear in a work, and what the writer omits may be as important as what he includes. Many of these traits help define the characters in the Twelve, especially those that deal with speech, behavior, attitude, and the past.

3. *Types of Characters in Literature*

The first thing an interpreter needs to decide when examining types of characters is whether the author chooses to say much or little about a figure. Characters about whom the writer tells only a small amount are normally called 'flat' characters, while a character about whom much is revealed is usually designated as a 'round' character. Laurence Perrine explains:

> The flat character is characterized by one or two traits; he can be summed up in a sentence. The round character is complex and many-sided; he might require an essay for full analysis (1959: 87).

A round character may be explained by himself, the narrator, and other characters, and have all or most of the aspects Macauley and Lanning list utilized to divulge who he is, what he does, and the reasons for who he is and what he does. A flat character, on the other hand, would not receive extensive treatment.

Just because a character is flat or round, however, does not determine that person's effectiveness or importance to the plot. Perrine rightly claims that

> both types of characters may be given the vitality that good fiction demands. Round characters live by their very round-ness, by the many points at which they touch life. Huck Finn breaks out of the novel Mark Twain put him in for new adventures in the endless territory of the human imagina-tion, while scholars and critics debate his moral develop-ment. Flat characters, though they touch life at only one or two points, may be made memorable in the hands of an expert author through some individualizing detail of appearance, gesture, or speech. Ebenezer Scrooge... can be summed up in the two words 'miserly misanthropy', but his 'Bah! Humbug!' makes him live vividly in every reader's memory (1959: 87-88).

It is just as true that a major or minor character may fail mis-erably to fit the needs of the piece's plot. Any persona, then, may be vital to what takes place in a story line, so each charac-ter must be evaluated for an exegesis of a work to be complete.

In good plots characters interact. Though round characters usually serve as a piece's major figure or figures, flat charac-ters must help determine the course of the story line for the work to be consistent and believable. Every individual charac-ter, or group of characters, should help the plot move from beginning to resolution, and should aid the growth of other characters. John Howard Lawson argues that the quality of a literary work depends on such interaction, for 'even if a few lines are spoken in a crowd, the effectiveness of these lines depends on the extent to which the individual is a part of the action' (1949: 283). How much impact a work exerts on a reader grows out of how well each character becomes a vital part of the plot.

A second aspect of character type that deserves attention is whether a character changes or remains the same during the course of a work. Perrine explains:

> All fictional characters may be classified as static or developing. The static character is the same sort of person at the end of the story as he was at the beginning. The developing character undergoes a permanent change in some aspect of his character, personality, or outlook (1959: 88).

The same is true of non-fictional characters as well, since historical narratives are also shaped by the level of flexibility each personage exhibits. How great the change in a figure may vary according to the needs of the plot, but it must be a change that alters the person and the shape of the story. Obviously a writer cannot develop every character to the same extent, so it is important to understand what figures do change, since it is those individuals that most often affect the piece's plot, mood, and themes. Without developing characters a work becomes tedious. Yet if a plot has only developing characters, it becomes convoluted and chaotic. Again, how well the author balances the interaction between round and flat, as well as static and developing, characters will determine a story's strength in the area of characterization.

4. *Characterization According to Genre*

Within each separate genre, characters function according to the needs of the specific type of literature. Developing characters change in a quite different way in tragedy than in comedy, and static characters often play a larger role in comedy than in tragedy, though this tendency is not universal. A brief look at how characters operate in comedy and tragedy will illustrate this principle.

Tragedy's most evident trait is the depiction of its main character—the tragic hero. Northrop Frye describes the tragic hero as -

typically on top of the wheel of fortune, halfway between the human society on the ground and then something greater in the sky. Prometheus, Adam, and Christ hang between heaven and earth, between a world of paradisal freedom and a world of bondage (1967: 207).

Tragic heroes are normally morally, emotionally or physically superior to other characters. Still they are not equal to divine beings. Thus, they hang between heaven and earth. Though they lack the weakness of other people, they also lack the strength of the gods. Because of this humanity, the hero usually falls through some personal flaw. Achilles' flaw is anger, Hector's is pride, and Faustus' is a desire to have divine knowledge. In tragedy the gods often attempt to bar the hero from ascending to their status, while human beings try to make him sink to their level. There are, of course, many variations of these patterns.

Minor characters illuminate the hero's story in tragedy. Some reveal the strengths and weaknesses of the hero, while others exist to move the plot, such as stock characters, symbolic characters, etc. Normally one persona acts as foil, or opposite, to the hero. This character is usually the hero's enemy, and has a different personality, goal, and function in the plot.

Comedy is the foil of tragedy in many ways. Instead of building the piece around one heroic figure, comedy utilizes a number of individuals to present its plot. As opposed to the tragic hero, the comic hero often has a pliable, neutral personality so he can change as the story takes shape. This does not mean the hero has no goals or standards, just that he is open to positive change. He is not bound by fate like his tragic counterpart. Other characters are more important in comedy, because they seek to aid or hinder the hero's desires. For instance, in a romantic comedy the hero may receive help in his efforts to marry a certain girl by a clever friend, but be thwarted by an ill-mannered, stubborn father of the girl. Thus, other characters help determine the success or failure of the hero.

As in other genres, prophecy portrays characters in a way that enhances its main goals. Therefore, it is likely that the characterization in the Twelve reflects the book's emphasis on sin, punishment, and restoration. Some justification for Yahweh's anger with Israel and the nations must reside in their attitudes and actions, unless the Twelve pictures God much differently than the rest of the Bible. Likewise, there must be something in the personalities of the remnant and the Lord that initiates forgiveness and renewal. If these various traits appear throughout the minor prophets, then the Twelve's unity grows even more plausible.

Characterization in the Twelve

Certain boundaries for this section need to be set at the outset of the study. First, because of the impossibility of examining every single character that appears in the minor prophets in only a portion of one chapter, only major figures receive extensive treatment, and even then the complexities of those personae will not be fully delineated. Less significant characters will be mentioned when they greatly affect the characterization of major figures. Second, since it is impractical to attempt to convey everything each one of the books of the Twelve says about characters only major parts of characterization contained in the minor prophets will be, or can be, covered. Certainly, areas of characterization inherent in the Twelve will be neglected, but hopefully the most vital concerns will get the treatment they deserve.

The initial task of a study of the Twelve's use of characterization is to pick the characters that need to be analyzed. Certainly, Yahweh stands at the head of any list of characters in the Twelve that ought to be discussed. Indeed, every other figure in the book draws its personality from reacting to God. Apart from the Lord, however, the picture clouds a bit, since few individuals appear in the story. Instead, certain groups take on the qualities of a single figure. Israel, though a whole race of people, becomes a single entity in the eyes of the prophets. The nations likewise coalesce into one body that receives condemnation or blessing. Even the prophets are invisible as individuals at times, though they all work together to present the Twelve's message. One more important persona that is really a composite character is the remnant, which, like Israel, the nations, and the prophets, operates as one person. At

the same time, Hosea, Gomer, Jonah, etc. are well-developed
individual characters, and the messianic figures in Haggai–
Malachi are apparently individuals, though one could interpret them as different sides of a single image.

For the purposes of this study, Yahweh, Israel, the nations,
the remnant, and the prophets will be treated as single players
in the plot of the Twelve. When individual parts of those com-
posites arise, such as Jonah among the prophets, they will aid
an understanding of the group as a whole. Though this
methodology of examining groups of people as one is more
problematic than discussing a single individual, it is nevertheless in keeping with the style of the Twelve and, indeed, of
much of the Old Testament.

Discussing the personality and nature of Yahweh normally
falls into the area of Old Testament theology. Since that discipline covers such a vast array of subject matter, there will be
no attempt here to duplicate the achievements of that field.
Rather, the comments of Old Testament theologians will be
used when applicable to the Twelve, but not otherwise.

1. *Yahweh*

In the Twelve, Yahweh develops as a character in a number of
definite directions. The Lord is depicted as husband, sovereign
and judge in one way in Hosea–Zephaniah, and plays these
roles quite differently in Haggai–Malachi. God moves ahead
as a character much as the plot develops through all of the
nuances of the sin, punishment, and restoration motifs. This
movement of character becomes apparent when one surveys
the individual books of the minor prophets. Every possible
manner of revealing character indicates that the Lord is an
ever-growing, ever-more-important persona in the Twelve.

The characterization of Yahweh begins in Hosea with words
and actions, so those means of interpreting character are the
best place to begin. Yahweh's first action is to call Hosea to the
prophetic office by asking him to take 'an adulterous wife and
children of unfaithfulness' (1.2). This strange request helps
illuminate God's relationship to Israel, for Yahweh proceeds to
say this order comes 'because the land is guilty of the vilest
adultery in departing from Yahweh' (1.2). Thus, the very first

verses of the Twelve portray the Lord as the husband of an adulterous Israel. So important to the message of Hosea is this image that John L. McKenzie claims: 'Nothing is needed to interpret any saying of Hosea beyond the fundamental insight that the relations of Yahweh and Israel are analogous to the relations of husband and wife' (1974: 101). While perhaps a bit overstated, McKenzie's comment gets to the heart of Hosea's message. Family imagery continues in 1.9, though in a different direction, where the Lord declares that Israel is 'not my people'.

Hosea's clearest statement of the husband-wife metaphor of God and Israel comes in 2.14-20. The basis of this 'marriage' also appears in this pericope. Encased in the book's comparison between Hosea's family and Yahweh's 'family' in ch. 2 is God's decision to take Israel back to the desert where the nation can once more become a faithful wife. In 2.16, after God makes Israel like she was upon going out of Egypt, the text says ' "In that day", declares the Lord, "you will call me 'my husband', you will no longer call me 'my master' " ' . The word for husband in this verse is בעלי, an obvious play on the idol name 'Baal'. God wants to wipe out every semblance of idolatry and at the same time open a new relationship with Israel. Hans W. Wolff explains that

> this saying announces that Israel will not just respect Yahweh somewhat reluctantly, since he is its legal lord, but it knows itself to be placed in a completely new, loving relationship with him (1974: 49).

Yahweh completes the marriage imagery by promising to 'betroth' Israel in 'faithfulness' (2.20). All subsequent references to Israel's harlotry against the Lord (4.1, 12, 15, etc.) stem from these initial declarations that Yahweh is Israel's husband.

When did this marriage between God and Israel take place? Hos. 2.14-20 indicates that this union dates at least from the time Yahweh delivered Israel from Egypt (2.15). As a pledge of the marriage covenant, the Lord promises five blessings to Israel: righteousness, justice, love, compassion, and faithfulness (2.19). These terms are indicative of God's desire for a special relationship with Israel. James Luther Mays observes:

> These concepts represent, on the one hand, what Yahweh
> had a right to expect from Israel as his covenant people (cf.
> 4.1; 10.4, 12); on the other hand, they sum up what Israel
> could look for from its covenant Lord. But Yahweh commits
> himself to give them as the price of wedding Israel, although
> the old covenant is broken and finished (1969: 51).

The rest of Hosea, whether discussing sin, punishment, or the
hope of restoration, builds on this covenant-marriage
imagery. Mays continues:

> It is the promise of a great and unexpected grace. The reality
> of the concepts will find expression in such actions as those
> described in 2.6f.; 14f.; 17; 11.8f.; 14.4-6 where Yahweh over-
> comes and heals the faithlessness of Israel and renews the
> old history of the Exodus and wilderness for the sake of
> restoring his people (1969: 51-52).

At times, Hosea's characterization of Yahweh changes from
that of Israel's husband to that of Israel's parent. For example,
in 11.1-4 Israel is depicted as the Lord's 'son' (11.1), though
this relationship is also based on the Exodus experience (11.1).
God's love and kindness are also featured here, so the emotional ties between Yahweh and Israel remain similar.
Though the new metaphor alters the characterization somewhat, the status of Israel is still that of dependence on God, the
status of God is as provider for Israel, the covenant remains
the foundation for Yahweh and Israel's expectations of one
another, and God's love for the straying chosen people continues to motivate future actions.

As husband-father of Israel, the Lord has every right to
denounce the evil actions of His nation-wife-child. Hosea's
presentation of the sins of the elect country stems from the
notion that, just as Hosea should chafe under the constant
adultery of Gomer, so Yahweh resents the wanderings of the
covenant spouse. Still, the Lord forgives Israel, which Hosea
symbolizes by pardoning his wife.

Though the Twelve's characterization will return to the
covenant imagery again, the portrayal of the Lord takes a
new turn in Joel. Because of the emphasis on the Day of the
Lord and its catastrophic implications, and due to the claim
that Yahweh will judge foreign nations, Joel pictures God as
the ruler of the universe. Thus, Yahweh is more than the hus-

band of one group of people. In fact, all nations answer to God. Apparently Joel, like Hosea, feels Yahweh's relationship to Israel is linked to the covenant (2.12, 17), so the basis for the Lord's anger at Israel's iniquity continues to be that Israel has broken faith with God.

Joel's depiction of the day of the Lord highlights the sovereign side of God's nature, since on 'that day' Yahweh alone will dispense justice. Leslie Allen focuses on this feature of God's personality, noting that 'Joel stresses the sovereign freedom of God: He cannot be coerced to do man's will. He does not surrender to the plausible logic of man's theology, but remains the supreme arbiter of man's destiny' (1976: 37). Because of worldwide disobedience, God has decided to devastate the world, beginning with Israel. Literal locusts devour the foliage in the land (1.2ff.), while a swarming locust-like military force may invade the country (2.1). Why? So Israel will choose to return to her Lord (2.12-17). When Israel does repent, Yahweh dispenses favours that remind the reader of the covenant pledges of Hos. 2.14-23.

God's sovereignty reaches to the ends of the earth. Joel 3.11-12 drives this idea home quite forcefully. Here Yahweh taunts the foreign countries and leads them into destruction:

> Come quickly, all you nations from every side and
> 	assemble there...
> Let the nations be roused;
> let them advance into the Valley of Jehoshaphat,
> for there I will sit to judge
> all the nations on every side.

Only a God with the ability to create, rule and judge the entire earth can make such claims.

It is patently obvious that a ruler with such consummate authority has every right to censor the action of covenant and cosmic people. Whether God judges as covenant spouse and parent or as sovereign ruler over creation does not ultimately matter. What concerns Joel most is that Yahweh has the moral right and physical power to carry out threats of punishment, and that, in the words of Willem Prinsloo: 'The accent is on Yahweh's mighty initiative. He brought about the crisis' (1985: 124). God controls the nations.

Amos continues both strands of the characterization begun by Hosea and Joel. In the opening oracles against the foreign nations (1.2–2.3), the prophet stresses that Israel's neighbors must answer to Yahweh for their cruelty to one another. Nowhere does Amos mention any specific covenant binding these countries, but apparently certain levels of civil behavior are expected of every kingdom. Judah and Israel's transgressions seem worse, for they represent extreme breaches of the Sinai covenant. The prophet says punishment will come upon the people because 'they have rejected the law of the Lord' (2.4), because they forgot who brought them out of Egypt (2.10-12), and because their worship does not even equal that of the wilderness period (5.25). Perhaps the best summary of Yahweh's relationship with, and opposition to, Israel comes in 3.1-2, where the prophet declares:

> Hear this word which the Lord speaks against you, O sons of Israel, against the whole family which I caused to come up out of Egypt:
>
> 'You only have I known
>   from all the families of the earth
> Therefore I will punish you
>   for all your sins'.

Here Israel appears as God's own family that has dishonored the tribal name.

Yahweh acts as a punishing spouse-parent in Amos. Israel will share the judgment of the nations on the Day of Yahweh. Though some of the people expect good things on that day, they will be sorely disappointed (5.18-20). Amos chronicles so many violations of the covenant relationship that the reader fully believes the visions of 7.1-9 and 8.1-3 that predict disaster for Israel, as well as the declaration in 9.10 that all sinners 'will die by the sword'.

Despite the justice of the punishment detailed in chs. 7–9, the picture of Yahweh as a restoring deity returns in 9.11-15. As in Hosea, a hint of forgiveness breaks through the strong condemnation and summation of Israel's sin that dominates the book. Even an angry, punishing family leader wants to eventually reunite the family, and Amos places the Lord in this role. Once more God acts as provider for Israel, while at the same time remaining the ruler and judge over the nations. The two relationships stay separate.

Obadiah and Jonah re-emphasize the image of God's role as king of all the earth. Obadiah's second verse reveals who is in charge of history, for Yahweh tells Edom, 'Behold, I will make you small among the nations/you will be greatly despised'. Evidently, the ability to set up and put down nations resides within the Lord's power. From this lofty position, God lists Edom's faults, such as pride (v. 3), violence against Judah (v. 10), and oppression (vv. 13-14), for which the nation will be judged. Israel, on the other hand, will receive blessings. While Edom will suffer on the Day of Yahweh (vv. 15-16), Israel will be restored (vv. 17-21).

A new side of God's ruling personality presents itself in Jonah. As in Obadiah, Jonah characterizes the Lord as the ruler of all nations, this time of mighty Assyria. In a new twist, however, Yahweh demonstrates love for the creation under condemnation. God does not desire even Nineveh to perish. There is no covenant with foreign countries, but there exists a desire to redeem the world. The sin described in the book belongs to Israel, the chosen people who refuse to share their God with sinful humanity.

Micah gathers the various threads of Yahweh's character that have already been mentioned. The day of the Lord breaks out as early as 1.3, and the reason given for the coming of 'that day' is that the covenant wife has lived like a prostitute, forsaking her husband for 'the wages of harlotry' (1.7). Thus, though God led Israel during the Exodus, or covenant-making period (6.4-5), judgment will now take place (6.9-16). All hope grows out of the possibility that the chosen people will once more accept what God requires of them, which is to 'act justly, love mercy, and walk humbly with... God' (6.8). Sin, though, stands between the people and forgiveness, so the judging spouse-father rises above the restoring spouse-father. With great intensity the two images contrast and complement one another.

Regarding the non-covenant countries, Micah notes that Yahweh rules as one who offers the 'heathen' a chance to worship at the 'mountain of the Lord's temple' (4.1). At the temple all nations will learn the ways of God (4.2), accept divine rule (4.3) and enjoy peace (4.3). Still, wicked groups receive the condemnation of an angry sovereign (5.5-6; 7.8-13). Therefore, the same tension that exists in the covenant context also exists in the cosmic sphere.

At this point, a summary of Yahweh's characterization is in order. Yahweh's personality is portrayed as both grieved and loving spouse of Israel. At times, the family metaphor shifts to that of parent, but the familial imagery still predominates Hosea–Micah. God's covenant with Israel provides the foundation for this characterization, and that covenant relationship puts the elect group in a separate category from the Gentiles. If anything, breaking the covenant makes Israel's sin worse than the nations. Throughout these six books the authors present Yahweh as the ruler of the Gentiles. Sometimes benevolent, always in control, the Lord judges the non-covenant peoples as their king more than as their family leader.

When family imagery characterizes Yahweh, the sins of the covenant people are normally elaborated in Hosea–Micah. When kingly metaphors appear, the nations' iniquity is usually highlighted. Therefore, the sin motif that moves throughout these prophecies stressing covenant and cosmic transgression corresponds to the characterization of a God who maintains covenant and cosmic relationships. Even as the sin portion of the Twelve's plot works on these two major planes, the characterization of Yahweh develops in a similar, unifying fashion.

Much as one would expect after Micah, the portrait of God as a punishing spouse-parent or king is given almost full expression in Nahum–Zephaniah. Every aspect of the righteously indignant deity emerges in this punishment section. At various points in Hosea–Micah, the prophets speak about Yahweh's nature (cf. Hos. 4.1-3; Joel 1.13-15; Mic. 1.2-5, 8-14), and, at other times, God speaks directly of personal traits (cf. Hos. 2.14-23; 4.4-15; Joel 2.19-20; Amos 1.3-5, etc.; Obad. 2-18; Mic. 6.1-5). In this section, however, God's *actions* provide the material of characterization. Threats, by both the prophet and the Lord, turn into realized deeds. Thus, God's character develops from a family leader or ruler who promises judgment in order to turn the world away from its sin into a leader or ruler who brings that punishment in hopes of effecting changes in the nations.

Nahum demonstrates how the personality of Yahweh determines the Lord's actions. In 1.1-8 the prophet introduces his message by listing the benevolent aspects of God, such as the fact that 'the Lord is slow to anger' (1.3), 'good' (1.7), a 'refuge in times of trouble' (1.7), and a help 'for those who trust in him' (1.7). From these images one is reminded of Hosea and Jonah, where God's grace towards Israel and the Gentiles is evident. But because of this goodness, Nahum believes the Lord is 'jealous and avenging' (1.2), a punisher of the guilty (1.3), the ruler of the earth (1.3-5), a God who expresses wrath (1.6) and a dogged pursuer of foes (1.8). Chief among these foes, at least in Nahum, stands Nineveh, the major city of Assyria. The most prominent characterization of Yahweh here has to be that of ruler and judge of the whole earth. Besides 1.3-5, vv. 9-11 of ch. 1 depict Nineveh as a group of people plotting against their governing master. Because of such plots, Nineveh 'will have no descendants' (1.14).

Because Assyria is under divine rule, Yahweh has every right to punish that place like any other nation. Since God rules all nations and armies, an idea fully documented in Joel, Amos, Obadiah, Jonah, and Micah, an attacker is dispatched to destroy Nineveh (2.1-10). This attack proves Yahweh's words are reinforced by deeds. Carl Armerding comments that in 2.1-10

> The judgment of God is not merely an abstract principle or rhetorical threat, as evidenced already in the natural phenomena that display his power. The judgment decreed in chapter 1 is now worked out with terrifying actuality (1985: 240).

Nahum completes his depiction of Yahweh as the sovereign ruler of Assyria by quoting the Lord's disdainful comments about Nineveh found in 3.5-7. Those who plot against the king inevitably fail.

Israel fares better than Nineveh in Nahum. In fact, the destruction of the wicked city encourages Israel, who has suffered at the hands of this powerful enemy (1.1-15). Jacob will be restored and no longer suffer at the hand of the oppressors (2.2). This benevolence towards Israel stands in direct contrast to God's attitude and actions towards Nineveh, and thereby illustrates the opposite sides of the two main characterizations of the Lord.

Habakkuk brings together the various strands of the Twelve's characterization, much as it also brings the plot to its climax. Here the family leader punishes the wicked Israel by sending Babylon against the covenant people (1.6), thus demonstrating sovereignty over the nations at the same time. When the prophet protests this decision as a continuation of the prospering of the wicked (1.12–2.1), Yahweh replies that Babylon will also be judged (2.8), which once again proves that God's will dictates history. Even with all the punishment imagery, though, the fact that the book concludes with the prophet rejoicing in the saving power and strength of God indicates that Habakkuk felt Yahweh's impulse to judge in no way dismisses the Lord's loving nature (cf. 3.18-19). Along with the plot, the divine characterization reaches a high point in Habakkuk from which it must either remain static or progress.

In Zephaniah the Twelve's image of Yahweh as punishing ruler and angry covenant spouse reaches its fruition. Here Yahweh is, overwhelmingly, more a character of deeds than of words. This emphasis on action first means the coming of the Day of Yahweh. When the Lord tires of covenant and cosmic sin, the decision is made to 'sweep away everything from the face of the earth' (1.2). Those who complacently theorize that God will do nothing about their sin (1.12) will be surprised (1.13). Yahweh's great power leads to decisive action. The prophet's comments support Yahweh's statements. Zephaniah first warns the nation to fear the 'Sovereign Lord' (1.7-8) who prepares a sacrifice consisting of wicked people. His second speech declares that God's action originates from extreme wrath, and will result in darkness and destruction (1.14-16). Next, the prophet includes foreign nations in Yahweh's wrath (2.4-7). After a short word about the destruction of idols in 2.11, Zephaniah's penultimate speech shows the comprehensive nature of God's devastating work. Lastly, the prophet exalts the Lord's salvation (3.14-17). Each of the prophet's oracles stresses what God *does* or *will do*. These actions span all areas of the Lord's judging impulses.

Despite Yahweh's justifiable desire to punish both Israel and the nations, mercy is a major component of Zephaniah's characterization of the Lord. George Adam Smith disagrees by writing:

> Note the absence of mention of the Divine mercy. Zephaniah has no gospel of that kind. The conditions of escape are sternly ethical—meekness, the doing of justice and righteousness. So austere is our prophet (1929: 58).

Smith's view overstates the remnant's repentance, for it is God's decision to cleanse them through the Day of Yahweh. Yahweh's willingness to spare anyone represents a great mercy in Zephaniah, since the heinous nature of worldwide corruption is so well documented. From this mercifully spared remnant a new people will arise, for whom Yahweh will defeat all enemies, eliminate all problems, and restore all fortunes (3.11-20). There is even mercy for Israel's enemies, since all these can call on the Lord's name (3.9). Therefore, expectation springs out of punishment. Thus, after, and because of, judgment, the merciful nature of God emerges.

After Nahum–Zephaniah, Yahweh's judgment appears complete. The covenant family has been purged down to a remnant, and the subjects of Yahweh have shrunk to only those who will call on God and serve the Lord alongside Israel. Yahweh's many-faceted personality has reached its fullest potential—except for the renewing aspects of that personality. This characterization of Yahweh fits the emphasis of the plot of these three books, since the punishment of the earth is carried out by the punishing figure, Yahweh.

After the climactic events of Nahum–Zephaniah, it may be easy to assume the Twelve has very little more to say about God's character. For example, in an otherwise noteworthy study of the characterization of God in the Old Testament Dale Patrick asserts:

> The prophetic rendering of Yahweh died out in the early post-exilic literature. In its place we find anonymous proto-apocalyptic passages in the prophetic books. In these, Yahweh's communication with his people at a specific moment

in time is progressively replaced by descriptions of Yahweh's coming intervention, interspersed with prayers and words of warning and comfort spoken anonymously. Portrayals of the destruction of foreign nations and enemies abound, and obscure allusions to world-historical or mythological dramas replace the concrete details of contemporary history. The outcome of these changes is the apocalyptic literature, which renders God as hidden and remote in history, dramatically, cataclysmically present in the unfolding drama of the end. It is as if the biblical God had no more role to play in the exile than to bring the fulfillment of the divine promises given earlier (1981: 24-25).

While Patrick's outline of the growth of apocalyptic is accurate in many respects, to say that God's activity in the post-exilic books is relegated to that of a 'hidden and remote' personage is overstated. Surely Yahweh's work in restoring Jerusalem and judging the wicked in Zechariah places the Lord very close to the action indeed. Also, to claim that the characterization of God as restorer is more colorless than God as judge seems prejudiced. The last three prophecies in the Twelve provide the completion of Hosea–Micah's depiction of God as family leader and cosmic ruler, and, further, give the rationale for Yahweh's actions in Nahum–Zephaniah. Without these books, then, the full development of Yahweh's character remains misunderstood.

Haggai marks a return to the portrayal of God as a benevolent figure. Somewhat simply, Haggai shares the divine demand for a new temple, and the new generation responds. Here there is no long (cf. 2.5) dissertation on the importance of the covenant relationship. Rather, the reader assumes that the presence of the people in the land after the exile signals the kinship between Israel and Yahweh. When God reveals that the community does not prosper because the temple lies in ruins (1.5-6), the reader understands that the nation must comply with the command to rebuild the house of worship if it is to keep its covenant commitments.

When Israel builds the temple, the Lord's desire to bless (a role filled by the family leader) surfaces. Yahweh encourages the people by strengthening their leaders (2.4), renewing the covenant (2.5), and promising that divine glory will fill the new house of worship (2.6-9). Further, the Lord notes that the people's repentance will restore the land (2.10-19). Finally, their leader receives a special blessing (2.20-23). At all times in Haggai, God fulfills the position of the restoring husband, much as that role is displayed in Hos. 2.14–3.5. Yahweh has brought Israel back from the wilderness (cf. Hos. 2.14-15), remarried Israel (Hos. 2.16-20 and Hag. 2.5), and cared for Israel's needs (Hos. 2.21-3.5; Hag. 2.15-19). This renewed relationship results from the drastic events of Nahum–Zephaniah, which testifies to the wholeness of the Twelve's characterization of God.

Zechariah moves beyond the notion of God as a restoring family member, which in Haggai relates exclusively to Israel, to the characterization of a ruler who restores every inch of a fallen kingdom. Most of the book does deal with the restoration of Jerusalem, as was delineated in Chapters 3 and 4, but there is also a definite strand of thought that emphasizes the eventual renewal of the Gentiles as well.

Yahweh reveals great love for the chosen people and the nations at the outset of the prophecy. Zechariah notes that God is 'very jealous for Jerusalem and Zion' (1.14), 'angry with the careless nations' (1.15), full of mercy for Jerusalem (1.16), and ready to 'comfort Zion and choose Jerusalem' (1.17). This intense concern for the covenant people (cf. 1.2-6) leads to the visions of cleansing in chs. 2–6, the promises of blessing in chs. 7–8, the offer of divine intervention in chs. 9–10, and the ultimate restoration of all things in chs. 10–14.

Various passages illustrate the familial love of God, but chs. 9–10 may be the high point of these images. In 9.8 the Lord declares, 'I will defend my house', and therefore the chosen people will no longer fear the oppressor. Once more, the basis of Israel's status as God's people and the temple as the Lord's house stems from the 'blood of my covenant with you' (9.11), The summary of the reason for Israel's restoration comes in 10.6, where God decides:

> They will be as though
> I had not rejected them,
> for I am the Lord their God
> and I will answer them.

Every hint of hope found in Hosea–Zephaniah reaches reality now as God completes every obligation expected of a tribal leader in Zechariah.

Yahweh's benevolence as the ruler of all nations likewise emerges in the prophecy. As early as 2.11-13 Yahweh makes the astounding declaration that the restoration of all things means the merging of the Lord's covenant and cosmic roles: 'Many nations will be joined with the Lord in that day and will become my people' (2.11). This possibility is buttressed by the claim in 8.20-22 that peoples from all lands will seek the Lord, as well as the hope that the Lord 'will proclaim peace to the nations' (9.10). In fact, 14.16-19 portrays the nations as co-celebrators with Israel of the Feast of Tabernacles! Zechariah characterizes God as using all-encompassing power as ruler of all things to decree that the Gentiles be included in the restoration of Jerusalem. The scope of Zechariah's renewal is thus worldwide. Yahweh's family is also worldwide (cf. 2.11). Again, this emphasis on God as restoring ruler grows out of such texts as Zeph. 3.8-9, which states that Yahweh's wrath will produce a global society of true worshipers. No longer is the Lord Israel's family head and the world's regent; now Yahweh stands as the familial provider for both.

Malachi couches his whole book in terms that describe the covenant obligations of Yahweh and Israel. The prophecy allows for rich characterizations of both parties, because the question-answer format forces the characters to back up verbal descriptions with action. From the very beginning the prophecy holds that the covenant proves God's love for Israel and motivates the blessing of the post-exilic community. Joyce Baldwin observes:

> Since Malachi's ministry is to Israel (verse 1), it is fitting that his book should begin with an affirmation of God's continuing love for the covenant nation. The skepticism with which it is greeted indicates that the sermon is relevant. The atrophy of human love in the community (2.13-16) has undermined confidence in the divine love, and there is no appreciation of the providential overruling of God which has made possible the return to Jerusalem and the rebuilding of the Temple (1972: 221-22).

Since Israel's first question challenges the existence of God's love for them (1.2), God reminds the people that Jacob was specially chosen over Esau to bear the covenantal promises (1.3). Beyond that, God displays love by keeping Edom from harming Israel further (compare Obad. 10-14 and Mal. 1.4-5).

Due to Israel's obstinacy, Yahweh almost becomes the judging family member again. God must denounce such problems as poor sacrifice (1.7-14), poor priests (2.1-10), and poor ethics (2.10-16), thus endangering the desired program of restoration. What occurs here is a family argument between a loving leader and a straying clan, and what saves the relationship is Yahweh's willingness to once more serve as provider, this time providing two special leaders (3.1-5; 4.5-6) who will teach the people how to serve properly. Because of covenant love, the Lord maintains the role of restoring family head, thereby enabling the Twelve's plot to close with the hope that not only is the temple, Jerusalem, and the world able to be restored, but that the hearts of the people can likewise be permanently renewed (cf. 4.5-6). Within that hope resides the only chance for lasting restoration. God's character—as seen in this dogged determination to keep the new people intact—guarantees that needed permanence.

Throughout the Twelve, Yahweh's character grows, develops and evolves from new husband and ruler of nations to the unifying family head of all creation. This universal family can only emerge because God's personality includes a punishing component, nonetheless the task is completed. Each change in the tenor of God's characterization mirrors the developments of the Twelve's plot. Yahweh as spurned spouse and ignored regent matches the plot's emphasis on sin; Yahweh as judge matches the story line's discussion of judgment; Yahweh as restoring leader matches the plot's promise of restoration (cf. the chart at the end of this chapter). Plot and character thus coincide where the major story elements and the story's major figure appear.

2. *The Prophet*
Next to Yahweh of course, the most important personae in the Twelve are the prophets themselves. Sometimes prominent,

sometimes elusive, sometimes invisible, these characters are the originators of the book and shapers of its plot. How they present themselves helps the reader understand the Twelve's message and unveils the prophetic self-image. This study does not attempt to offer a portrait of each prophet, particularly since many of the books offer little personal data about these confidants of the Lord. Still, every book contributes something to a composite interpretation of the prophetic character. At least three characterizations of the prophets emerge in the Twelve, though numerous other lesser aspects are also noticeable. The prophets act as symbol, messenger, and co-revelator, depending on the needs of the plot, and how they carry out these functions in part determines how the reader perceives every vital segment of the whole book.

Undoubtedly, the prophet's role as messenger dominates many of the books of the Twelve. After all, the formulaic expression 'thus says Yahweh', an explicit claim that the prophets have a message that comes directly from God, appears in every minor prophet but Habakkuk and Jonah. In both of these books, though, the Lord speaks directly to the prophet, so these books do not really deviate from the pattern set by the others. What does it mean to speak for God? In the early days of Old Testament prophecy it meant in part for the prophet to lose all awareness of the world around him as he received and recited God's oracle (cf. 1 Sam. 19.23-24). In the Twelve, however, with the possible exception of the vision scenes in Amos and Zechariah, the prophets are given messages that relate to the events of their day and openly display the preacher's personality. Apparently the prophets had to apply the 'word' from God, since their individual qualities were not obliterated. Still, the message conveyed originated with Yahweh and at times the Lord appears as one speaking directly. That the prophets spoke words attributed to the Lord indicates they were willing to take the responsibility for recounting those words accurately.

At times the prophets acted not only as oral messengers of God but also as physical symbols of the Lord's communications to Israel. Hosea's marriage to Gomer is an example of such symbolic prophecy, as is Jonah's descent to Tarshish, descent into the boat, descent into a fish, and descent into prejudice.

When Zechariah assumes the persona of a poor shepherd he does so to *show* the people what he has been telling them. In this way the 'word of Yahweh' cannot be misunderstood even if it is disobeyed.

Also closely related to the messenger side of the prophetic characterization, yet somewhat different, is the prophet's work as co-revelator of the divine word. As was stated above, the prophets often apply oracles they receive to their situation (through God's direction) thereby acting as interpreters of what Yahweh says. At other times they speak a word with which the Lord concurs and elaborates further. So the prophet does not speak his own word as such, but neither does he serve as a mechanical mouthpiece for the Lord. In fact, the prophets occupy a high position. They are the friends of God, the interpreters of God's will and words, and the best, if not only, hope the covenant and cosmic people have of knowing how to have a proper relationship with Yahweh. Amos best explains this exalted position when he notes in 3.7-8 that

> surely the Sovereign Lord does nothing unless
> He reveals His plan to His servants the prophets.
> The lion has roared, who does not fear?
> The Sovereign Lord has spoken, who cannot
> prophesy?

Hosea introduces the many facets of the prophet's characterization by portraying all three of the traits described above. First his life and his family's serve as a powerful symbol of how Israel has broken its covenant with God. Without any apparent reluctance Hosea obeys the direct command of God to take 'an adulterous wife' and raise 'children of unfaithfulness' (1.3). He even names his children to reflect God's displeasure with the acts of Jehu (1.4-5), to announce the end of the Lord's mercy for Israel (1.6-7), and to declare that the covenant nation is no longer the elect (1.8-9). Even the terrible adultery on Gomer's part provides a stark picture of how Israel disregards all promises made to Yahweh. Just as importantly, the reconciliation between Hosea and Gomer described in 3.1-5 represents a future restoration of the relationship between God and Israel. That Hosea plays the part of Yahweh

in this drama demonstrates the notion that the prophet serves
as the Lord's representative to the nation.

After ch. 3, Hosea moves on to the verbal roles of messenger
and co-revelator. First, the prophet is the herald, the messenger who delivers God's 'charge against Israel' (4.1). It is only
in 4.1 and 11.11 that direct statements like 'Hear the word of
the Lord' and 'says the Lord' appear, so the messenger aspect
of Hosea's characterization does not receive much treatment.
Hosea mostly acts as God's interpreter and co-revelator in chs.
4–14, since the reader must sort out the speeches of the Lord
and of the prophet by first and third-person references instead
of by noting the occcurrences of formulaic statements like
'says the Lord'. It is not always easy to decide whether Yahweh or Hosea is speaking, especially since the Lord intones His
own name at times (cf. 4.10). Still, it is fairly evident in passages like 5.1-7, for instance, that God denounces the wicked
in 5.1-3 (Who else can discipline the 'rebels'?), and that the
numerous third-person references to the Lord in 5.4-7 indicate that Hosea denounces the people even further in those
verses.

Various aspects of the prophet's role as co-revelator surface
in Hosea. First, the prophet agrees with Yahweh's statement
about Israel's sin. In 4.16-19 Hosea follows God's complaints
about the prostitution of Israel with comments about the stub-
bornness, shameful practices, and future punishment of the
covenant people. Though these observations are closely related
to Yahweh's sermon, it is significant that the prophet's position
is high enough for his words to be placed alongside Yahweh's.
Second, the prophet focuses on the possibility of repentance.
God closes a speech in 5.15 with the promise that He will not
deal with Israel until they admit their guilt. Hosea then
explains in 6.1-3 how that repentance can take place and how
much God will bless that repentance. Here the prophet does
not only repeat Yahweh's words in a new way, rather, he
provides a good bit of new information from a hint in God's
oracle. Third, the co-revelator does offer hope in passages like
11.10, where Hosea speaks of the return of the exiles. So every
vital theme in the prophetic genre flows from the direct speech
of the prophet in Hosea. The book does not need various
formulae to separate the messages of Yahweh and the

prophet, then, because the prophet not only speaks accurately when he quotes Yahweh but also when he speaks *for* Yahweh. Gerhard von Rad highlights the significance of this aspect of the prophetic character when he writes:

> It is hardly possible to overrate the importance of the prophet's share, for without it the word the prophet receives does not reach its goal and therefore cannot be fulfilled. What makes it such a tremendous responsibility is the fact tht the prophet is thus the one who puts the will of Yahweh into effect: Yahweh thereafter commits himself to stand by the decision of his ambassador (1965: 73).

Hosea mentions other facets of the prophetic personality that at least should be noted. Much like Ezekiel does later (cf. Ezek. 3.17; 33.6-7), Hosea casts the prophet as the 'watchman' over God's people (9.8). Indeed, in 9.8 the prophet plays this part 'with' or 'alongside' Yahweh, which, if the text is not corrupt here, testifies to the co-revelatory status of the prophet. Hosea complains that,though the prophet merits a lofty position, the people are so steeped in sin that they think the watchman is a 'fool' or 'madman' (9.7). So the prophet is unappreciated by the very people he hopes to help. How foolish and ungrateful this attitude towards the prophet is becomes clear in 12.13, where Hosea states that 'by a prophet the Lord brought Israel out of Egypt/and by a prophet he cared for them'. With Moses viewed as a prophet, Hosea's depiction of the prophets reaches added heights. According to Hosea, the prophets brought Israel out of bondage, gave them the covenant, and now watch out for their safety by pointing out their sins, thereby safeguarding their relationship with Yahweh. Moses embodies the major characteristics of a prophet, since he was God's messenger, co-revelator, symbol, watchman, and leader. Hosea claims that the prophets still share those qualities and should therefore maintain a prominent position in Israel.

Much as it introduces the structure and plot of the Twelve, Hosea sets forth all the basic character traits of the prophet. Whether as symbol, messenger, or co-revelator, the prophet stands within the finest tradition of Yahweh worship. Without the prophet, the covenant nation exists devoid of the essentials of faith that please God. The rest of the Twelve display variations of the prophetic characterization begun in Hosea, but they hardly surpass the efforts of this initial prophecy.

Joel develops the characterization of the prophet as co-revelator along the lines mentioned above, and exhibits the same high view of prophecy evident in Hosea. Though 1.1 alerts the reader to the fact that what follows is a 'word of the Lord', the book does not quote Yahweh or have the Lord speak directly until 2.12, at which point the prophecy's only use of 'says Yahweh' occurs to note the change of speakers from prophet to deity. Rather, the prophet simply begins the book with his declaration about the coming punishment (1.2-12, 15-20; 2.1-11) and a call to repentance (1.13-14). This willingness to craft his own oracle, albeit at Yahweh's behest (1.1), demonstrates Joel's confidence that he can accurately transmit Yahweh's warning to Israel. So close to God is the prophet that, like Hosea, he can initiate a message to which Yahweh responds.

Co-revelation continues after the Lord speaks in 2.12. The characters alternate their speeches with the intention of declaring the guilt of the nations (Israel's guilt has already been established in 1.2-2.1) and offering a bit of hope to Israel. After Yahweh breaks the suspense of 1.2–2.11 by mentioning repentance in 2.12, the prophet swiftly counsels the nation to turn to God (2.13-18). God then promises forgiveness (2.19-20), followed by Joel's song of blessing in 2.21-24. The prophet's quick transformation from preacher of doom to herald of hope shows that the purpose of the prophet, as hinted in 1.13-14, was always to bring the nation back to God. Consequently, the prophet's desire to restore over-matches his desire to point out transgression, which befits the character of one so closely aligned with a God of restoration.

How highly Joel values the prophetic tradition becomes obvious in Yahweh's speech in 2.25-31. When the Spirit of God falls on the people after the Day of Yahweh the most blessed thing that happens to the people is that they take on the qualities of the prophets (2.28). From the greatest to the least (2.29) and the oldest to the youngest (2.28) the people will 'prophesy', 'dream dreams' and 'see visions' (2.28). Each of these functions describes the work of a prophet, so the highest possible relationship the people can enjoy is that maintained by Yahweh and the prophets. Once more, the privileged position of the prophet emerges, this time in a direct declaration by Yahweh.

The final revelatory function of the prophet in Joel is as a predictor of the Gentiles' doom. God announces the subject in 3.17, the prophet responds with a proclamation that calls all nations to assemble for judgment (3.9-11), the Lord next describes judgment in terms of a bloody harvest (3.12-13), and finally the prophet sums up the judging of the world by saying 'the Lord roars from Zion, and thunders from Jerusalem' (3.16). The full counsel of God has therefore been announced, interpreted, and repeated for the covenant and cosmic people's benefit. Joel represents the prophets well, because he characterizes the group as confident, accurate, and well rounded in their work.

Clearly the prophetic characterization in Hosea and Joel fits with, and relates to, the character of Yahweh and the plot of the Twelve. Yahweh's case against Israel is supported by a member of the covenant people. More specifically, God's anger at Israel's sin is supported by individuals who are deeply concerned about the nation's past, present, and future (cf. Hos. 12.13), and who have been rejected along with the Lord (Hos. 9.7-8). The case against the nations receives confirmation from Joel, who stands in a close relationship with God. Just as Hosea and Joel introduce the problem of the Twelve's plot, these books also describe the general characterization of the prophets that governs the rest of the prophecies. The problems associated with sin are announced by a covenant and cosmic God who verifies His assessments of the nature of Israel and the nations through the actions and words of the prophets. The very closeness of God and the prophets best reveals the major aspects of the prophets' personalities.

No better example of the prophet as messenger exists in the Twelve than appears in the portrayal of Amos. At least 21 times Amos uses the term 'says the Lord' (נאם יהוה), and another 21 times utilizes some form of the phrase 'thus says the Lord' (כה אמר יהוה). He also has visions that include direct conversation with God (cf. 7.1-9; 8.1-3). This preponderance of claims that Yahweh speaks suggests that, though the prophet cannot be characterized as an automaton, it is still as God's messenger that Amos desires to be remembered. Perhaps 3.7-

8 illustrates Amos' self-concept, for that passage states that the Lord tells His plans to the prophets and they speak, just like when the lion roars everyone nearby is afraid. When God speaks Amos carries that message to the people.

Amos may be the most intense figure among the minor prophets. He preaches about sin, punishment, and restoration with a starkness of detail that distinguishes him from the others. When he condemns the actions of the nations in 1.2–2.3, the frequent reminders that these are words from God creates an insistent, almost staccato, rhythm in the text that exudes the urgency of what Amos shares. Other images Amos uses, such as comparing women with cows (4.1), reveal his impatience with generality. The sin of Israel is so great (6.7) and the day of the Lord so awful (5.18-20) and near (4.12), that Amos cannot mince words. Even the restoration passage (9.11-15) is written in clipped, sharp language.

Three passages reveal the attitude of Amos towards prophecy and further help unlock the book's characterization of the prophets. First, Amos notes in 2.10-12 that Yahweh has sent the prophets (along with the Nazirites) to speak because of concern for Israel's wellbeing in the promised land. As in Hos. 9.7-8 and 12.13, then, the prophets are sent as caretakers of Israel's relationship with the Lord. They are a token of God's covenant love. Like the Hosea texts, Amos 2.10-12 also reflects the rejection of the prophets. If Yahweh is a spurned spouse, then the prophets are emissaries of the husband equally despised by Israel. Second, as was mentioned earlier, 3.7-8 argues that the prophets are Yahweh's most intimate associates. They are the people who must explain God's 'roaring' to the people. Third, and perhaps the most revealing of all, in 7.10-17 the book describes an event in Amos' life. When derisively called a 'seer', Amos replies that God took him and sent him to speak, and then he gives the Lord's message to his accuser. Again, the characterization of Amos follows the pattern of the prophet going where he is sent and saying what he has been told to speak.

The messages Amos relates carry so much weight that he rarely presumes to add to them. They are so clear he rarely needs to interpret them. Taken as a whole, however, these simple, direct ethical exhortations comprise some of the most telling literature in the Old Testament. Amos humbly presents himself as the messenger of a higher authority, but in doing so the prophet lays bare covenant and cosmic sin in a fashion unsurpassed in the prophetic canon.

Obadiah follows Amos' pattern of characterizing the prophets as messengers of God. Punctuated by reminders that the words are from Yahweh (vv. 1, 4, 8), the first 18 verses convey the Lord's anger with Edom. God's speech ends in v. 18 when the text concludes that 'Yahweh has spoken', a different phrase than those found earlier in the book. Obadiah changes from messenger to co-revelator/interpreter in the last three verses of the book, stressing that Israel will someday inhabit the land of its enemy Esau (v. 19). This short book illustrates the fact that the prophets possess special knowledge about world events, for though Edom oppresses Jerusalem now that mistreatment will be turned against her in the future.

Jonah reverts to the depiction of the prophet as symbolic picture of God's dispute with Israel. Hosea acted the part of the Lord in his prophecy, and was thus a positive image, but Jonah represents some of the least desirable attitudes of the prophets and people of Israel. Until now the characterization of the prophets uniformly praises them as the friends of God and as individuals who support the accusations the Lord makes concerning covenant and cosmic sin. Though they hope for repentance, the prophets denounce sin from a perspective of personal righteousness. Here, however, the prophet personifies Israel's wickedness.

Jonah's disobedience does not stem from any lack of privileges the other prophets are afforded. He receives a word from God (1.1), has obvious preaching ability (3.1-5), and communicates with Yahweh directly (4.1-11). Apparently Jonah's problem begins with those to whom he must minister. Even when forced to preach to Nineveh, Jonah delivers a five-word (in Hebrew) sermon and retires to look down on the people and hope for their destruction. Other unsavory aspects of Jonah's character emerge in the story, including rash anger and a tendency to pout (4.9). Some of the other canonical prophets, most notably Jeremiah, complain because they cannot see the positive side of God at work (cf. Jer. 12.1ff.), but, ironically, Jonah becomes angry because those qualities are too evident (4.1-2). Thus, Jonah, as a prophet, fully understands the person and purposes of God. Put quite simply, he does not want God to show as much concern for cosmic sin as for covenant sin.

Nowhere in the Twelve does the prophet represent the sin problem in Israel so graphically. Symbolic prophecy always deals with some major transgression in the minor prophets (cf. Hos. 1–3 and Zech. 11.4-17), but the prophet *embodies* that iniquity only in Jonah. Through this symbolic characterization, then, the plot and a major character are inextricably linked. The prophet is Israel, and the prophet has sinned. The story also reveals that the prophets are not gods themselves. They only represent God to other people. In this whole process the reader is confronted with all the dimensions of the Twelve's message in Hosea–Micah. Sin exists in the covenant people, the Gentiles, and in the prophets, and the problem of disobedience to Yahweh seems insoluble.

Micah's characterization greatly resembles Hosea's in style and Amos' in scope. Like Hosea, Micah exchanges speeches with Yahweh throughout the book, even explicitly distinguishing between what 'I said' (3.1) and what 'Yahweh says' (3.5). Each of the occurrences of 'says the Lord' (4.6; 5.9) and 'thus says the Lord' (2.3; 3.5) functions more as an aid to the reader than as any sort of messenger formula. Micah uses his position to chide poor prophets, leaders, priests and judges (e.g. 3.1-4, 8-12). The prophet also predicts the ultimate restoration of the remnant in 5.3-9, tells Israel Yahweh's requirements for holiness (6.6-8), and petitions the Lord concerning Israel's future (7.18-20). Like Amos, the book draws together the various motifs contained in earlier books. Micah's interests range from sin to punishment to restoration, from leader to lowest social strata, from the past to the future and from Israel to other nations. A great co-revelator must handle all the significant facets of prophecy to deserve the right to serve in this capacity, since the co-revelator claims to say what God would say had He spoken directly. Micah's main interest, though he obviously has others, is to bring every element of Israel's society face-to-face with its breaking of the covenant with Yahweh. No other co-revelator achieves this goal with any more telling accuracy than Micah.

Whether as symbol, messenger, or co-revelator, the prophets are characterized in Hosea–Micah as individuals who mirror the attitudes of Yahweh, either in speech or deed, about Israel and the nations. As God's associates, they also condemn sin and point out that only extreme repentance can stave off coming judgment. Even Jonah's actions, as rebellious as they are, reinforce the nature and plan of God. Therefore, the characterization of these prophets meshes with that of Yahweh, and with the plot of the Twelve as well. Though the prophets warn the nations, the world is bent on self-destruction. Except for Yahweh, no one cares for Israel like the prophets, so only God is pained more by their iniquity.

Despite the negative views of some scholars towards Nahum already noted in this book, the prophet merely delineates the next logical step in Yahweh's plans for creation. Though Jonah certainly proves the existence of negative feelings about Nineveh among even the prophets, it must also be recognized that such particularistic attitudes are condemned in Jonah. It would definitely be odd, then, for the canon to include both Jonah and Nahum if the latter's theology was at variance with the mainstream of the Twelve's theology. Consequently, Nahum does act as a herald of doom, but that doom only comes after Nineveh's perpetual disregard for other nations and not simply because of Nahum's nationalistic prejudice.

Like Obadiah and Habakkuk, the inscription of Nahum says the book is a 'vision', in this case a vision that consists of a sermon against Nineveh. Unlike Obadiah's 'vision', however, Nahum's book contains mostly commentary by the prophet instead of quotations of what God has said. In fact, perhaps only 1.12-14; 2.13, and 3.5-7 come from the Lord directly. The first passage agrees with Nahum's assessment of Nineveh and comments that Judah's affliction will soon end. Each of the last two texts begin with ' "I am against you", says the Lord Almighty', with both giving authority to preceding messages of the prophet. Perhaps 3.8-19 belongs to Yahweh, but the lack of a direct indication of that fact, such as appears in the other passages, argues against that possibility.

Because of Nahum's prominent speaking role in the prophecy, his characterization is as co-revelator instead of as messenger. Of course Nahum's sermon grows out of what he learns from God (1.1), but the picture of the prophet is still of an individual who understands Yahweh's will well enough to state it directly. The oracle the prophet delivers is of major importance, since it announces the end of Yahweh's call for repentance and the beginning of unstinting judgment. Though his predecessors in the Twelve stress the sins of the world's countries, they also emphasize the need for change and hint at restoration in the future. Where Nineveh is concerned, Nahum offers no such hope, so the nature of the prophetic co-revelator shifts from a warning figure to a herald of doom. This shift coincides with Yahweh's reluctant change from pleading to punishing parent. Both characters have tried to avert the necessity of hastening judgment, as is evident in Hosea–Micah, but once again both Lord and prophet agree on what must take place.

Habakkuk represents a crucial point in the characterization of the prophet in the Twelve. Until this point all the prophets except Jonah accept the words and deeds of the Lord almost uncritically. Perhaps the prophets did not demur as long as some chance for repentance lingered, or as long as it was a foreign nation that was earmarked for destruction, but when the punishment comes to Judah, thus including the prophets themselves, questions arise. Habakkuk asks some very difficult questions of the Lord about why God does certain things, why the evil prosper, and how the righteous can survive punishment they do not deserve. In the process he explodes any notion that the prophets are somehow wooden, lifeless characters, and may reveal how the prophets forged their orations. By any standard Habakkuk is a character of great depth and force who, because of these traits, pushes the Twelve's plot to its climactic point.

The development of Habakkuk's character is achieved, as is the development of the Twelve's plot, through his complaints. At first Habakkuk merely expresses the common complaint of the righteous that the wicked prosper more than they do (1.2-4). God's answer incites the prophet even further, since the notion that Babylon will conquer Israel is hardly welcome! How anxious the prophet becomes emerges in 2.1, for, after registering his objection at Yahweh's answer (1.12-17), he retreats to his 'watch' to see what God will do. Of course, the prophet is supposed to serve as watchman (Hos. 9.8), so his stance is sound. Once the Lord explains that judgment will come on all nations, though, Habakkuk expresses his satisfaction with the will of God in a closing hymn (3.11-19). During this process of testing the mind of God, the prophet develops from frustrated supporter (1.2) of the Lord to a satisfied, informed confidant of Yahweh (3.2, 18-19).

Through his personal development Habakkuk answers some very logical questions for the reader. First, his actions show that co-revelation does not come easily or in a historical vacuum. Habakkuk's report on God's actions comes after much searching and sacrifice. His message will cause him pain along with the rest of Israel. Second, the prophet's probing of Yahweh's will dispels any thought that the Lord may not judge covenant and cosmic sin equally. The wicked of all nations will be punished. Third, Habakkuk's confidence in the future (cf. 3.16-19) means any righteous reader can have the same confidence. No doubt Habakkuk is a co-revelator of a different stripe, since the book's question-answer format varies from the style of Hosea, Micah, etc. Because of the way he gains his knowledge, however, Habakkuk takes the reader into the council of God (cf. Jer. 23.18) and demonstrates the process of how God 'reveals His plan to His servants the prophets' (Amos 3.7). Therefore, Habakkuk serves as revealer, interpreter, and guide, even as he fulfills the traditional functions of a prophet (2.1).

In Zephaniah the prophet is characterized in three ways: interpreter of God's wrath, proclaimer of worldwide destruction, and herald of coming restoration. Like Yahweh, his character develops as the plot progresses, but, unlike Yahweh, he develops most prominently in the middle of the book rather than at the beginning or end. The author thereby balances the plot by making the prophet prominent when the Lord is less involved.

Zephaniah's initial comments come between Yahweh's first two, very wrathful, speeches. The prophet quickly explains that the people must be still because 'the Day of the Lord is near' (1.7). This explanation of God's anger shows Judah the gravity of its sin. After God's second caustic speech, the prophet describes Yahweh's day more fully (1.14-16). No doubt is left about the severity and comprehensiveness of the approaching punishment. In both his speeches the prophet's role is to explicate Yahweh's wrath to the audience.

In his next three speeches the prophet reaches his full stature as a character by gradually assuming the role of co-revelator. He no longer only interprets the Lord's speeches, instead he informs the reader of nations beyond those mentioned in Nahum and Habakkuk that will suffer punishment. It is also Zephaniah who mentions the hope for the remnant (2.3, 7), thus aligning himself with earlier prophets who counsel that repentance leads to restoration (cf. Hos. 14.1-3; Joel 2.13-14, etc.). It is the prophet who denounces the old enemies Philistia and Assyria, claiming that both will be desolate (2.4-7; 2.13-3.5). Zephaniah still stresses, though, that it is God's judgment he announces (cf. 2.2-3, 11, 13; 3.5). Yahweh remains the story's principal figure. Yet, the prophet takes on the added dimension of an original proclaimer of judgment rather than remaining just an interpreter of God's anger.

Lastly, the prophet serves as herald of Yahweh's merciful restoration of Judah and the nations (3.14-17). Like a choral leader, the prophet encourages Judah to sing of God's redemption (3.15) and love (3.17). Once more he interprets the message of God, but this time the message emphasizes the glory that follows the purging of the day of the Lord. Zephaniah's final role develops from its start to its finish, for in 1.7 he counsels silence because of sin, but in 3.14 calls for a song of victory. The gloom of 1.14-16 changes to the exultation of 3.14-17. Clearly, Zephaniah gets to play the part all the prophets from Hosea to Habakkuk want to play. Though he must take the covenant and cosmic peoples through the furnace of judgment, he is allowed to ultimately reveal the lasting grace of God. Indeed, he leads the nation in celebrating the end of punishment. His character, long considered by scholars a gloomy individual, actually provides the means for leading the people to better times.

As with the depiction of Yahweh, Zephaniah's characterization fits the flow of the Twelve's plot. His changing character matches the evolving nature of the minor prophets' conflict and resolution. It is his happy privilege to reveal that punishment has done its work and that restoration will soon begin. Habakkuk acts as a bridge between the punishment of Judah and the Gentiles, while Zephaniah serves as a bridge between the total devastation he and Habakkuk picture and the restoration that begins in Haggai.

Practically every aspect of the characterization of the prophets in Nahum–Zephaniah works with that of Yahweh to provide an upturn in the Twelve's story line. Yahweh gets angrier and more inclined to judge in these books, and so do God's servants, God's co-revelators, the prophets. At the same time the disgust of both characters eases when judgment does its work. One feels at the end of Zephaniah that Lord and prophet are both ready for better things. New tension arises, of course, when one has to consider the readiness of the covenant and cosmic nations for that restoration.

Yahweh starts the restoration process by speaking to the covenant people through Haggai. That Haggai is character-ized as a messenger becomes evident in his first speech to the nation, for the very day of the prophet's reception of the word is noted (1.1), and every segment of the message is described as coming from the Lord (1.1, 2, 3, 5, 7, 8, 9). If that initial speech were not enough, the text explicitly calls Haggai 'the Lord's messenger' in 1.13, and the previous verse observes that the prophet's sermon was heeded because the people felt 'God had sent him' (1.12). Three other dated 'words' are recorded in Haggai (2.1-9, 10-19, 20-23), with each having the same emphasis on the prophet sharing a message from God rather than interpreting the mind of God. Therefore, as a character Haggai stands in the strong tradition of messenger prophets represented by Amos and Obadiah. These messengers are blunt, forceful and quite intense. Their oracles cannot wait if their hearers are to survive.

Haggai achieves more success with his audience than any of the prophets, exept perhaps for Jonah. Some of the response occurs because of the status of Haggai as God's representative (cf. 1.12-13), but much of the positive reaction stems from the change in the people themselves. Joshua and Zerubbabel are definitely higher-quality leaders than many of their predeces-sors, and this remnant of Israel that survives the Day of Yah-weh has learned not to reject a word of the prophet. Without the continuing faithfulness of the prophet in transmitting the will of God, however, such actions would not be possible. Haggai's obedience determines the fate of the nation and makes the rebuilding of the temple a reality. Like Amos, nothing deters Haggai from dispensing his duties as the messenger of the Lord. The prophet's love for Israel is thereby demonstrated in this diligence.

Given the depth and intensity of the book of Zechariah, it is not surprising that the characterization of the prophet displays a number of facets. At some point in the book the prophet acts as messenger, symbol, and co-revelator. Only Hosea shows the reader so many sides of the prophetic character. Each aspect of characterization helps drive home the restoration motif, so once more the prophetic figure works in conjunction with the character of Yahweh to create the Twelve's plot.

Though Zechariah does develop all phases of the prophet's character, by far the most prominent of these phases in the book is the prophet as God's messenger. On at least 47 occasions the text punctuates its statements with a form of 'says the Lord' or 'thus says the Lord'. Every chapter except 14 mentions that Zechariah shares what God has told him. Like Haggai, Zechariah receives messages on specific days (cf. 1.7; 7.1), but, unlike Haggai, these dated 'words' come in the form of 'visions'. Very dutifully the prophet recounts what he 'saw', and each of these visions relates some aspect of Jerusalem's restoration (cf. the sections on Zechariah in chs. 3–4). In 7.1 Zechariah receives several short messages for the people dealing with the nation's sin and Yahweh's plans to eradicate that iniquity and to subsequently bless Jerusalem (7.1–8.23). At every change of subject in these two chapters the prophet notes either that this word of God 'came' to him or that the message is something God 'says' (cf. 7.1, 4, 8; 8.1, 3, 4, 6, 7, 9, 14, 18, 20, 23). Zechariah 1–8 never deviates from this messenger pattern, which indicates that the book desires to set forth a concrete, clearly understood theme of Jerusalem's restoration that is viewed as coming directly from God. Because of its origin, the veracity of these oracles and visions cannot be questioned. Any further ideas forwarded by the prophet grow out of this undeniable authority.

Once an unshakable foundation for the restoration of Jerusalem has been laid by God's messenger, the characterization of the prophet switches to that of co-revelator in 9.1–11.3. In these verses the prophet answers some implicit questions about barriers to Israel's restoration. Two difficulties are handled in 9.1-13. First, the prophet (9.1-4) and Yahweh (9.5-8) jointly declare that any enemy that attempts to attack Jerusalem will fail. Next, Yahweh states that the poor leadership Judah has endured will be replaced by a messianic figure who will establish a reign of peace in the land (9.9-13). Zechariah completes this positive note with assurances of God's blessings in 9.14-17. Chapter 10 begins a rebuke of the leaders of Israel that finds first the prophet (10.1-2) then the Lord (10.3-12) denouncing the sorry 'shepherds' of Israel. Zechariah concludes that these shepherds will meet a terrible end (11.1-3). This section devoted to co-revelation shows that Zechariah is not only a visionary, for he understands that the nation's practical problem is terrible leadership. If the blessings promised in chs. 1–8 are to become a reality, then holy leaders are needed. This co-revelation also introduces further comments on the destruction of Israel's enemies (ch. 12), the sins of the people and prophets (ch. 13), and God's reign on earth (ch. 14). As co-revelator, the prophet realizes the difficulties associated with renewing the temple, the land and the people.

Zechariah's most vehement words against Israel's 'shepherds' come when he becomes a symbol of those individuals in 11.4-17. At first Zechariah serves the flock well (11.4-7), but when the flock rebels the prophet symbolically breaks two staffs that represent God's covenant with the nations (11.10) and the covenant with Israel (11.14). In the end the worthless shepherds are blamed for the termination of both covenants (11.17). What the prophet says here is that the covenant and cosmic people are far away from God, which makes their restoration that much greater. Also, the pericope demonstrates that renewal is totally the work of God, since the Lord both removes the wicked shepherds and provides new ones. When the prophets act as symbols, they usually portray a negative side of Israel, as is evident in Hosea and Jonah, and Zechariah's role certainly takes on that distinction.

In the last three chapters Zechariah plays the part of messenger again (chs. 12–13) before concluding the story as co-revelator. As in chs. 1–8 and 9.1–11.3, chs. 12–13 provide the authority of a message from God before the prophet interprets that message in the last chapter. God's word is that Israel's enemies will be defeated and a new remnant will emerge that will serve the true shepherd, Yahweh. Zechariah believes that these events lead to the complete emergence of Jerusalem as the holy city of God (14.1-21).One other way Zechariah characterizes the prophets must be mentioned, which is the fact that the book describes the prophets directly at several points. Passages like 7.1-14 and 8.9 relate the value of past prophets, but 1.1-6 and 13.1-6 provide an especially helpful contrast between good and bad prophecy. Chapter one observes that the good prophet warns the people about their sins (1.4), shares only God's word (1.5), and has his predictions come true (1.6). Zechariah embodies these qualities. On the other hand, the wicked prophet speaks lies (13.3), deceives the people (13.4), and deserves rebuke (13.5-6). Such are worthless shepherds. Whether as co-revelator, messenger, or symbol, Zechariah achieves the level of status enjoyed by the 'earlier prophets' (1.4). Few prophets work harder than Zechariah to achieve this standing, for his reputation is earned by serving as the complete prophet. Because he functions as complete prophet, he preaches all the major motifs of the prophetic genre, but the book makes it clear that, at this point in the Twelve, the most complete word concerns the Lord removing all obstacles to the redemption of all creation.

One need only know that Malachi's name means 'my messenger' to begin to understand his characterization. Though scholars may argue whether Malachi is an actual name or not, the significance of the term is that the reader should attribute to the book all the authority that is due a message from God. Malachi's style differs from that of the other messengers due to his employment of a question and answer scheme. Every part of the book comes as a direct statement of God, with the possible exception of introductory phrases like 2.17 and biographical notes like 3.16. The questions Malachi uncovers resemble Zechariah's messages in some significant ways, since their intent is to remove any sin that hinders the restoration of Israel.

What message does Malachi bring the people? It must first be recognized that Malachi focuses on the restoration of the people's spiritual life rather than on the rebuilding of Jerusalem and the temple. His message simply states that covenants with God (1.2–2.9), family (2.10-16), and one another must be kept. God cannot be robbed if restoration is to come (3.6-15). On the other hand, the prophet reports that God will provide, as was promised in Zechariah 9.9-13, the leaders who will cleanse the people's cult (2.17–3.4) and change their hearts (4.6; 3.24 in Hebrew). Again all obstacles to restoration will be removed. The sobering news for the people of course, is that, if *they* are obstacles to renewal, then they will be purged (3.2-4). So the final messenger of the Twelve brings news of restoration. That news comes as no surprise, even though Malachi's message reminds Israel that they may not share in that time of blessing.

When the reader finishes Malachi, the final word is that three authoritative messengers, Haggai, Zechariah, and Malachi, have been commissioned by God to tell the covenant and cosmic people through much searching and hard work, that restoration will overshadow even their punishment. This good news becomes known because they have had special access to the benevolent, covenant God of Israel and ruler of the nations. As God's special servants they act out (symbol), transmit (messenger), as well as interpret and explicate (co-revelator) the will, purpose and word of God. Though their themes differ from the earlier nine books, these prophets certainly draw their characterization from their predecessors. Not one of the twelve prophets fails to demonstrate some side of the prophetic character, and each one cooperates with the other characters in developing the story of the Twelve.

3. *Israel as Rebel and Remnant*
Besides the two most critical personae, Yahweh and the prophet, other, more minor, characters also exist in the Twelve. Most of these figures are flat, or static, appear less frequently than the prophets and the Lord, and draw most of

their characterizations from their relationship to the major characters. Israel is definitely the most significant of these characters. One special problem that arises in the study of Israel's characterization is that the nation's personality takes on at least two sides as the Twelve proceeds. One side presents the rebellious, sinful actions of the covenant people, while the other portrays the nation as a righteous remnant that does what God commands. At times the contrasting images converge, indeed appear to confront and battle one another, thereby providing a sense of tension in the depiction of the character.

Like the prophets, Israel assumes a composite nature in the Twelve. Whether as rebel or remnant, the nation is pictured as one figure acting as a whole. As may be expected, Israel's characterization is in response to what Yahweh and the prophets say; consequently, much that relates to this character has already been covered. The nation is depicted as an unfaithful wife, prostitute, rebellious child, covenant-breaker and hater of neighbors in Hosea–Micah. In Nahum–Zephaniah Israel appears as both object of destruction and bearer of slender hope for the future. Haggai–Malachi changes the metaphor to portray Israel as the remnant struggling to be what the prophets say it must be. Quite obviously, Israel's characterization develops along with, and is governed by, the Twelve's plot.

The Twelve's initial assessment of Israel is quite unflattering to say the least. Represented by Gomer in Hosea 1–3, Israel is definitely the covenant people of God, but is just as definitely a covenant 'wife' who has other lovers (2.2), bears illegitimate children (2.4), and must be wooed to come back home (2.14–3.5). Relentlessly, Hosea continues noting unfaithfulness (ch. 4), corruption (ch. 5), worthless worship (ch. 6), etc., to build his case, or charge, against the covenant people.

Hos. 11.1-4 describes Israel as a child that flees from its father when asked to come home. In fact, Yahweh intones: 'the more I called Israel, the further they went from me' (11.2). Consequently, attempts by the prophet to call the nation to repentance (cf. 6.1-3) utterly fail. Even at the end of the book the writer asks Israel to change (14.1-3), but no guarantee of such a needed reversal appears.

Joel adds to the gloomy description of Israel by showing that the nation is sinful from top to bottom. Elders (1.2, 14), priests (1.13; 2.17), and lowest citizens (1.5) alike are encouraged to weep and fast before the Lord. Because the duty of keeping a sacred covenant does not motivate Israel to serve the Lord, Joel predicts that the day of the Lord (1.15) will bring a vicious enemy to punish the people (2.1-11). Joel's urgent commands in chapter one to all levels of society indicate that the nation wallows in spiritual malaise. The covenant people have become lazy and complacent. So, in Hos. 1.1 through Joel 2.11, Israel acts like an ungrateful, rebellious group whose actions verify Yahweh's charges. Worse yet, there is no sign of any change in this pattern of behavior.

Some relief from this bleak characterization of the elect nation comes in Hos. 2.14–3.5; 11.8-11; 14.4-8 and in Joel 2.28-32; 3.17-21. God promises that in the future the people will return to Yahweh and enjoy the blessings He has always wanted to give them. Yet, these promises refer more to future times than to the present generation, almost as if the Lord knows the contemporary group will not repent. As for Israel, there remains no hint of a changed heart. Nowhere does either book chronicle any move towards God on the part of Israel. It is still as rebellious child and straying wife, then, that Israel acts after Joel.

Amos just confirms what the two previous prophecies claim about the chosen people. Based on the Exodus covenant (2.9-16; 3.2; etc.) Israel owes Yahweh special allegiance, but has refused to obey the Lord so long as 'they do not know how to do right' (3.10). Like Joel, Amos warns that the day of the Lord will purge sin from the land (5.18-20), yet again Israel remains unmoved. Perhaps 6.1 best summarizes the mental, emotional and spiritual state of Israel. There the prophet hisses:

> Woe to you who are complacent in Zion,
> and to you who trust in Mount Samaria,
> You notable men of the foremost nation,
> to whom the house of Israel comes.

Amos elaborates on this complacency in 6.4-6, charging that the rich eat the best food (6.4), lie on the nicest beds (6.4), enjoy the finest music (6.5) and consume the choicest wine (6.6), all without worrying even a tiny bit about the decay of the nation. Therefore, Amos concludes, these leaders will lead the way into exile. All sin breaks the covenant, but the sin of self-satisfaction blocks the repentance that could erase the coming punishment.

Despite the promise of restoration that closes the book (9.11-15), there is no reason to think judgment will not overwhelm the covenant people. In fact, the renewal Amos describes must come *after* exile (9.14). The impression the Twelve conveys to the reader at this point is that Israel is a hopelessly callous adulterer who cares neither who has been hurt nor what the future may bring. More importantly, Israel will soon learn how unacceptable the actions that result from this attitude have become to Yahweh.

Though Obadiah chastises Edom for its cruel treatment of Israel instead of offering any direct characterization of the chosen people, the truth of Amos' threats becomes evident in the fact that Jerusalem indeed has been destroyed. No longer do the leaders of Israel harm and oppress others, instead they are now victimized by their enemies. Once more, Israel receives promises of blessing (vv. 19-21), but again those predictions refer to a distant future when exiles shall come back to Palestine and occupy the land.

Jonah furthers the characterization of Israel as a spoiled, complacent, sedentary figure. Through Jonah, the prophetic symbol, the book's author demonstrates that the covenant people run from God's commands (cf. Hos. 11.2 and Jon. 1.3), exhibit the same unconcern for others inherent in the 'heathen' (cf. Amos 1.3–2.3 and Jon. 1.1-3), and all the while take the mercies of Yahweh for granted (cf. Amos 6.1-7 and Jon. 4.5-11). At the conclusion of the prophecy Jonah sits hoping for the destruction of Nineveh, confident at the same time that he, as a prophet of God, rests outside the wrath of God (Has he forgotten his experience inside the fish?). Like Israel, Jonah does not fulfill his obligations and he does nothing positive, even in the face of imminent judgment. This book does not improve the image of the covenant people. If anything,

Israel is at its worst here, and deserves punishment at least as much as Nineveh does.

Micah almost exhausts himself trying to make Israel realize its transgressions and get the nation to renounce those sins. The prophet begins his message with an urgent cry to 'look', that is to realize that God will come to judge iniquity (1.3-5). Later he cries 'woe' (2.1) and asks the leaders to 'listen' (3.1; 6.1) to his important warnings. After lengthy attempts to rouse Israel, the people's rejection causes the prophet to complain:

> What misery is mine!
> I am like one who gathers summer fruit
>   at the gleaning of the vineyard.
> There is no cluster to eat
>   or early figs my soul craves (7.1)

Even Micah's final hopes are pinned more on God's grace than Israel's repentance. Apparently, the prophet speaks to either a deaf or an uncaring people. Israel does not even protest its innocence or argue with Micah, as it does in Amos 7.10-17 and Malachi. Rather, the chosen nation accepts the prophetic assessment, yet somehow believes its status as an elect nation will provide an escape from catastrophe.

After Hosea–Micah it is extremely difficult to mount any case whatsoever against Yahweh's plan to punish the covenant people. Not even the prophets believe Israel should be pardoned. Certainly Amos intercedes for Israel (7.1-9), but God's final decision is to 'spare them no longer' (7.8). One cannot blame Yahweh for this attitude nor the prophets for their comments, since Israel seems determined to disregard its familial obligations to the Lord, to continue to mistake mercy for indulgence, to keep sinning against one another and neighboring countries and to remain complacent in all these wrongdoings. The covenant people act like a wicked, frivolous wife, in other words, like Gomer, so the punishment of Hosea's wife will become the chastisement of Israel (Hos. 2.1-13).

Nahum–Zephaniah proves to be the turning point in the Twelve's characterization of Israel, for in these books a gradual shift in the nature and identity of the chosen people takes place. In Nahum the elect nation does not play a major part.

When Israel does appear it is to hear the future promises of God (1.12-13, 15) or to rejoice with the other nations at Nineveh's downfall (3.19). In Habakkuk, however, the first concrete signs of Israel's punishment emerge. Because the nation will be destroyed, thus forcing the righteous to suffer with the wicked, God must start over with a new group of people, if Israel is to have any place in the world's future. Yahweh's comment that in difficult times 'the righteous will live by his faith' (2.4) indicates that a small segment of the people will survive the inevitable coming judgment. It is also fairly safe to assume that the segment that survives will take God and the covenant seriously.

Earlier in the Twelve, Micah argues that, though Judah must be destroyed, Yahweh will ultimately 'bring together the remnant of Israel' (2.12). In this verse Israel is a scattered flock of sheep that Yahweh will father and take back to its pen. Only if God acts as shepherd of this 'remnant' can Israel survive, as James Luther Mays comments:

> Hope lay alone in the possibility that the title of shepherd represented a dimension of YHWH which transcended his wrath and judgment. Here the good shepherd promises to fulfill his office in sentences spoken as the firmest assertions (1976: 75).

Micah later states that the lame, injured remnant of Israel will become a significant group (4.7), will triumph over its enemies (5.7-8), and will be the recipients of God's forgiveness (7.18). Though he does not elaborate on the personality of that remnant, Micah establishes the fact that only this remnant will receive the blessings mentioned in Hos. 14.4-8; Joel 2.28-32; Amos 9.11-15 and Obad. 19-20.

Interspersed between the Day-of-Yahweh oracles in Zeph. 1.2–3.11 are hints that a remnant will survive the covenant and cosmic punishment, and be the nucleus of a new people of faith. Certainly, Zephaniah continues to characterize Israel in a very negative fashion in the early speeches, but in 2.3, 7, 9 a new note creeps into the picture. The prophet exhorts the 'humble of the land' to 'seek the Lord' and thereby escape 'Yahweh's anger' (2.3). Further, when the Gentiles are condemned, the remnant receives assurances that one day it will inherit Philistia (2.7), Moab (2.9), and Ammon (2.9). Even with these positive images, however, God does move ahead with judgment, so what will become of the remnant?

The climax of Zephaniah takes place in 3.8-13, where God reveals that the day of the Lord will purge the earth (3.9), leaving alive only those who call on, and serve, Yahweh (3.9). Since all rebellious people are removed, the faithful remnant can serve Yahweh without hindrance. Zephaniah now characterizes the remnant as meek, humble, trusting, righteous, honest and bold (3.12-13). One could hardly fail to note the contrast between this Israel and the one described in Hos. 1.1 through Zeph. 2.2. Yahweh also reacts differently to Israel now, for it is once more possible, because of the cleansing nature of judgment, to show the love towards Israel that was exhibited in the past (cf. Hos. 11.1-4 and Zeph. 3.17). Due to the fires of judgment, the complacent, adulterous nature of Israel disappears, and a new, holy Israel emerges. Therefore, the characterization of the covenant people at this point reflects the vision Micah foresaw, and the process of the adulterous wife becoming faithful predicted in Hos. 3.5 is now complete. The rebel has been reborn as a righteous follower of Yahweh.

Without a doubt, before Haggai any change of personality on Israel's part came only because such alterations were forced on the nation. After all, it takes the ravages of the Day of Yahweh to melt away the wicked segment of the chosen people and bring forth the remnant. In Haggai, however, both because of the lessons learned through judgment, and due to the higher moral fiber of the remnant, Israel willingly makes changes in its pattern of living. As Zephaniah predicted (3.12-13), the nation has taken on the characteristic of obedience, and, as a result, now enjoys the favor of the Lord.

Clearly Haggai believes the post-exilic (post-judgment) community must be the remnant Micah and Zephaniah describe. He comes to this conclusion after the leaders and people heed the call to work on the temple, for, based upon their obedience, he specifically refers to them as the 'remnant of the people' (1.12-14). God also acknowledges their obedience, since they are blessed with the divine presence in the temple, promises for the future, and approval of their leader (2.1-23). Such adherence to God's will is unthinkable in

Hosea through Zeph. 2.2. At this stage in the Twelve, Israel makes every effort to be God's righteous remnant: they hear, they obey (1.12), they fear God (1.12), and they work on Yahweh's house (1.14).

Zechariah only calls Israel 'the remnant of this people' three times (8.6, 11, 12), but the location of these references is very significant. Poised after the prophet's visions and messages concerning the cleansing and restoring of the chosen people (1.1-8.23), and before the glorious portrayal of the world's future (9.1-14.21), Zechariah's characterization of Israel as the remnant in ch. 8 unifies the book's various strands of thought on the nature of the chosen people. Each of the three recitations of Israel as remnant contributes something vital to Israel's characterization. In 8.6 the Lord promises to collect the elect from the far corners of the earth, which illustrates the suffering of the far-flung group. Next, 8.7-11 declares that since the nation plans to rebuild the temple, God will return safety to the people. Yahweh's solemn pledge is to 'not deal with the remnant as... in the past' (8.11). Thus, the people receive a fresh start with their God. Finally, 8.12 states that the heavens and earth will bless Israel as 'an inheritance to the remnant of this people', and the following verse offers Israel a prominent place among the countries of the world. Evidently, 8.6 describes the immediate past work of Yahweh, 8.11 relates to the present efforts of God on Israel's behalf, and 8.12 covers what the Lord will do for the people in the future. So 8.6 corresponds to Zech. 1.1–8.6, 8.11 sums up 8.7-23, and 8.12 looks forward to 9.1–14.21.

Slowly, almost inexorably, in Zechariah the remnant ceases to be a remnant simply because righteousness will spread to *all* of Israel and from there to the whole earth. From humble beginnings, the remnant grows until it includes covenant and cosmic people alike (14.16-21). Therefore, by the end of the prophecy Israel is characterized as a righteous, blessed remnant that obeys the Lord and takes Yahweh's message to the nations. In short, Israel now functions as God has always intended.

Malachi's picture of Israel develops not only from the promises of what the remnant can be, but also out of the harsh reality of what the nation actually *is*. Doubtless, the prophet understood God's intentions for the nation or he would not have spoken as he does in 4.1-6. Yet he also knows of present iniquity perpetuated by the people, or he would not have mentioned the problems delineated in 1.2-3.15. In the light of this tension, the interpreter must decide which, if either, tendency best characterizes Israel.

Very much as Haggai does, Malachi lists the sins of the remnant before noting any blessings for them. In Mal. 3.16, the righteous segment of Israel that follows Yahweh once again emerges. Out of the rebellious post-exilic community a remnant-within-the-remnant exerts itself and consequently receives the promises of God (3.16–4.6; 3.16-24 in Hebrew). It is this remnant that ultimately represents the elect group's only hopes for the future, since it is this remnant that will trample the wicked (4.3; 3.21 in Hebrew) and respond properly to 'Elijah' (4.5-6; 3.23-24 in Hebrew). Just as Haggai's listeners respond to the command to rebuild the temple, so Malachi's hearers who fear the Lord (3.16) heed his demands for repentance. At the close of the Twelve, then, Israel continues to strive to be the holy remnant of God. The sins recounted by Malachi indicate that Zechariah's vision of a universal remnant must await fulfillment, but the fact that there is a segment of Yahweh followers at all shows a marked improvement in Israel's character.

The Twelve's characterization of Israel presents the covenant figure as a developing character. Though not as multi-faceted as Yahweh or the prophets, this persona starts as an unfeeling adulteress, becomes an object of destruction that finally wakes up to its difficulties, and finishes as a person that, although not without imperfections, follows her covenant Lord-husband. While Israel certainly deserved the punishment described in Nahum–Zephaniah, the character at least has enough intelligence to learn from its experiences. Or does it? Malachi points out the danger of slipping back into sin while noting with relief the group's repentance. So the nation continues on the route of Zechariah's ambitious program, but the fulfillment of the remnant's potential does not come easily.

Though running the risk of slipping into redundancy, it must be recognized that the Twelve's depiction of Israel fits well with the characterizations of Yahweh and the prophets.

Israel acts rebelliously in Hosea–Micah, suffers the punishment requisite for that sin in Nahum–Zephaniah, and finally
acts like a new person in Haggai–Malachi. God's actions are,
at least in part, brought about because of the covenant people's
deeds. Likewise Israel, especially after the Day of Yahweh,
reacts to what the Lord says and does. Nothing in the characterization of Israel itself contradicts the findings of the
prophets either, which lends further unity to the actions of the
Twelve's characters. In this coherence of characterization a
coherence of plot is also quite evident.

4. *The Nations*

Of all the vital characters in the Twelve, the nations, or Gentiles, receive the briefest treatment. At times the group seems
void of definitive personality, almost as if this figure has no
particular significance to the plot. It is important to recall,
though, that every character in good literature has a definite
function, even if that purpose is only to bring out some aspect
of another character. The nations certainly fulfill this role,
and, at times, exhibit some interesting traits of their own.

Joel 3.1 through to Amos 2.3 represents the first important
characterization of the Gentiles in the minor prophets. Here
the group, like Israel, is presented as a sinful figure worthy of
punishment. Chief among the character traits the prophets
mention is cruelty. First, Joel charges that the nations have
mistreated Israel. Indeed they have scattered the covenant
people to the corners of the earth (3.2), divided Israel's land
(3.2), and sold Jewish children into prostitution for a drink of
wine (3.3). For these and other transgressions Yahweh will
punish them (3.4-16). Second, Amos lists a number of offenses
the Gentiles have committed against one another. These
crimes include every possible heinous act from ripping open
the wombs of pregnant women (1.13) to defiling the remains
of the dead (2.1). Yahweh vows to punish every one of these
atrocities. At this juncture in the story the Gentiles have been
characterized as cruel, savage, without conscience or human
compassion and totally devoid of any moral awareness. Put
another way, the nations are depicted as the stereotypical
enemy of the Jews.

Obadiah continues the portrayal of the nations as an unfeeling monster. Edom, one of Israel's most despised foes, helps Babylon destroy Jerusalem and even kills the fugitives of the city (v. 14). Julius Bewer captures the sense of this characterization of Edom when he writes that Obadiah

> sees the Edomites full of malicious joy over Judah's calamity, hears their words of scorn and ridicule, sees them coming into the city to loot and plunder, sees them cutting down fugitive Jews at the crossroads, and overmastered by his emotion he breaks forth into passionate warnings, as if Edom were even now doing these things (1911: 11).

Because of such cruelty to its 'brother Jacob' (v. 10), God's judgment will come against Edom (vv. 15-16). As Edom has done to Israel, so God will do to the Edomites (v. 15).

Jonah and Micah likewise portray the Gentiles as gross sinners, but these books also offer a trace of hope for them as well. In Jonah the 'heathen' characters are certainly sinful, since the sailors in 1.6 recognize the validity of a number of gods, and the city of Nineveh is too wicked to tell its right hand from its left (4.11), yet they seem more responsive to Yahweh than the stubborn prophet (cf. 1.16; 3.5-10). Though idolatrous, the Gentiles can change. Though cruel and unjust (cf. Nahum), Ninevah can repent. The willingness of the cosmic group to turn to the Lord should make the covenant people ashamed of their continual disobedience.

Micah characterizes the foreign countries as lurking outside Jerusalem, hoping to conquer the weakened city. The enemies of Israel gloat at her weakness (4.11) and lay siege to Zion (5.1). Further, the prophet claims the nations practice witchcraft (5.12), worship idols (5.13-14), and disobey Yahweh (5.15). As vassals of the sovereign Lord, the cosmic peoples owe allegiance to Yahweh (5.15). Despite their wickedness, Micah believes the heathen will someday approach the mountain of God to learn of God's ways and 'walk in His paths' (4.2). Once more, the situation of this character may be bleak, though it is not totally desperate.

Except for the oracles of hope, almost every reference to the non-covenant character depicts that persona as cruel, especially to Israel, vindictive, and without moral scruples. Like

Israel, the Gentiles obviously deserve judgment. Until they recognize their responsibility to bow before the Lord on the holy mountain, they can only look forward to devastating punishment (cf. 4.1-5). Certainly, this depiction coincides with the condition of Israel, so the whole earth must prepare for destruction.

Nahum simultaneously presents the most devastating portrayal of the nations and announces the punishment of that group. Nineveh's sins are many, and include such crimes as plotting against God (1.9, 11), idolatry (1.14), vile behavior (1.14), shedding blood, lying, plundering (3.1), enslaving nations (3.4), presumption (3.8), and cruelty (3.19). In fact, Nineveh symbolizes the evil nature of all the enemies of God. Though a mere vassal of God, the proud Assyrians rebel against God (1.9, 11). Nahum indicates that Yahweh will put Nineveh in its proper place, just as Assyria once humiliated Israel.

Because there exists no apparent positive character traits in the foreign figure at this point in the Twelve, the prophet notes that judgment will now commence. Edward Dalglish interprets the significance of God's punishment when he writes that

> The epiphany of Yahweh confronts such immorality with condign judgment and metes out the sentence of doom to the cruel Assyrian nation which has built its kingdom, not on the inalienable rights of men and nations, but upon irresponsible power structure. It will further demonstrate the impotency of the Assyrian gods and temples... The vivid battle scenes and tragic defeat of the Assyrians are but a mirroring judgment of the war crimes and barbarities which have characterized the reprehensible aggression of their militarism (1972: 235).

After Assyria's downfall the once proud character becomes pathetic, 'pelted with filth' (3.16), a byword (3.7), and one whose destruction causes the whole world to rejoice (3.19). The magnitude of Assyria's punishment matches the depths of its sin.

Just as Habakkuk provides the crisis point of the Twelve's plot and the characterizations of Yahweh, the prophets, and Israel, so it also marks the highest point of Gentile power and arrogance before it punishes that pride and oppression. When Yahweh answers Habakkuk's first complaint He describes the Babylonians as 'feared and dreaded', 'a law to themselves', militarily strong, 'bent on violence', and haughty (1.7-11). In short, they represent the epitome of heathen power, lawlessness and ruthlessness. Mighty Babylon does not concern itself with mercy, nor does it believe destruction will ever come its way. God further charges that Babylon has destroyed nations and shed blood (2.8), has built a kingdom based on injustice (2.9), and has acted like a nation full of criminals (2.12). As with Nahum's portrayal of Nineveh, this depiction of Babylon intends to portray the Gentiles as totally rebellious against God. Indeed, the Gentile persona has no redeeming traits. If anything, the character has grown in wickedness since Joel introduced it.

When the Lord deals with Babylon it is as its sovereign king. It is Yahweh that dispatches the country across the earth (1.5-6), which demonstrates God's mastery over this proud power. It is also Yahweh who will punish this vassal for cruelty, oppression, and bloodshed. Because Babylon is 'puffed up' (2.4), 'arrogant' (2.5), 'restless' (2.5), and 'greedy' (2.5), God decides to reverse the nation's fortunes. Yahweh declares: 'Because you have plundered many nations, the remaining people will plunder you' (2.8), and predicts that Babylon 'will be filled with shame instead of glory' (2.16). Like Nineveh, Babylon will become a shadow of its former self, thus negating its intense pride. The once arrogant, lawless terrorizer of Yahweh's other vassals will be put in its place.

Zephaniah continues to chronicle the judgment of the nations, though the emphasis shifts somewhat from major powers to the smaller neighbors of Israel. Assyria, so vain as to claim: 'I am and there is no one else besides me' (2.15), will be totally desolate on the Day of Yahweh (2.13-14). Also crushed at the time of punishment are Israel's ancient enemies Philistia (2.4-7), Moab and Ammon (2.8-11), as well as Ethiopia (2.12). More than any other trait, the sin of pride characterizes this group (cf. 2.8-15). They believe that the weakness of Jerusalem can be equated with the impotence of Yahweh. Thus God will judge them. Regardless of the size or might of the country in question, the Twelve pictures the nations as

totally outside the will of God. Zephaniah characterizes the
Gentiles as unwittingly being collected, like Israel, to serve as
sacrifices on Yahweh's Day of retribution (cf. 1.7).

Quite miraculously the day of the Lord purifies the nations
and allows them to serve Yahweh (3.8-9). Unlike Israel,
whose restoration is led by the remnant mentioned in 2.3, 7, 9,
and 11, the Gentiles' renewal comes without much warning.
God simply decrees, as their king, that they will worship Him.
This sudden change in character without explanation in the
text makes the nation a flat, passive character on one level,
since no development is discernible. On another plane, though,
the character's passiveness clearly demonstrates its relationship to Yahweh. God can and does order the nations as their
king, which is illustrated by their sudden transition. However,
the reader does not enjoy the gradual transformation evident
in the other figures in the Twelve, though the fact that the
heathen come to the Lord at all proves God's love for the cosmic people as well as Yahweh's determination to bless the
whole creation. Throughout Hosea–Zephaniah the fate of the
nations mirrors that of Israel. After sin comes inevitable, and
deserved, judgment, then the most rudimentary beginnings of
restoration. These stages of the Gentiles' history are not
emphasized as strongly as the same phases of Israel's story,
but they are evident nonetheless. In Haggai–Malachi a similar pattern persists, with Israel continuing to play the major
role, though the nations do not disappear.

Only the barest trace of the Gentiles appears in Haggai, but
Zechariah portrays the non-Jewish peoples in the traditional
manner as the enemy of Israel, and at the same time promises
that they will ultimately embrace Yahweh. As early as 2.11,
Zechariah optimistically characterizes the nations as part of
the people of God. The Lord will dwell among them even as He
lives in the midst of Israel. Zechariah sounds a less positive
note in 14.12-15, however, when he describes a Gentile army
cursed by God for besieging Jerusalem. This passage reminds
the reader of the angry characterizations in earlier books concerning the cruelty of the nations towards Israel. Unlike the
previous prophecies, which use the inhumanity of the Gentiles
to argue for their punishment, Zechariah turns this invasion
into an opportunity for the conversion of Israel's enemies

(14.16-21). Once God gives victory to the covenant people, the cosmic people share that triumph. God unites the earth's countries into one family. Thus Zechariah and Zephaniah combine to portray the Gentiles as an adopted child of God. After all, they are now the Lord's people (2.11) and share the feast of the tabernacles with Israel (14.16-19). From being a bitter foe of Israel and rebellious servant of Yahweh, the Gentiles have become as blessed as the original covenant people.

Except for an unflattering picture of Edom that relates more to its past than its future, Malachi adds little to the portrait of the nation's character. Since their restoration depends more on Yahweh's work than on an extensive renovation of lifestyle in the Twelve, it is not unexpected that Malachi fails to stress the nations' new status. Apparently, the Twelve wants to leave the reader with the impression that the renewal of the cosmic group is a certainty that awaits future fulfillment.

Whatever the reasoning behind the text as it stands, the gradual change of the Gentiles from fierce opponents of God to part of Yahweh's people clearly parallels the Twelve's plot. Along with Israel, the nations rebel, suffer, and come to God. The sin of the non-covenant countries is extreme, but no more so than that of the covenant people. Likewise, their restoration is just as dramatic as their foil's. Though not as significant a character as Israel, the Gentile figure helps to display the worldwide authority of God, and this character's renewal demonstrates the Lord's desire to rehabilitate the whole universe. So the nations help to illuminate the personality of Yahweh, and to demonstrate the evil side of Israel, and thereby they emerge as an effective minor persona in the overall scheme of the Twelve.

Conclusion

Some questions linger at the end of this chapter. Quite obviously, not every aspect of characterization in the Twelve has been covered. Perhaps the chief gap that must be filled at this point concerns the relationship of the development of the book's characters to its plot. Though the events of the Twelve affect the figures and *vice versa*, a summary of this intersecting of plot and character is in order at this point.

Within the U-shaped, comic story line of the Twelve, Yahweh serves as the individual for whom and through whom the events take place. God is the hero in that it is His desires, the obstacles to those desires, and the overcoming of the barriers to those wishes that constitute the plot of the Twelve. Yet the Lord is never seriously threatened by any foe, whether that enemy is Israel or one or all of the nations. Thus, God does not depend on anyone else to resolve the plot, which separates the Lord from typical comic heroes. All setbacks to the ultimate goals of Yahweh are removed by Yahweh alone.

Israel and the Gentiles function more like normal comic foils. They oppose one another at every turn, attempt to thwart the plans of the other, and try to achieve a higher rank than their opponent. Ironically, after the whole exhausting struggle, Zephaniah and Zechariah put them both on equal footing. As Habakkuk wisely observes:

> Has not the Lord Almighty determined that the people's labor is only fuel for the fire, that the nations exhaust themselves for nothing? For the earth will be filled with the knowledge of the glory of the Lord as the waters cover the sea (2.13-14).

Though ancient foes, Yahweh molds both covenant and cosmic peoples, mostly through judgment, into a single unit.

How the prophets fit the comic mold is more problematic. Maybe they are the friends who help overcome the crises of the plot, or perhaps they represent both God and the defeated enemies. Sometimes symbol, sometimes co-revelator, other times frustrated messenger, at all times the prophets are Israel's best hope to survive the Day of Yahweh. Perhaps this ambiguity of character provides a final clue to the prophets' personality, since they were often rejected by the very people they tried to serve. Yahweh, though, almost always seems pleased with 'His servants the prophets'.

Therefore, the development of the character of Israel and the nations from rebellious family and vassals to co-heirs of God's glory fits the sin-punishment-restoration pattern of the plot. Even God and the prophets adapt to the needs inherent in the story line. Yahweh is the spurned clan leader or king, the punishing father and sovereign, or the restoring deity depending on the stage of the plot. The prophets link themselves to the action by communicating and interpreting God's message to their audience, whether that message contains woe or joy. Yahweh's attitudes and actions grow out of the words and deeds of the covenant and cosmic peoples, so the characters mesh effectively. No major individual figure remains static in the Twelve, since all the personae must react to the ebb and flow of the plot. Consequently it is safe to argue that the structure, plot, and characterizations of the Twelve work harmoniously.

Chapter 6

THE TWELVE'S POINT OF VIEW

Introduction: Major Aspects of Point of View

Few areas of literary criticism are as complex as point of view. Numerous methodologies have been forwarded for examining the subject, many of which vary a great deal. Point of view is the process of discovering who tells a story, how it is told, how accurately it is told, and with what amount of knowledge and understanding it unfolds. All these aspects help reveal the vantage point from which an event is seen and narrated. As can be ascertained from the preceding definition, two subjects comprise the major concerns of point of view: who tells the story and how it is told. The first concern is usually handled under discussions about narrators and their audiences, and the second under the many types of narration.

In the past twenty to thirty years so many studies of point of view have appeared that the interpreter must select and use only those facets of the discipline that best illuminate the literature under scrutiny. Wallace Martin's excellent survey *Recent Theories of Narrative* demonstrates the current explosion of interest in the whole area of narration. In his chapter on point of view Martin notes four aspects that have normally characterized studies of the subject since Anne Barbauld's 1804 analysis of Samuel Richardson's fiction. Martin believes that

> though writers have discovered new methods of narration since Barbauld's time, her conceptual distinctions survive in recent criticism. First there is that of *grammatical person* or *voice*: who writes? Apart from experimental fiction, the narrator tells either a story about others... or one in which he or she is involved... Second, there are different *kinds* of *discourse*: narration, dramatic presentation (quoted dialogue or

monologue), and a catchall category often called 'comment-ary' (exposition, interpretation, judgment and possibly digressions interpolated by the narrator). *Access to con-sciousness* is a third basis of classification. The narrator may be able to enter many minds... or only one... and of course has the option of keeping the story in the outer world. *Time* and *tense* are also indispensable axes of analysis (1986: 131).

Each of these elements deals with the initiators of stories. In other words, they are concerned with the examination of how a plot unfolds from the storyteller's point of view.

R. Alan Culpepper shows that three terms are crucial to defining a storyteller's role in a plot: real author, implied author, and narrator (1983: 15-16). The real author is the individual who actually pens the contents of a literary piece. In the case of the Twelve one would have to uncover the historical figures who wrote the books and the person or persons who fixed the canonical order of the minor prophets to produce a real author of the work. For the purpose of this study there is no need to argue the authorship of each book. Such studies have been done, and done well, so the author's identity is not a trivial matter, but this book strives to analyze the literature the writers have produced rather than the writers themselves.

An implied author is the person the author chooses to embody thoughts, feelings, and values in a story. This figure speaks from outside the story rather from within it. Wayne Booth says: 'The "implied author" chooses, consciously or unconsciously, what we read; we infer him as an ideal, liter-ary, created version of the real man, he is the sum of his own choices' (1961: 74-75). Booth elaborates on this definition of the implied author when he argues that

> even the novel in which no narrator is dramatized creates an implicit picture of an author who stands behind the scenes whether as stage manager, as puppeteer, or as an indifferent God, silently paring his fingernails. This implied author is always distinct from the 'real man'—whatever we may take him to be—who creates a superior version of himself, a 'second self', as he creates his work... (1961: 151).

So the implied author represents the writer conceived by the reader, or the writer as implied by what a story stresses. The real author and implied author may or may not hold similar beliefs depending on the needs of the story. Sometimes there can be a gap between what a real author actually believes and does and the authorial image he projects in a work.

A narrator actually tells the story. Unlike the implied author, the narrator operates within the text as storyteller and, most times, interpreter of events. At least three types of narrators appear at some point in the Twelve. A first-person narrator, who refers to himself as 'I', speaks in biographical–symbolic passages like Hos. 3.1-5 and Zech. 11.4-17. This narrator reports as an eyewitness. Another kind of narrator is the third-peson narrator, who describes characters in the story as 'he', 'she', 'it', or 'them'. Jonah exhibits this brand of narration. The third-person type is often called an omniscient narrator, since this type speaks as more than an eyewitness, indeed speaks as an all-knowing chronicler of events. Adele Berlin describes the third-person narrator:

> In the case of biblical narrative, the narrator has a potentially omniscient perceptual point of view. He can be anywhere and everywhere, even inside the minds of the characters. The reader's perception is formed by what the narrator reveals of his omniscience and the way it is revealed. Thus, although the narrator potentially knows more than the reader, for practical purposes the perceptual viewpoints of the narrator and the reader coincide—the reader comes to see what the narrator sees (1983: 52).

As Berlin suggests, there are levels of knowledge that the omniscient narrators choose to reveal. Again, what the reader is allowed to learn grows from the special needs of each individual plot.

Besides the overt use of a narrator, many works present their story by using a dramatic approach. Here no intrusive voice arises in the text or presentation. Rather, the speeches and actions of characters create and explain what happens in a story. Edgar V. Roberts explains the dramatic approach when he notes that

> a writer using the *dramatic* point of view confines his work mainly to quotations and descriptions of actions. He avoids

> telling you that certain characters thought this or felt that,
> but instead allows the characters themselves to voice their
> thoughts and feelings... The key to the dramatic point of
> view is that the writer presents the reader with action and
> speech, but does not overtly guide the reader toward any con-
> clusion (1973: 57).

Large portions of the Twelve utilize this category of narration.
God and the prophet speak, each one taking a turn giving and
then interpreting messages. It is often possible to separate the
speeches only by noticing when Yahweh speaks in the first
person and when the prophet refers to the Lord in third person. At times, phrases like 'thus says the Lord' act as an
indicator for the reader that the speaker has changed.
Perhaps this point of view most involves the reader's own
thoughts and imagination.

Literary works vary as to how much the implied author or
narrator knows and tells. One first-person storyteller may be
more intrusive than another. A third-person narrator may
possess more knowledge and depth of understanding than a
like narrator in a different story. Some works are more effective proponents of dramatic presentation than others. The
reliability and authority of narrators also differ. Due to higher
knowledge, information, morality, understanding, or motives
some narrators are superior to their counterparts. For
instance, the opinions of Malachi are more accurate than
those of Israel in that book. When the type of narrator
emerges, his attitudes and accuracy can also be checked. In
short, how the story is told can be examined. These are the
core concerns of narration. It is not adequate to identify the
narrator without understanding his narration, or narrative
technique, as well.

Wayne Booth holds that the distance an implied author or
narrator maintains from the intended reader helps determine
a work's narrative technique, and lists five ways this distance
reveals itself. He asserts that:

> 1. The *narrator* may be more or less distant from the
>   *implied author*. The distance may be moral, intellec-
>   tual, or physical.

2. The *narrator* also may be more or less distant from the *characters* in the story he tells. This distance can be morally, intellectually, temporally, or emotionally.
3. The *narrator* may be more or less distant from the *reader's* own norms.
4. The *implied author* may be more or less distant from the *reader* intellectually, morally, or aesthetically.
5. The *implied author* (carrying the reader with him) may be more or less distant from other *characters* (1961: 156-58).

Each of these items can alter the plot and mood of a work. In the Twelve, it is especially important to concentrate on differences between the implied author and the narrator's norms and those of their audience. Likewise, there is often quite a distance between the perspective of the Lord and the prophets as opposed to that of Israel and the nations. Such narrative tensions help create the conflicts in the plot.

The preceding discussion has focused, obviously, on those telling the story. Just as obviously, however, these narrators must give their messages to an implied audience or narratee. If the implied author and the narrator have a purpose in what they say, then it is also true that they aim at a certain kind of audience. The implied audience is that group of people that seems to be the target of the narration. They are the recipients of the proclaimed values of the narrator or implied author.

One key to discovering, and interpreting, the minor prophets' implied author, narrator, and implied audience is to chart the distance between these parties. Booth observes, 'From the author's viewpoint, a successful reading of his book must eliminate all distance between the essential norms of his implied author and the norms of the postulated reader' (1963: 157). Many of the norms held by the characters in the Twelve have already been noted in earlier chapters, but will be reinforced now. In the minor prophets the implied author attempts to convince the audience of a way of thinking about, and reacting to, Yahweh that is foreign to their current behavior, but that is not foreign to what they should agree is correct. Through this effort much of the personality of the storytellers is revealed.

From this brief introduction three areas of analysis emerge that will help research on the unity or disunity of the Twelve. First, it is necessary to describe the goals, aims, and moral values of the implied author, since this figure's profile is vital to the interpretation of the other narrative participants. Second, the type of narration inherent in the Twelve must be handled. Within this area falls all types of narration and narrators. Third, the implied audience must be discussed. This audience's position, moral norms, and goals require exploration if the implied author and narrator's roles are to have any value. Without an audience the storytellers speak in a vacuum. After these aspects of the minor prophets have been introduced their relevance to the unity of the Twelve will be assessed.

It should be noted that this chapter makes no attempt to peel back the redactional layers of the Book nor to theorize about the editors of those layers. Various authors, beginning with R.E. Wolfe (1935), have tried to produce such studies, so redactional analyses of the minor prophets do play a role in minor prophets study. Once more, however, it is the final form of the Twelve that is in question here. This final text represents the only redactional level we possess for sure, is the text endorsed by the believing community, and is important enough on its own merit to warrant explication. However these books were passed down to the present day, the final result is the text as it now stands.

The Twelve's Implied Author

As Booth suggests, the implied author is the individual 'who stands behind the scenes' (1963: 151), the narrative persona who sets the tone for a work by creating its agenda. This agenda may include praise or condemnation of the reader, and could either hope to change the audience for the better, or desire to lay that group open for destruction. After all, Jonah preached to an audience without wanting it to repent, Nahum spoke of a nation he knew would not change, and Haggai addressed people who he saw mend their ways. The distance between the implied author's agenda and the characters in the story's attitudes and actions helps produce a portrait of the

implied author and the implied audience. Thus these aspects
are highlighted below.

The shape of the Twelve and the historical references contained in the text obviously point to a post-exilic date for the
final form of the minor prophets. Otto Eissfeldt observes that
Jesus ben Sira (49.10) mentions the Twelve prophets, notes
that the collection could not have been gathered until the last
of the books was written, and concludes the earliest date for
the collection would be 300 BC (1966: 383). Eissfeldt reasons
that

> the lower limit is provided by the above-mentioned passage
> in ben Sira at the beginning of the second century, so that we
> may consider the collection to have come into being as a unit
> in the course of the third century. Probably the redactor no
> longer knew the twelve books as independent entities. It is
> likely that some of them had already, at an earlier time, been
> gathered into smaller collections, just as smaller collections
> underlie the books of Isaiah, Jeremiah, and Ezekiel.
> Nothing more precise than this can be said, since the
> evidence which is relevant here is capable of more than one
> interpretation (1966: 383-384).

Even if one places the completion of the final form of the book
closer to the date of Malachi, the result is the same: the Twelve
took its present form during post-exilic times, or, more
specifically, from 400-300 BC. The significance of this conclusion for the discussion of the Twelve's implied author is that
the interpreter must start from the vantage point of the post-
exilic community. It is impossible to act as if the exile had
never occurred, and quite probably the books are ordered to
impact post-exilic Israel and all future readers.

At the very outset of the minor prophets the high moral
standards of the implied author emerge. Indeed this figure
strives to hold the same perspective as the Lord. Hosea 1–3
introduces the values of the implied author even as it offers an
outline of the plot and characters of the Twelve. Because the
minor prophets begin with Hosea, the persona behind the text
evidently believes Israel has consistently prostituted its
covenant with the Lord. The presence of Hosea's prediction of
the exile and return in 3.4-5 indicates that the implied author
blames this prostitution for the catastrophic events of the

destruction of Jerusalem and the resulting exile, as well as for the fall of Samaria. Further, the implied author presents the Lord and the prophet as working together as co-revelators in chs. 4–14 in an attempt to bring the nation to repentance. Despite these efforts, though, Israel never responds.

In Joel, the sins of the nations are added to those of the covenant people (cf. 3.1-16). It would be redundant to enumerate the sins of Israel and the Gentiles again here, but it is appropriate to declare that the implied author is in total agreement with Yahweh's assessments of the iniquities of the covenant and cosmic peoples. Nowhere is there any underlying protest of anyone's innocence in Hosea–Micah. Consequently, whatever judgment God levies meets with the approval of the implied author, and, except for the probing questions of Habakkuk, which are fully answered, the punishment described in Nahum–Zephaniah is accepted. What is significant about the implied author's opinions on sin and punishment is that these viewpoints are meant to teach the post-exilic community (and future readers) why the exile took place. Just as importantly, these lessons from the past may help the Book's audience avoid the mistakes of pre-587 Israel.

Despite his opinions on sin, the implied author emphasizes that God's ultimate goal for Israel is to restore and bless the nation. Hints that obedience can ward off destruction abound in Hosea–Zephaniah. Beginning with Hos. 3.4-5, which claims Israel will be restored after a time of dwelling 'without king or prince, without sacrifice or sacred stones, without ephod or idol' (3.4), Hosea consistently offers opportunities for Israel to repent. The prophet encourages the people to 'acknowledge' Yahweh so they can be forgiven and blessed (6.1-3), claims that the Lord will refuse to give up Israel (11.8-11), and predicts a time of future restoration will come (14.4-8). Joel furthers the restoration theme by declaring that every segment of Israel's society will be filled with God's Spirit in 2.28-32. Eventually, Joel believes, Israel will be blessed above all nations of the earth since Israel will flourish while the Gentiles will languish in judgment (3.17-21).

Even the prophecies that are most adamant about the guilt of Israel and her neighbors offer passages on hope. Amos says that after the Day of Yahweh the Lord 'will restore David's fallen tent' (9.11-15), Obadiah thinks that, though Jerusalam has been destroyed, there remains a future for the covenant people (vv. 17-21), Jonah notes that there is even hope for the Gentiles, and Micah believes that 'in the last days' (4.1), many nations will join with Israel in the worship of the Lord (4.1-5). The punishment section likewise reflects hope, since Nahum claims Nineveh may fall, but the elect nation will eventually stand (1.15-2.2), Habakkuk looks forward to redemption (3.12-19), and Zephaniah lists numerous blessings for Jews and Gentiles alike after the day Yahweh purges the earth (3.8-20). Of course, Haggai–Malachi begins the process of restoration all these texts describe.

Evidently, the implied author believes in the importance and probability of restoration because of a strong confidence in the mercy of God, the ability of the Day of Yahweh to achieve its purpose of cleansing the earth, and the desire of the remnant to accomplish the tasks God sets for it. Certainly the mercy of God emerges at several places in the minor prophets, including during calls to repentance (Hos. 11.8-11) and times of punishment (Nah. 1.3, 7-8). Likewise, the presence of the restoration section of the Twelve shows how much confidence the implied author places in the redemptive nature of God's universal purging of sin. Speaking as a post-exilic figure, who has hopes for the remnant of which he is a part, the implied author's inclusion of passages revealing the obedience of Israel (Hag. 1.13-15; Zech. 1.6; Mal. 3.16) demonstrates his belief that the chosen people have learned not to ignore God. Because of the exile, they are more apt to follow the advice of the prophets as well. Throughout the Twelve the implied author expresses the conviction that when the remnant finally survives the Day of Yahweh it will provide Israel with leadership pleasing to the Lord. Micah thinks that once the remnant is gathered (2.12) it will both receive God's blessings and be a blessing to other countries (5.7-8). Zephaniah furthers the picture of the group by claiming that all hope for the world rests in the creation of a holy remnant (3.8-20). Clearly Haggai presents the people of his day, especially their leader Zerubbabel, as at least the beginnings of a faithful nation. Perhaps the only shade of doubt arises in Malachi, where many problems are mentioned, but even there it is the faithful remnant's repentance that leads to the ultimate hope of 'Elijah's' coming (3.16–4.6; 3.16-24 in Hebrew). At no point, then, does the implied author cease to believe that the nucleus for the kind of nation Yahweh desires already exists within the people. A better future depends on the actions of the remnant in the present.

When the above-mentioned traits are collected at least a thumbnail sketch of the implied author can be made. Who stands 'behind the scenes' of the Twelve? An individual who decries the sins of the covenant and cosmic people, agrees with their judgment, and just as adamantly clings to the promise of their renewal. This person is pro-remnant and therefore pro-Judah, but also teaches that God has a plan for the whole creation. As a post-exilic persona, the implied author thinks the covenant group has learned from its mistakes and envisions a glorious future for them. Despite such enthusiasm, however, the implied author knows the faults of the community, as Malachi aptly attests. The message to the remnant is that God's blessings are a certainty, but it is only so to the generation that serves the Lord. Thus, realism balances hope, and hope guides realism.

In many ways the implied author corresponds closely to the character of Yahweh, After all, behind every prophetic messenger and co-revelator stands the Lord. Indeed if Yahweh dwells among the people (cf. Hag. 2.5), then He shares the perspective of the righteous remnant of post-exilic times. The implied author agrees with Yahweh's position on sin, punishment, and restoration, and trusts in the influence of the messianic figures Haggai, Zechariah, and Malachi mention. By tying the implied author so closely to the picture of the Lord, the Twelve takes the first step in unifying narration and characterization.

Types of Narrators and Narration in the Twelve

Because of its diverse background and purpose, the Twelve utilizes more than one form of narration. In keeping with its portrayal of many-faceted characters, the Book develops more than one narrator. Though each narrator and narrative type works to produce a coherent story, part of the richness of the literature grows out of the Twelve's deft usage of narrative materials. This section attempts to chart the occurrences of first, third, and dramatic forms of narrative presentation and to introduce the kinds of narrators such forms produce.

Hosea 1–3 familiarizes the reader with all three types of narration and, thus, with all three narrators. Chapter 1 tells the story of Hosea's marriage in third person. Hosea is referred to as 'him', so no autobiographical account appears. Similarly the narrator is not a character in the story, so there exists some distance between the action and the storyteller. What distance there is, however, occurs between the norms of the narrator and the audience rather than between the values of God and the narrator. In fact, the narrator seems to share Yahweh's displeasure with Gomer's and Israel's sin. Third-person narrators have often been called 'omniscient', because they can know what a character does and why the character acts in that manner. In this chapter, though, as in much of biblical narrative, the author presents a scene and allows the reader to judge a character's motivation. The psychological reasons for a persona's deeds are not directly explained. As Robert Alter says, the narrator's

> typically monotheistic decision is to lead us to know as flesh-and-blood knows: character is revealed primarily through speech, action, gesture, with all the ambiguity that entails; motive is frequently, though not invariably, left in a penumbra of doubt; often we are able to draw plausible inferences about the personages and their destinies, but much remains a matter of conjecture or even of teasing multiple possibilities (1981: 158).

Certainly, Gomer's actions are bad enough, as are those of Israel, so bad in fact that the motivation behind them matters little. Hosea presents the action as a life drama and reports how the prophet's life and the nation's sin coincide.

Chapter 2 of Hosea displays the most prevalent type of narration in the Twelve. This passage uses direct speech, this time by Yahweh, to convey the prophetic message, a method that dominates chs. 4–14. God explains Israel's chastisement (2.1-13), and then enumerates the nation's future blessings (2.14-23). In chs. 4–14, as in Joel, Obadiah, Micah, Nahum,

Habakkuk, Zephaniah, and parts of Zechariah, God shares the speaking with the prophet, which illustrates the dramatic nature of the presentation still more. Even Amos (except for 7.10-17), through a messenger-style book, and Malachi, which uses a question-answer format, unfold through direct, dramatized speeches. Only Jonah and Haggai of all the Twelve have no alternating speeches, so it is plausible to conclude that dramatic narration is the most important narrative mode in the minor prophets. Indeed Alter argues that Old Testament narrators in general, after 'beginning with narration'

> move into dialogue, drawing back momentarily or at length to narrate again, but always centering on the sharply salient verbal intercourse of the characters, who act upon one another, discover themeselves, affirm or expose their relation to God, through the force of language (1981: 75).

This dramatic narration does not allow for third-person intrusion. Only the characters reveal who they are and what they are doing.

Finally, ch. 3 presents the Hosea–Gomer, Yahweh–Israel story in autobiographical fashion. The prophet himself notes that 'the Lord spoke to me' (3.1), 'I bought her' (3.2), 'I told her' (3.3), and 'I will live with you' (3.3), and mediates the future of Israel directly (3.4-5). Hosea's personal narration parallels the personal concern the Lord has for Israel. In fact, ch. 3 parallels ch. 2, since God restores His 'wife' in 2.1-23, while Hosea recovers Gomer in 3.1-5. Zechariah explains his visions and symbolic acts in the first person, and Habakkuk also speaks in the autobiographical mode, so the form occurs elsewhere. Probably the most significant point about first-person narration is that it allows the reader to identify with the emotions of the prophets. Otherwise they can become almost god-like themselves instead of the reader's fellow struggler.

When first- and third-person narration occurs some specific aspects of the prophetic office surface. More specifically, the prophets either act as symbols or present their messenger visions in first- and third-person narration. Hosea illustrates the symbolic purpose, since both 1.1-11 and 3.1-5 characterize the prophet as a representative of God's relationship with Israel. Amos' short biographical pericope (7.10-17) serves a similar function. Like the whole sinful nation, Amaziah, the priest, rejects the prophetic message from Yahweh (cf. 2.12; 7.12-13). Consequently, the priest bears the punishment his sins warrant, but his punishment takes on a national perspective, for, after sentencing Amaziah, Amos predicts: 'And Israel will certainly go into exile, away from their native land' (7.17). Fitted between other sections dealing with Israel's destruction, this passage uses an event from Amos' life to demonstrate that the nation will fall because of the sins of its people.

Clearly Jonah's third-person narrated story also casts the prophet in a symbolic light (cf. ch. 5). Again, though told through a narrator who does not participate in the story, very little authorial intrusion arises in Jonah. Jonah's actions and speeches speak for themselves, and, without the Lord's question about the prophet's right to be angry (4.9), the reader would be left to ponder Jonah's motives alone. Very little narration really occurs. Jonah's speeches and activities are reported with a subtlety that bids the audience to think in order to ascertain the finer details of the plot. Whatever the intent of the narrator, though, Jonah's status as sinner can hardly be questioned. His story proves the cosmic scope of sin through the iniquity of Nineveh, as well as the covenant side of sin through his own disobedience and hatred. The most telling fact about Jonah's life is that it symbolizes the total depravity of Israel, for, if the prophets, God's special envoys, are corrupt, the nation has sunk low indeed.

Habakkuk deserves a special category all its own in many of the literary aspects of the Twelve this book describes. Always a pivotal book, the work employs a unique narrative system. Though both Yahweh and Habakkuk speak in the book, autobiographical material also appears. Habakkuk asks: 'How long, O Lord, must I call for help, but you do not listen?' in (1.2), declares 'I will stand at my watch' in 2.1, and begins the final chapter by stating: 'Lord I have heard of your fame; I stand in awe of your deeds' (3.2). At least two symbolic purposes are served in Habakkuk's first-person sections. First, Habakkuk represents the confusion the righteous remnant feels at the coming of the Day of Yahweh. Though no sin of theirs has precipitated judgment, they must learn to live by faith (2.4) and wait for salvation from the Lord (3.6). A second symbolic, or representative, feature of Habakkuk's struggles is that the reader observes how the prophet receives his oracle. The give and take between the Lord and the prophet chronicled in Habakkuk shows God's word was not produced outside the arena of human pain. So Habakkuk represents the prophets' desire to gain a message from God, and the attempt of the righteous to grasp the ways of Yahweh.

Zechariah's symbolic passage (11.4-17) condemns the foolish shepherds of Israel. Throughout the prophetic section of the canon, priests and prophets who mislead the people are denounced. Here such leaders are blamed for a breach in the relationship between Yahweh and all creation. This representative act shows the wickedness of both covenant and cosmic groups, and reminds the reader of earlier negative symbolic texts like Hosea 1–3 and the book of Jonah.

Various prophetic visions are narrated in first or third person. Amos 7.1-3, 4-6, 7-9, and 8.1-3 begin with the phrase: 'This is what the Lord showed me' or a similar caption, and 9.1 claims 'I saw the Lord'. These judgment oracles assume more power because of the visual effects the reader gains by imagining the prophet standing in the presence of God while receiving the messages. Haggai notes when the word of God 'came' to the prophet, what the prophet said, and how the people responded, all in the third person. Though not technically visions, Haggai's 'words' have the same form as Zechariah's early dated visions. Haggai's story is basically told without comment, which reveals the narrator's desire to display the excellence of Haggai's work as an effective messenger of God. As with the Amos oracles, the first-person narrated visions of Zechariah gain an authentic tone because they are eyewitness accounts. Lest the audience doubt the veracity of such odd descriptions of God's message, the prophet explains what he saw and heard. Zechariah's reception and sharing of visions characterized him, along with Haggai, as one of Yahweh's true messengers, so the storyteller links narration to one of the book's chief characterizations of the prophet.

Though it is impossible to pinpoint the identity of the non-dramatic narrator with absolute accuracy, it is likely that the figure seeks to highlight the role of the prophets. Whenever first or third-person narration surfaces it does so to emphasize the symbolic or messenger facets of the prophetic character. Both traits occur to grab the audience's attention by *showing* them God's word or by alerting them to the fact that a sermon has come directly from Yahweh's mouth. That these are important messages becomes even more evident when the reader realizes the normal narrative pattern has been broken to offer these warnings.

Very seldom, if ever, does any striking narrative voice appear in the majority of the Twelve. Of course an implied author stands behind even dramatic narration, but all other information on plot, themes, and characters comes from the personae themselves. Therefore, much of the minor prophets' viewpoint on those literary categories has already been discussed in Chapter 5.

Despite the fact that the chapter on characterization helps explain the viewpoints of the Book's major figures, the role of the prophet in dramatized narration deserves some mention. Whether as symbol, messenger, or co-revelator the prophet mediates the thoughts of Yahweh to other human beings. The prophet either narrates God's word directly, with comment, elaboration, or further revelation, or by action. Each of the prophets stands between the Lord and the world, both having communion with God (Amos 3.7-8) and living among the people (cf. Haggai). Wayne Booth calls narrators who speak from within a story either 'observers' or 'narrator agents'. He explains that

> among dramatized narrators there are mere observers (the 'I' of *Tom Jones, The Egoist, Troilus and Criseyole*), and there are narrator agents, who produce some measurable effect on the course of events (ranging from the minor involvement of Nick in *The Great Gatsby*, through the extensive give-and-take of Marlow in *Heart of Darkness*, to the central role of Tristram Shandy, Moll Flanders, Huckleberry Finn and—in the third person Paul Morel in *Sons and Lovers*) (1961: 153-54).

Certainly, some prophets impact their dramatized works more than others, yet each reacts more as an involved narrator agent than 'mere observer'. The speeches of Hosea, Joel, etc. help move the plot from exposition to resolution, though clearly Hosea has more impact on the Twelve's overall plot than Obadiah, for instance. Unlike Yahweh, the narrator agents are not all-knowing, instead they must react to impulses from God to develop their speeches. Just as they depend on the Lord to know how to speak, so also the nation relies on the prophet for knowledge of how to please Yahweh. As neither deity not ordinary worshiper, the prophets have the opportunity to build bridges between heaven and earth.

The narrator agents live through and explain the cycles of sin, punishment, and restoration Israel experiences. Hosea and Amos suffer through the self-destructive transgressions of Samaria. Habakkuk puzzles over how God punishes sin. Malachi struggles to help the post-exilic community be the remnant of Yahweh. In the midst of problems, however, God's narrator agents declare better times to come. Though the Lord's complaint is not ultimately with the prophets, it is their task in the Twelve to bear the responsibility of reconciling Creator and creation. The prophetic speeches in the minor prophets give evidence of the power and conviction that typified the prophets' attempt to carry out the mission.

Because each type of narration found in the Twelve focuses on the prophet's task, the Book's narration relates to the characterization of the prophets much as the implied author's identity seems closely tied to the depiction of Yahweh. Much of the time the dramatized prophet acts as co-revelator, or narrator agent, in short, as the individual who fulfills Amos 3.7-8. Though very little commentary exists in the first- and third-person sections, the intent of the narrator seems to be to focus on the prophets' messenger and symbolic qualities. Certainly, the perspective the reader gains is that of the prophet whether a passage stresses sin, condemnation, or renewal. It is the prophet's mediated message that appears in the text. Far from making the Twelve redundant, however, this interlacing of narration and characterization rather creates an indissoluble bond between the story and its storyteller. By presenting the narrator as prophet, the text also gains an authority and credibility that surfaces simply because the prophets, those God always consults, stand behind the entire literary piece.

The Twelve's Implied Audience

It is not always easy to identify a work's implied audience. Different works vary as to how much they identify their reader. Because of the audience-oriented nature of prophecy, though, the group the Twelve addresses is more obvious than in other literary pieces. Two items are vital to the discussion of the minor prophets' implied audience. First, the distance between the implied reader and the Book's implied author and narrator helps identify the intended audience. Second, because of its position in the canon and historical background Malachi's message may reveal some characteristics of the implied audience.

There are several ways a narrator and/or an implied author may create distance between himself and an audience. In fact, it is possible for there to be distance between a narrator and an implied author, but that situation does not arise in the Twelve. Wayne Booth suggests that a writer may separate himself from a reader in at least three ways: intellectually, qualitatively, or practically (1961: 125). The first term relates to the idea that a reader may not possess as many facts as the author (1961: 125). The second item means that readers expect certain plot elements in a work, such as cause and effect in the story line, conventional forms like a certain number of lines in a sonnet, basic artistic patterns like balance, symmetry, etc., and some individual artistic qualities (1961: 125-28). Finally, the third term is concerned with the moral aspects of the characters and audience (1961: 131). In a work so closely related to moral values as the Twelve, it is natural that the piece's main focus is on practical, or moral distance. How great a gap exists between what both God and the prophets teach and do and the thoughts and deeds of the nation, Israel, and the remnant determines the status of the implied audience.

In Hosea–Zephaniah the writers attempt to instruct the audience about a variety of vital concerns. Foremost among these interests is the debilitating effect of sin, a theme which dominates Hosea–Micah. From these books, post-exilic Israel learns why the nation has suffered the judgment of God and thus how to avoid that punishment in the future. Just as the pre-exilic group could have repented and avoided the Day of the Lord (Hos. 6.1-3), so the new people can serve God whole-heartedly and, thereby, continually enjoy the Lord's blessings (Mal. 3.17-18). Nahum–Zephaniah warns Israel of the devastating nature of judgment, since the post-exilic audience did not live through that time period. Beyond the lessons of judgment, the text seeks to alert the audience that they can receive the restoration of fortunes delineated in Zeph. 3.14-20. This generation must be the body that accepts the covenant and assumes the role of the remnant.

Haggai, Zechariah, and Malachi are very instructive in the area of how well the present covenant group is fulfilling the predictions of Zephaniah. Though Hag. 1.13-15 and Zech. 1.6 reflect progress in Israel's responsiveness to God, Malachi's messages reveal some barriers to their full restoration. Malachi warns that the people have slipped back into living as if God does not love them (1.2-5). In other words, they have regressed to the point of becoming like Gomer again (cf. Hos. 2.1-23). The covenant means little to them, as their blemished sacrifices, careless priests, and unfaithfulness attest. Unless the community changes, the whole cycle of sin, punishment, and restoration may start anew (Mal. 4.1-6). Therefore, Malachi reveals that the implied audience is having difficulty acting like the remnant. But there are still individuals who fear God (3.16-18), so the situation is not hopeless. The constant warnings and promises that dot the whole body of the Twelve likewise point to a group that can still repent before fresh judgment comes.

Several kinds of distance exist between the implied author and his audience. First, and perhaps most importantly, the audience's norms are not always those of the storyteller. In Hosea–Micah there is no evidence that the readers accept the standards set forth by these prophecies. Israel never repents (though Nineveh does in Jonah), never changes and never follows Yahweh. Apparently the people have their own standards of conduct, as the presence of the Jeroboam cult in Amos

7.10-17 indicates. Even in Haggai–Malachi it is not possible to tell if the implied audience embraces God's ways or not. If Malachi best represents the post-exilic situation, the limited obedience recounted in Haggai and Zechariah may serve to spotlight present iniquity. In this scheme, the earlier returning Israelis act more appropriately than their later counterparts.

Another gap between the implied author and reader revolves around the future. In Haggai and Malachi the people behave as if the nation has no future. As a country composed of returned exiles a lack of hope has engulfed the people. No one takes the temple or its cult seriously, because they believe God's love has left them (Mal. 1.2), and because they have had little financial success (Hag. 1.5-11). Anyone else surveying the scene would call the situation hopeless, but each of the three books, especially Zechariah, envisions a bright future for Israel as the key to the restoration of the whole earth (Zech. 14.16-21). God promises to bless the remnant (Hag. 2.10-19; Zech. 8.6-13; Mal. 3.16–4.6). What the implied audience seemingly cannot understand is that they are to be that remnant.

Finally, the implied audience differs from the implied author intellectually in that they have failed to grasp the significance of the overall sweep of Israel's history. Because of their situation, the post-exilic community focuses on the present. Malachi notes that the people have lost all sense of Yahweh's historical covenant with Israel (1.2-5), have not learned the importance of temple sacrifice (1.6-14), and have forgotten the most basic commandments (2.10-16). It is hard to tell where indifference stops and ignorance begins. Only a few of the people understand the ramifications of the Day of Yahweh and live accordingly (3.16-18). To erase this lack of understanding the potential remnant must study all the major motifs of the Twelve. Once grasped, the message of the minor prophets will educate Israel about the past, present, and future.

What can be surmised, then, about the implied audience? From the collected information the implied readers are part of the post-exilic community. This group now enjoys some of the blessings promised to the remnant, such as land, temple, safety, etc., but it has slipped into sin due to negligence and indifference. The prophets teach that restoration is inevitable, yet they always emphasize that the Lord is not bound to carry out this renewal in *their* generation. All restoration belongs to the faithful remnant through whom even the 'heathen' will come to Yahweh (Zech. 2.11-13). Undoubtedly there remains some hope that the implied audience may yet fulfill its great potential. For audiences beyond post-exilic times the message remains the same: God will aid those who change their ways and worship Him alone.

Of all the characters in the Twelve the implied audience relates the closest to the remnant. This observation is particularly accurate if the remnant is expanded to include all, regardless of race, who 'call on the name of the Lord and serve Him shoulder to shoulder' (Zeph. 3.9). The group in post-exilic Israel that would derive the most encouragement from identifying with the implied audience would be the remnant, and the remnant's numbers could swell if the implied audience takes its warnings seriously. In some ways, however, the implied audience also identifies with the nations and sinful Israel because of the Twelve's constant calls to repentance in each of its major sections. It is the sinful, after all, who need to join the remnant. All in all, the implied audience requires instruction, encouragement, chastening, and guidance. Each of these needs brings the reader not to Yahweh or the prophet, but to those who ought to respond to the message those characters present. So, even here the Twelve unites narration and characterization.

Conclusion

Every feature of the Twelve's narration has some close connection with its characterization (cf. Chart 3). The ultimate viewpoint of the minor prophets strives to match the intentions of the Lord. Thus, the implied author, the person behind the whole book, is the Lord, as the prophets themselves would claim. As for the narrator, the person who mediates the message of the implied author to the audience, that role falls to the prophets. They are God's narrator agents. Since sinful Israel, remnant Israel, and the sinful and remnant Gentiles are

God's foils in the story, it is logical that these figures represent the implied audience. These correspondences give the text symmetry and coherence.

Two factors have contributed to the brevity of this chapter. The initial reason is that much that the narration reveals has already been covered. A study that focused primarily on narration would doubtlessly cast those items in a different manner. This analysis begins with genre instead of narration, so other literary facets have helped abbreviate the explication of narration. A second, more important, factor is that the preponderance of dramatic narration in the Twelve somewhat limits the extent of narrative scrutiny. Even when the minor prophets employ first and third-person storytelling the events are normally presented without extensive commentary. Therefore, even narrated prophecy exhibits dramatic tendencies. Where the implied author and narrator choose to remain totally anonymous the interpreter should allow them that privilege.

Chart 3: Narrative Features in the Twelve

Narration	*Characterization*
The Implied Author	Yahweh
The Narrator	The Prophet
The Implied Audience	Covenant and Cosmic Remnant

Chapter 7

EPILOGUE

Needless to say, it is my conviction that the minor prophets are arranged as a unified literary work. If I understand the prophetic genre in at least a rudimentary way—by no means an established conclusion—the structure, plot, characterization, and narration of the Twelve, indeed most of what makes a literary piece a coherent construction, operate together. The structure and plot present a story, the characters give life to that story, and the narrative framework provides an audience for whom the story is intended.

A number of things could improve an understanding of the Twelve's unity. More work needs to be done on the structure of the prophecies. Perhaps a chiastic framework can be found that will better explicate the books' interrelatedness. The plot, too, deserves more treatment. Only the most basic elements of the story line are covered here, and, due to the length of the study, many subplots, digressions, and foreshadowings had to be omitted. I sense that many parts of the plot are much more interrelated then I have presented. For instance, Hosea's introductory book seems to have many parallels with Malachi's closing prophecy.

As for characterization, the role of other minor figures could be considered. Obadiah mentions an 'envoy' (1.1), Joel may include individuals in his presentation (cf. 1.10?), Gomer is an intriguing figure, and certain players in Jonah, because of their membership among the Gentiles, could aid the perception of the cosmic people's place in the Twelve's overall scheme. How the prophets are characterized needs elaboration so the prophetic movement can be better grasped. Surely Amos is a different kind of messenger than Zechariah, and Hosea's co-revelation does not mirror Zephaniah's. Even the means by which the prophets say they received their messages could become clearer through some in-depth studies of Amos, Habakkuk, Haggai, and Zechariah.

Some attention needs to be paid to the effect of dramatic narration in the minor prophets. Scholars often mention the presence of alternating speeches in the prophecies, yet few explain why this pattern makes any difference in the presentation of the oracles. Also, the functions of non-dramatic narration need exploration. Especially in books like Zechariah, where all types of narration occur, there must be some reason the text shifts from one format to the next. Through such studies perhaps even some of the roles of prose and poetry in prophecy may be at least partially revealed.

Many of the aesthetic qualities of the Twelve have been left out so the basic aspects of the work could be included. Irony, poetic imagery, dialogue, and setting are just a few of the items that deserve development. These elements of the Twelve should be analyzed so that the artistic abilities of the authors can be highlighted.

Besides all these considerations, the historical data surrounding the canonical order of the books, slight as it is, may require some re-evaluation. Particularly important in this area is the Septuagint's ordering, because it varies from the Hebrew tradition. Yet, the last six books are positioned the same in both versions. No doubt the first six prophecies can serve as a chronicle of sin in either tradition. It is also possible that the Greek text reflects an early attempt to place the books in some historical order, a task foreign to the logic behind the Hebrew canon. If studied alongside other variations between the Hebrew and Greek Bibles, perhaps some new light on the canonical process could surface.

There is absolutely no way to verify that the pattern I have proposed was *exactly* what the original shapers of the Book of the Twelve had in mind. Because of the literary evidence, however, I do not believe this pattern is a contrived scheme forced on the text. The task has been at least in part an exegetical one, so the evidence for my theory's validity, or lack thereof, resides in the text itself. Certainly there could be other reasons these prophecies have always been considered one book, but the literary intentionality of the text argues that whatever further unity surfaces will probably grow out of its stylistic symmetry.

BIBLIOGRAPHY

BOOKS

Alden, R.
> 1965   'Malachi', *The Expositor's Bible Commentary*, Vol 7. Grand Rapids: Zondervan.

Allen, L.C.
> 1976   *The Books of Joel, Obadiah, Jonah and Micah*, The New International Commentary on the Old Testament. Grand Rapids: Eerdmans.

Alter, R.
> 1981   *The Art of Biblical Narrative*. New York: Basic Books.
> 1985   *The Art of Biblical Poetry*. New York: Basic Books.

Aristotle
> 1974   *Poetics*, trans. S.H. Butcher. *Dramatic Theory and Criticism: Greeks to Grotowski*, ed. B.F. Dukore. New York: Holt, Rinehart & Winston.

Armerding, C.E.
> 1985   'Nahum', *The Expositor's Bible Commentary*, Vol. 7. Grand Rapids: Zondervan.

Barker, K.L.
> 1985   'Zechariah', *The Expositor's Bible Commentary*, Vol. 7. Grand Rapids: Zondervan.

Baldwin, J.
> 1972   *Haggai, Zechariah, Malachi*, Vol. 7. Grand Rapids: Eerdmans.

Berlin, A.
> 1985   *The Dynamics of Biblical Parallelism*. Bloomington: Indiana University Press.
> 1983   *Poetics and Interpretation of Biblical Narrative*. Sheffield: Almond.

Bewer, J.
> 1911   *A Critical and Exegetical Commentary on Obadiah and Joel*, The International Critical Commentary. New York: Scribner's.

Blenkinsopp, J.
> 1977   *Prophecy and Canon: A Contribution to the Study of Jewish Origins*. Notre Dame, In.: University of Notre Dame.

Booth, W.C.
> 1961   *The Rhetoric of Fiction*. Chicago: University of Chicago.

Bullock, C.H.
    1986   *An Introduction to the Old Testament Prophetic Books.* Chicago: Moody.
Carroll, R.P.
    1986   *Jeremiah*, Old Testament Library. Philadelphia: Westminster.
Childs, B.
    1980   *Introduction to the Old Testament as Scripture.* Philadelphia: Fortress.
Clements, R.E.
    1976   *One Hundred Years of Old Testament Interpretation.* Philadelphia: Westminster.
Cohon, B.D.
    1939   *The Prophets: Their Personalities and Teachings.* New York: Scribner's.
Craigie, P.C.
    1984   *Twelve Prophets*, Vol. 1. Philadelphia: Westminster.
Culpepper, R.A.
    1983   *Anaatomy of the Fourth Gospel: A Study in Literary Design.* Philadelphia: Fortress.
Driver, S.R.
    1901   *Joel and Amos*, Cambridge Bible. London: Cambridge University Press.
    1906   *The Minor Prophets*, Vol. II, The Century Bible. Edinburgh: Jack.
Duhm, B.
    1922   *Das Buch Jesaia.* Göttingen: Vandenhoeck & Ruprecht.
Eissfeldt, O.
    1966   *The Old Testament: An Introduction*, trans. P.R. Ackroyd. Evanston: Harper & Row.
Fowler, A.
    1982   *Kinds of Literature.* Cambridge, Ma.: Harvard University.
Frye, N.
    1967   *Anatomy of Criticism.* New York: Atheneum.
    1982   *The Great Code: The Bible and Literature.* New York: Harcourt Brace Jovanovich.
Good, E.H.
    1981   *Irony in the Old Testament*, 2nd edn. Sheffield: Almond.
Hammershaimb, E.
    1970   *The Book of Amos: A Commentary*, trans. J. Sturdy. Oxford: Blackwell.
Harper, W.R.
    1905   *A Critical and Exegetical Commentary on Amos and Hosea*, International Critical Commentary. New York: Scribner's.
Hillers, D.R.
    1984   *Micah*, Hermeneia Series. Philadelphia: Fortress.
Holman, C.H.
    1972   *A Handbook to Literature*, 3rd edn. New York: Odyssey.

Kaiser, O.
  1977   *Introduction to the Old Testament: A Presentation of its Results and Problems*, trans. J. Sturdy. Minneapolis: Augsburg.

Keil, C.F.
  1980   *The Minor Prophets*, trans J. Martin, Commentary on the Old Testament, Vol. 10, 1869, rpt. Grand Rapids: Eerdmans.

Kelley, P.H.
  1984   *Micah, Nahum, Habakkuk, Zephaniah, Haggai, Malachi*, The Layman's Bible Commentary, Vol. 14. Nashville: Broadman.

Kerr, W.
  1967   *Tragedy and Comedy*. New York: Simon & Schuster.

Kugel, J.
  1981   *The Idea of Biblical Poetry*. New Haven: Yale University.

La Sor, W.S., D.A. Hubbard & F.W. Bush
  1985   *Old Testament Survey: The Message, Form and Background of the Old Testament*. Grand Rapids: Eerdmans.

Lewis, C.S.
  1959   *A Preface to Paradise Lost*. London: Oxford University Press.

Lindblom, J.
  1962   *Prophecy in Ancient Israel*. Philadelphia: Muhlenberg.

Lowth, R.
  1829   *Lectures on the Sacred Poetry of the Hebrews*, trans. G. Gregory. Andover: Codman.

McKenzie, J.L.
  1974   *A Theology of the Old Testament*. Garden City, NY: Image Books.

Macauley, R. & G. Lanning
  1964   *Technique in Fiction*. New York: Harper & Row.

Martin, W.
  1986   *Recent Theories of Narrative*. Ithaca, NY: Cornell University.

Mays, J.L.
  1969a   *Amos*, Old Testament Library. Philadelphia: Westminster.
  1969b   *Hosea*, Old Testament Library. Philadelphia: Westminster.
  1976   *Micah*, Old Testament Library. Philadelphia: Westminster.

Mitchell, H.G., J.M.P. Smith & J.A. Brewer
  1912   *A Critical and Exegetical Commentary on Haggai, Zechariah, Malachi and Jonah*, International Critical Commentary. New York: Scribner's.

Motyer, J.A.
  1974   *The Day of the Lion: The Message of Amos*, The Bible Speaks Today. Downer's Grove, Ill.: Inter-Varsity.

Moulton, R.G.
  1899   *The Literary Study of the Bible*, rev. edn. Boston: Heath.

Mowinckel, S.
  1979   *The Psalms in Israel's Worship*, Vol. 1, trans. D.R. AP-Thomas. Nashville: Abingdon.

Napier. B.D.
    1982   *Song of the Vineyard: A Guide Through the Old Testament*,
                rev. edn. Philadelphia: Fortress.
Paterson, J.
    1948   *The Goodly Fellowship of the Prophets.* New York: Scribner's.
Patrick, D.
    1981   *The Rendering of God in the Old Testament.* Philadelphia:
                Fortress.
Perrine, L.
    1959   *Story and Structure.* New York: Harcourt, Brace.
Petersen, D.L.
    1984   *Haggai and Zechariah 1–8*, The Old Testament Library.
                Philadelphia: Westminster.
Prinsloo, W.S.
    1985   *The Theology of the Book of Joel, BZAW* 163. Berlin/New York:
                de Gruyter.
Rad, G. von
    1967   *The Message of the Prophets*, trans. D.M.G. Stalker. New
                York: Harper & Row.
    1965   *Old Testament Theology*, Vol. 2, trans. D.M.G. Stalker. New
                York: Harper & Row.
Roberts, E.V.
    1973   *Writing Themes about Literature*, 3rd edn. Englewood Cliffs,
                NJ: Prentice-Hall.
Smith, G.A.
    1929   *The Book of the Twelve Prophets*, 2 vols. Garden City, NY:
                Doubleday, Doran.
Smith, J.M.P., W.H. Ward & J.A. Brewer
    1911   *A Critical and Exegetical Commentary on Micah, Zephaniah,
                Nahum, Habakkuk, Obadiah and Joel*, The International Crit-
                ical Commentary. New York: Scribner's.
Smith, R.
    1984   *Micah–Malachi*, Word Biblical Commentary. Waco, Tx: Word.
Snaith, N.H.
    1953   *Mercy & Sacrifice: A Study of the Book of Hosea.* London: SCM.
Thompson, J.A.
    1980   *The Book of Jeremiah*, The New International Commentary on
                the Old Testament. Grand Rapids: Eerdmans.
Verhoef, P.A.
    1987   *The Books of Haggai and Malachi*, The New International
                Commentary on the Old Testament. Grand Rapids: Eerdmans.
Watts, J.D.W.
    1966   *Studying the Book of Amos.* Nashville: Broadman.
    1975   *The Books of Joel, Obadiah, Jonah, Nahum, Habakkuk and
                Zephaniah.* London: Cambridge University Press.
    1985   *Isaiah 1–33*, Word Biblical Commentary. Waco, Tx: Word.
Wilson, R.R.
    1980   *Prophecy and Society in Ancient Israel.* Philadelphia: Fortress.

Wolff, H.W.
    1974   *Hosea*, trans. G. Stansell. Philadelphia: Fortress.
    1977   *Joel and Amos*, trans. W. Janzen, S. D. McBride Jr & C.A. Muenchow. Philadelphia: Fortress.
    1981   *Micah the Prophet*, trans. R.D. Gehrke. Philadelphia: Fortress.

PERIODICALS AND ARTICLES

Buss, M.J.
    1984   'Tragedy and Comedy in Hosea', *Semeia* 32, pp. 71-82.

Clements, R.
    1977   'Patterns in the Prophetic Canon', *Canon and Authority: Essays in Old Testament Religion and Theology*, ed. G.W. Coats & B. Long. Philadelphia: Fortress, pp. 42-55.

De Roche, M.
    Jan. 1980 'Zephaniah 1.2-3: The "Sweeping" of Creation', *Vetus Testamentum* 30, pp. 104-109.

Good, E.
    1984   'Apocalyptic as Comedy: The Book of Daniel', *Semeia* 32, pp. 41-70.

Gottwald, N.K.
    1962   'Poetry, Hebrew', *Interpreter's Dictionary of the Bible*. Nashville: Abingdon, pp. 829-38.
    1984   'Tragedy and Comedy in the Latter Prophets', *Semeia* 32, pp. 83-96.

Gunn, D.M.
    1984   'The Anatomy of Divine Comedy: On Reading the Bible as Comedy and Tragedy', *Semeia* 32, pp. 115-29.

Malchow, B.V.
    1984   'The Messenger of the Covenant in Malachi 3.1', *Journal of Biblical Literature* 103/2, pp. 252-55.

Muilenburg, J.
    1969   'Form Criticism and Beyond', *Journal of Biblical Literature* 88/1, pp. 1-18.

Pierce, R.W.
    1984   'Literary Connectors and a Haggai/Zechariah/Malachi Corpus', *Journal of the Evangelical Theological Society* 27/3, pp. 277-89.
    1984   'A Thematic Development of the Haggai/Zechariah/Malachi Corpus', *Journal of the Evangelical Theological Society* 27/4, pp. 401-11.

West, M.
    1984   'Irony in the Book of Jonah: Audience Identification with the Hero', *Perspectives in Religious Studies* 11, pp. 232-42.

White, H.
    1981   'The Value of Narrativity in the Representation of Reality', *On Narrative*, ed. W.J.T. Mitchell. Chicago: University of Chicago.

Wolfe, R.E.
    1935   'The Editing of the Book of the Twelve', *ZAW* 53, pp. 90-129.
Zakovitch, Y.
    1984   ' ⌒ and ⌣ in the Bible', *Semeia* 32, pp. 107-14.

INDEXES

INDEX OF BIBLICAL REFERENCES

INDEX OF AUTHORS